Teaching
for Meaning in
High-Poverty Classrooms

Teaching
for Meaning in
High-Poverty Classrooms

Michael S. Knapp

with

Nancy E. Adelman
Camille Marder
Heather McCollum
Margaret C. Needels
Christine Padilla
Patrick M. Shields
Brenda J. Turnbull
Andrew A. Zucker

for SRI International

Foreword by John I. Goodlad

Teachers College • Columbia University
New York and London

Published by Teachers College Press, 1234 Amsterdam Avenue, New York, NY
10027

This book is based on a study carried out under the sponsorship of the U. S. Department of Education, Office of Policy and Planning/Planning & Evaluation Service,
under contract LC880-54001.

Library of Congress Cataloging-in-Publication Data

Teaching for meaning in high-poverty classrooms / Michael S. Knapp . . .
   [et al.].
      p.   cm.
   Includes bibliographical references and index.
   ISBN 0-8077-3424-1. — ISBN 0-8077-3423-3 (pbk.)
   1. Socially handicapped children — Education (Elementary) — United
States.   2. Education, Elementary — United States — Curricula.
I. Knapp, Michael S. (Michael Sturgis)
LC4091.T436   1995
371.96′7′0973 — dc20   94-46779

ISBN 0-8077-3424-1
ISBN 0-8077-3423-3   (pbk.)

Printed on acid-free paper
Manufactured in the United States of America

01 00 99 98 97 96 95 94   8 7 6 5 4 3 2 1

For Mimi Stearns,
whose intelligence, insight, sense of humor,
and irrepressible spirit led the way

Contents

Foreword

The conventional view of children not learning assumes individual deficiency and deviancy — individual pathology in extreme cases. Historically, such children were written off, in effect, by educators and educational systems. The "slow learners" of the past were simply given more of the tasks they found hard to do, and those who didn't rise to the occasion, simply exited the school system, often at an early age. Generally, little heed was paid to the fact that learners experiencing such difficulties were concentrated in lower socioeconomic strata of society.

During the 1960s, as educators began to pay more attention to the problems children from low-income families might be experiencing in schools, programs proliferated that sought to remediate the perceived deficiencies in children's reading, writing, and mathematical skills. "Compensatory" education efforts, initiated at this time, persisted into the 1980s, when the problems of so-called at-risk children and youth surged once again onto the national educational agenda, and are alive and well in schools today. Such efforts, both those in specialized programs and in the regular classroom, have been guided by a remarkably consistent diagnosis. The problem, it is typically assumed, lies with the individual learner and the deficiencies of his or her background; accordingly, the learner is brought into the mainstream through more of what are assumed to correct unfocused learning habits: carefully sequenced curricula, drill and repetition, tight control by teachers, and so forth. This is what colleagues and I found in the regimen for "slow learning" children in the classrooms we studied in the late 1960s and again in the late 1970s. In later inquiry, we concluded that many classroom and school practices were putting children at risk, and that these practices disadvantaged even more those who already were disadvantaged by the circumstances beyond their individual effort and control (Goodlad & Keating, 1990).

The study on which *Teaching for Meaning* is based adds powerfully to the thesis that the methods of learning and teaching shown over and over to work best with students progressing normally work at least equally well with students doing poorly and especially in settings in which large numbers of such students are concentrated. The authors' argument challenges the wisdom of classroom routine that emphasizes drill, repetition, and exercises divorced from their context, which so often characterize "remediation" and even the main diet of regular classroom instruction in many schools, among them, the typical school available to children from low-income families. The team of researchers studying 140 classrooms across 15 schools over the course of a school year demonstrated that alternatives to conventional practices in mathematics, reading, and writing instruction, which place greater emphasis on meaning and understanding, have a great deal to offer the children of poverty.

This carefully executed work would be significant in its own right even if it were a first warning shot regarding the mindless folly of seeking to correct children's past and present learning difficulties simply by requiring that they repeat the circumstances in which they have had little success. But it adds significantly—indeed dramatically—to the message emerging from serious inquiry in many related fields: Individual development or progress, whatever the domain of endeavor, is ecologically connected to contextual circumstances. Careful interventions or adjustments in these circumstances often have the potential to powerfully change or accelerate the trajectory of individual development.

John I. Goodlad
July 1994

Preface

Our goal in writing this book is to advance the understanding of what is possible in schools and classrooms serving large numbers of children from low-income families. The book focuses on a range of instructional practices that, in varying degrees, promote children's *understanding* and build *meaning* into their academic learning experience. We approach this topic by describing and analyzing actual practices uncovered in a two-year investigation of 140 classrooms located in a variety of school settings. We offer the first comprehensive demonstration of what meaning-oriented instruction can achieve in schools in which educators have long believed that mastery of "basic skills" is the most desirable and realistic goal. What we have seen in these schools convinces us otherwise: Teachers and the policy makers who support that approach are capable of offering their students more powerful learning opportunities from which both high- and low-achieving students can benefit.

Our specific focus is on the enactment, impact, and support of curricula in elementary schools that serve children from low-income families. We concentrate on the three subject areas — mathematics, reading, and writing — that form the bulk of the students' instructional experience in grades one through six. Across these grade levels, we examine many facets of the teaching task — how teachers manage the classroom learning environment, construct academic tasks, engage learners in academic work, and respond to cultural differences in students' backgrounds — and we present evidence about the effects these activities have on student learning. In addition, we explore the ways in which schools supplement instruction in the regular classroom with other forms of instruction aimed at particular learning needs. Finally, we consider how schools and districts create conditions that support meaning-oriented instruction.

It is important to understand what this book is *not* about. We do not explore the theoretical underpinnings of meaning-oriented instruction, nor do we offer a how-to guide for this form of teaching. By the same token, we do not examine the experiences of individual learners. Rather, we offer a wealth of teaching examples based on different pedagogical assumptions and, through careful analysis, uncover the principles at work in many different settings.

In writing this book, we address a wide range of readers who are concerned about the quality of education offered to learners who grow up in impoverished circumstances. The descriptions and insights we provide will be particularly useful to those at any level of the educational system who design, guide, support, and coordinate educational programs aimed at "disadvantaged" learners, through both the regular school curriculum and specialized programs for targeted groups; policy makers in schools and districts who wish to improve the quality of learning opportunities; educators and their students in institutions that prepare new teachers or administrators for work in high-poverty settings; and scholars whose work focuses on curriculum, teaching, and the connections between policy and instruction. Practicing teachers will also find much in the book that broadens their perspective on what they can do and what their efforts may accomplish (though, as noted above, the book does not offer lesson ideas, particular curricula, or other forms of practical guidance).

To all these audiences we offer a systematic exploration of a major and growing challenge facing educators today. We do not offer prescriptions or recipes but rather a set of insights that can guide future efforts to meet this challenge. We hope that these insights will help a wide range of educators renew their efforts to provide high-quality learning opportunities in high-poverty classrooms. The children of poverty deserve the best we have to offer them.

Acknowledgments

This book is based on a study carried out under the sponsorship of the U.S. Department of Education, Office of Policy and Planning/Planning & Evaluation Service. Any opinions, findings, conclusions, or recommendations expressed in the book are those of the authors and do not necessarily reflect the views of the U.S. Department of Education. We are especially indebted to Carol Chelemer, Adriana deKanter, Alan Ginsburg, Mary Jean LeTendre, Martin Orland, and Val Plisko of the U.S. Department of Education for their vision, continuing support, and helpful criticisms during the conduct of the study.

Many other people contributed to the study and subsequently to the preparation of this book. Members of the field staff spent 2 years collecting data in classrooms and schools and provided both the raw material and many of the insights contained in the chapters of this book: Lee Anderson, Rebecca Benjamin, Carol Carlson, Norma Francisco, Janie Funkhouser, Grace Pung Guthrie, Susan King, Gary Lichtenstein, Beverly Matson, Ellen McIntyre, Laverne Middleton, Christene Petry, Beverly Pringle, Katherine Ramage, Ellen Renneker, Lisa Richardson, Debra Shaver, Deborah Swanson-Owens, and Choya Wilson. Other members of the study team carried out the complex technical and logistical work of managing databases, programming, coordinating testing, preparing manuscripts, and other administrative tasks too numerous to mention: Marion Collins, Carolyn Estey, Katherine Habina, Klaus Krause, Lucy Omo, Dorothy Stewart, Peggy Thompson, and Cynthia Williamson.

Various individuals located in universities, government agencies, and professional associations offered advice on study design, technical details of analysis, and the interpretation of results: Richard Allington, Beatrice Birman, Dale Boatwright, Jere Brophy, Gary Echternacht, Carolyn Evertson, Marcia Farr, Beverly Glenn, Pamela Grossman, Edward Haertel, Bruce Henderson, Andrew Porter, Marilyn Rauth, Robert Slavin, and Marshall Smith.

Finally, we are deeply indebted to the 140 teachers in California, Ohio, and Maryland who permitted us to observe their classrooms on numerous occasions, gave freely of their experience in interviews, and filled out daily classroom logs throughout an entire school year. To the principals and other staff in their schools and to the district staff who made the study possible, we also extend our thanks.

Teaching
for Meaning in
High-Poverty Classrooms

The Teaching Challenge in High-Poverty Classrooms

Michael S. Knapp

Schools that serve large numbers of children from low-income families face one of the most difficult tasks in education. Over the years, the teachers and administrators who staff these schools have learned to cope with high mobility among children, limited resources, inadequate facilities, and concentrations of children with diverse and hard-to-meet learning needs. Perhaps most difficult of all, each day these educators must deal with children who are not particularly well versed in the art of "doing school."

Most teachers try hard to make the best of the challenge before them; many wonder why it seems so hard to engage and maintain children's attention to learning tasks, communicate what often appears to be common sense, and show demonstrable achievement gains on conventional measures of learning. In their approach to their work, these teachers often settle for a curriculum that aims at the most "basic" elements of the content to be learned, on the assumption that no more can be managed and that mastery of the basics is an important accomplishment.

The children who attend such schools face an equally difficult task. From their point of view, it is not always obvious what they have to gain from being in school or from going along with what schools ask of them. For one thing, the culture and language of school are often unfamiliar, even if the children have grown up speaking English; for a growing percentage of children from low-income families, English is literally a foreign language. To complicate matters, what teachers expect of students in high-poverty classrooms is not always clear or compelling; indeed, it often appears to the students that relatively little is expected of them.

The result in these settings is an educational experience that lacks meaning and importance to the learners. Thus, children learn to work two-digit subtraction without understanding in some basic way what the two columns of figures represent or even what subtraction is, much less how it relates to their lives. Or these children learn to recognize letter sounds and syllables on the printed page but remain puzzled about what the text actually says or why it is important to read. Or they never get the experience of writing something coherent and readable to an audience with which they wish to communicate.

The difficult tasks of teaching and learning in high-poverty classrooms have prompted a continuing search over the years for effective teaching practices and curricula. At issue are questions about the capabilities of learners, the nature of learning itself, the content of challenging academic instruction, strategies for teaching, and ways to manage productive learning environments.

THE CHALLENGE TO TEACHERS

The reasons for the failure to teach the children of poverty to understand what they are learning are complex and go well beyond the nature of curriculum and instruction in the schools that serve this segment of the student population. Nor are the complaints about lack of meaning in education unique to the children of poverty; reformers have directed attention to these issues for schools serving all segments of society. But the problem is demonstrably acute in high-poverty classrooms, compounded by many conditions over which teachers have no control.

The Roots of the Problem

A familiar way of construing the teaching problem in high-poverty classrooms is to dwell on conditions in the children's homes and communities. Arguably, these conditions often put constraints on children's readiness to engage in the tasks that schools set for them, and there is no denying that economic hardship confronts these children's families with contingencies that make the basics of living difficult. Adequate (or any) employment is hard to find, and along with it stable and affordable housing. Such families move — or are forced to move — often and at unpredictable times. They often find themselves in community environments that are hostile or even overtly violent. As a direct consequence of limited family income, children in impoverished circumstances do not eat as well as, and are generally less healthy than, their more affluent counterparts. The stresses on families in such circumstances test the strength of relationships and support systems, and it is not surprising that most of the children of poverty find themselves in single-parent families, many of which are without extended family support networks nearby. To compound matters, families with limited means in American society are often those whose grasp of the English language and mainstream customs is equally limited.

All these conditions have manifestations in the high-poverty classroom, and it is tempting to see these symptoms as the core of the issue. It is true enough that students come and go during the school year; on any given day, some have not had breakfast; many do not have a full command of Standard English and get little practice using it outside of school; and so on. This way of construing the problem is somewhat one-sided, however, and fails to recognize the *relationship* that is struck between learners and teachers, between individuals from an often unfamiliar cultural background and representatives of an institutional setting.

When one takes an interactive, relational view of the encounter between teachers and the occupants of high-poverty classrooms, other matters become as important as the traits, needs, or apparent deficiencies that come through the classroom door. What does each party to the relationship know of the other's world? Do they explain to each other what they are thinking, or even try to find out? What assumptions does each make about the nature of such relationships, the ground rules for behavior, the purposes of their being together?

A good deal of research over the past decade has begun to spell out in conceptual terms the dimensions of the relationship between nonmainstream learners and mainstream schools. This body of research clearly identifies various roots of the educational challenge facing teachers in high-poverty classrooms, many of them attributable to educators' preparation, expectations, motivations, and imaginations. These traits, in turn, are often constrained by the working conditions in high-poverty schools, which do not always make it easy to construct high-quality learning opportunities: Insufficient resources, high pupil-staff ratios, and substandard facilities are commonly found in schools populated with large numbers of children from low-income backgrounds.

Managing the School Day and Teaching Specific Subjects

This book's task is to zero in on the elements of the teacher-learner relationship in high-poverty classrooms that are most closely related to curriculum and instruction, the matters over which teachers exercise the greatest day-to-day control. In this regard, two kinds of challenges present themselves; the first transcends the specifics of a particular subject area, and the second is specific to the subject matter being taught. Among the first set of challenges, two pervade the entire school day, cutting across all areas of curriculum: establishing classroom order and responding to cultural diversity.

Fundamental to any classroom is the creation of some order that aligns students' work with the teacher's agenda and thereby makes classroom life both predictable and productive. Threats to order are present in every classroom, but high-poverty classrooms are especially susceptible to disorder. Hungry children do not concentrate very well and are easily distracted. Children who experience a significant amount of violence in their lives outside of school are likely to see it as an acceptable solution within the classroom. Students newly arrived in midyear change the classroom chemistry and need to learn the routines that others mastered months ago.

High-poverty classrooms are often culturally diverse. At a minimum, the culture of children in such settings is likely to differ from the values, norms, and attitudes held by teachers. More likely, children sit beside classmates who look different and have been raised with different expectations. Often these seatmates speak different languages or English dialects. Not all high-poverty classrooms contain such diversity, however; some are numbingly homogeneous — for example, all students may be from the same neighborhood, minority group, and low-income bracket. But all high-poverty classrooms pose a challenge to teachers' culturally based notions of how to conduct the business of teaching and learning.

The demographics of high-poverty classrooms compound what is a fact of life in any classroom: Some children master school tasks quickly, and others appear less capable of carrying out these tasks. But in high-poverty classrooms, such differences are often sharply drawn, and the gap widens quickly as children progress through the elementary grades. Complicating matters is the difficulty of perceiving *actual* ability beneath the surface of low performance, which often reflects other conditions as much as a child's innate capacity for learning.

At the same time that teachers address issues of classroom order and cultural diversity, they face challenges inherent in the particular subject matter they are teaching. In the elementary grades, where numeracy and literacy dominate the curriculum, teachers are constantly translating mathematics, reading, and writing into terms that can engage learners and encourage growth in skills and content knowledge. Of particular concern to teachers in high-poverty classrooms — and to those who design school curricula or prepare teachers for their work — are questions about what to teach, how to teach it, and when to teach it.

In particular, faced with apparent learning deficiencies of all kinds, teachers in high-poverty classrooms wrestle with questions about how much they can or should emphasize "advanced" skills in mathematics, reading, and writing. They fashion strategies that vary the pacing, presentation, and design of academic learning tasks and the role of the teacher in controlling or guiding classroom activity (and the role of students in guiding their own learning). With high-poverty classrooms in mind, teachers are especially likely to evolve strategies that can capture and retain the attention of students who often seem disconnected from instruction. In addition, high-poverty classrooms tempt teachers to maximize the frequency with which content and skills are taught or retaught, so that children have as many opportunities to practice as possible.

TEACHING FOR MEANING: ALTERNATIVES TO CONVENTIONAL WISDOM IN HIGH-POVERTY CLASSROOMS

A fifth-grade mathematics class midway through the year highlights a common approach to the challenges teachers face in high-poverty classrooms:

> *Mr. Gates's mathematics lesson.* It is time for mathematics. Mr. Gates[1] asks the children to switch from the dictionary skills worksheet they have been working on to the mathematics homework. The students, a mixed group of Anglo and Hispanic children from a nearby housing project, fumble for their homework sheets. Some never find them; a few — primarily a handful of boys (mostly Hispanic) sitting in seats around the edge of the room — pay little attention to what is going on, but the teacher appears not to notice (for the moment, the nonparticipants are quiet). The next 15 minutes are devoted to a review of the homework, which involved long division. Mr. Gates proceeds in rapid-fire fashion, asking for the correct answer and providing it if some member of the class fails to give it. The students correct their own sheets and then sing out how many they got right. The class shifts to a 15-minute blackboard presentation by Mr. Gates on the finer points of long division with a two-digit divisor (which was the subject of the homework). Many students fidget during the explanation; the nonparticipating children are beginning to be louder and more noticeable. ("This class just doesn't seem to get it," he explains at the end of the class; his game plan appears to be to repeat the explanation "till they understand it.") The class ends with a period of seatwork — more practice with long division problems. The class works at this task, but the contingent of nonparticipating

---

1. The name of this teacher and all others appearing in vignettes throughout the book are pseudonyms.

boys does little. Once again, Mr. Gates pays little attention to them
(he explains later that he has tried hard to involve them and they
"just don't respond; they don't care about learning, so I don't spend
much time with them"). A few minutes later they and their classmates tumble out the door to recess.

This scene is typical of many days in a large number of classrooms
across the nation. Although instruction is taking place and the class is
under control for the most part, some important elements are missing
from the children's education. The students are being taught procedures
without meaning, and there is no compelling reason for them to learn
these procedures. What they are being taught lacks connection to their
lives. Not surprisingly, their response to instruction lacks enthusiasm. As a
class, they are not "getting it," even though by yearend they may manage
a reasonable score on the district's standardized tests. What is more, a part
of the class that is culturally different from the teacher has, in effect, been
written off.

Conventional Wisdom

There are already widely accepted answers about how to educate the kinds
of students in Mr. Gates's classroom, and his approach to mathematics
exemplifies many of them. These answers form an unstated but pervasive
"conventional wisdom" about curriculum and instruction in high-poverty
classrooms shared by large numbers of practitioners (see Knapp, Turnbull, & Shields, 1990; Knapp & Shields, 1991; Means & Knapp, 1991).

In brief, the conventional wisdom focuses on what children lack
(e.g., print awareness, grasp of Standard English syntax, a supportive
home environment) and seeks to remedy these deficiencies by teaching
discrete skills (e.g., decoding skills, language mechanics, arithmetic computation). Curriculum and instruction follow a fixed sequence from "basic" to "advanced" skills, so that students master simpler tasks as a prerequisite for the more complex activities of comprehension, composition, and
reasoning. To inculcate these skills, the conventional wisdom favors a style
of teaching in which instruction is fast paced and tightly controlled by the
teacher to maximize student time on task. In addition, this approach to
instruction differentiates what is taught, and how it is taught, by students'
proficiency: Especially in reading, high- and low-performing students
tend to be segregated into different "ability-based" groups, and the latter
are often assigned to one or more remedial programs that provide supplemental instruction aimed at deficiencies in basic skills. Conditions in the
school or district setting—including curricular scope and sequences, assess-

ment procedures or instruments, textbook choices, and supplemental program guidelines — often support this view of academic instruction.

There is considerable research support for this approach to teaching in high-poverty classrooms. Several decades of process-product studies, for example, point to the value of various elements of this approach (e.g., Brophy & Good, 1986). This research base rests its conclusions primarily on high correlations between generic teaching practices and scores on standardized tests (most of which capture students' mastery of discrete skills).

Teaching for Meaning

Significant alternatives to this conventional wisdom — in particular, what is widely described as "teaching for understanding" (e.g., Cohen, McLaughlin, & Talbert, 1993; Brooks & Brooks, 1993; Perkins & Blythe, 1994) — have attracted the attention of educators and scholars in the past decade. These alternatives share a family resemblance (Means & Knapp, 1991). Each, in its own way, deemphasizes the teaching of discrete skills in isolation from the context in which these skills are applied. Each rests on the assumption that knowledge is less discrete, less separable into distinct subject and skill areas. Each fosters connections between academic learning and the world from which children come. And each views the children's cumulative experience of that world as a resource for learning; whatever deficiencies may exist in their capabilities or life circumstances, the children are viewed as being capable and possessing useful knowledge. To accomplish these goals, alternative instructional strategies in each area draw from a common pool of techniques, among them emphasis on discussion and extensive opportunities for engaging in the activities to which skills relate (writing, reading, solving mathematical problems).

Of particular relevance to the situation illustrated by Mr. Gates's classroom is the attempt — common to this class of alternative approaches — to enhance the *meanings* that children find and construct in their instructional experiences. In specific terms, the proponents of these alternatives (and the authors of this book) assume that children derive greater meaning in their school-based academic work from three sources. First, when they are actively engaged in the attempt to make sense of things they experience in school, they are encouraged to be meaning makers. Second, they derive meaning from seeing the relationship of parts to whole, rather than being left with only parts. Opportunities to connect one concept or one skill to another increase their conceptual grasp of what they are doing, whether it involves communication, problem solving, appreciation of artwork, or carrying out projects. Third, they find meaning by connecting new learning experiences to their existing body of knowledge, assumptions, and meanings, much of which is rooted in their upbringing and cultural roots. We refer to teaching that seeks to maximize these three things as "teaching for meaning."

Although most of the work to date regarding teaching for meaning has been done with mainstream middle-class classrooms and children in mind, there is evidence that these approaches can work well in high-poverty classrooms. For example, research on "cognitively guided" mathematics instruction — in which teachers spend more time on word problems, deemphasize drill and math facts, encourage multiple solutions to problems, and draw heavily on children's prior mathematical knowledge — provides some evidence that inner-city "disadvantaged" children greatly improve their capacity for solving unfamiliar problems as a result of this kind of instructional experience (Villasenor, 1990; Peterson, Fennema, & Carpenter, 1991). Similarly, approaches to reading and writing instruction that grow out of a more integrated view of literacy have produced promising results in demonstrations within high-poverty settings, such as efforts to enhance children's "critical literacy" (Calfee, 1991) or to promote children's text comprehension through explicit teaching of comprehension strategies, as in "reciprocal teaching" models (e.g., Palincsar & Klenk, 1991). Similar evidence points to the potential of writing instruction characterized by explicit strategy-focused teaching, the use of prompts to stimulate more demanding kinds of thinking, and modeling of the composing process (Bryson & Scardamalia, 1991).

ONGOING QUESTIONS AND ONE SOURCE OF ANSWERS

The research to date suggests that teaching for meaning has promise and a compelling logic, but many questions remain about it and its place in high-poverty classrooms. Beyond the limited evidence available from existing demonstration studies, we know little about using these approaches in the variety of settings in which students from low-income families are taught. For example, many of the alternative approaches emphasizing meaning have been developed and promoted by scholars working in collaboration with a select group of practitioners. What form do these ideas take when imitated, adapted, or otherwise picked up by a wide variety of teachers working in more typical settings? What do these approaches demand of teachers, and are they up to the task? Do students in these settings actually improve their reasoning, comprehension, and composition skills? What about their mastery of basic skills? How are policies and other features of the school setting implicated in the delivery of instruction based on alternative principles?

These questions were among those that motivated the Study of Academic Instruction for Disadvantaged Students, a two-year investigation sponsored by the U.S. Department of Education (Knapp, Adelman, Marder, McCollum, Needels, Shields, Turnbull, & Zucker, 1992). It examined the teaching taking place in schools that serve large numbers of children from low-income families (the authors of this book were the principal members of the study team). In this book, we explore these questions by drawing on what we learned from the investigation about what was taught, how it was taught, the results of instruction, and the way instruction was supported in approximately 140 classrooms located within 15 such schools in three states (California, Maryland, and Ohio). The investigation concentrated on the three subject areas—mathematics, reading, and writing—that account for the majority of teaching and learning time in the elementary grades.

The research on which this book is based represents a study of "natural variation." In contrast with studies that "plant" a promising practice or program in a set of classrooms and study its effects with appropriate experimental comparisons, we investigated the range of practices that had developed in a less planned way in a variety of schools. We concentrated on schools that appeared to be performing well, as far as this could be judged by evidence from standardized testing measures. We assumed that important insights about effective practice could be derived by documenting, contrasting, and assessing the effects of the varying approaches to curriculum and instruction across a large number of classrooms in such schools.

The school and district settings differed considerably in the kinds of student populations served as well as the school and district environments surrounding academic instruction. The settings shared the characteristic that half or more of the students came from families in poverty (as defined by participation in the free or reduced-price lunch program). Three districts served primarily inner-city populations: one primarily African American children, another primarily African American and Hispanic, and the third a mixture of many ethnic and racial groups. A fourth district was located in a suburban setting adjacent to a large city and shared many of the characteristics of inner-city school districts. The remaining two districts were located in rural or semirural settings, one serving a population of white children and the other a mixed white and Hispanic population. Within these sites, classrooms of experienced teachers were selected to maximize the variety in instructional approaches undertaken (Appendix A provides more detail on sample selection).

The research team focused on instruction throughout the school year. By directly observing lessons, inspecting materials, testing students, examining school records, interviewing teachers and administrators repeatedly, and having teachers keep daily logs of their instructional activities, the researchers assembled in-depth portraits of instruction in combination with a profile of what was taught throughout the year (see Appendix A for an extended discussion of research methods). The research team studied all six grades in elementary school—grades 1, 3, and 5 the first year, grades 2, 4, and 6 the following year.

ORGANIZATION OF THIS BOOK

The first two chapters of the book examine the two challenges, discussed earlier, that pervade the school day: how teachers establish classroom order and respond to cultural diversity. Though these matters transcend the requirements of particular subject areas to some degree, Chapters 1 and 2 argue that they are intimately linked to decisions about subject matter and how it will be taught. In particular, certain approaches to classroom order and cultural diversity provide a foundation for meaning-oriented teaching; other approaches limit, or rule out altogether, the possibility of teaching for meaning.

Chapters 3, 4, and 5 describe attempts in the classrooms we studied to teach for meaning in mathematics, reading, and writing, as contrasted with more conventional skills-oriented teaching. Chapter 6 examines the contribution to high-poverty classrooms made by supplemental instruction and, in particular, the implications for meaning-oriented instruction. In Chapter 7 we summarize evidence regarding the effectiveness of meaning-oriented approaches in helping both high and low performers master advanced and basic skills of literacy and numeracy.

Chapters 8 and 9 show how characteristics of teachers, the nature of students in the classroom, and features of the policy environment support or inhibit the introduction of teaching for meaning in high-poverty classrooms. The Conclusion summarizes the book's argument and draws implications for students, teachers, teacher educators, and policy makers.

CHAPTER 1

Managing Academic Learning Environments

Heather McCollum

During the school day, teachers face the task of establishing order in the classroom in ways that support academic learning. The task has traditionally been viewed as one of "classroom management," but we find it more productive to treat it as intrinsically linked with the teaching of subject matter. After all, most teachers' attempts to "manage" children take place in the context of a particular learning activity and with some instructional goal in mind.

Although orchestrating the activities and whereabouts of 20 to 35 elementary school children all day long is no small feat in any setting, it is often particularly difficult in classrooms with large numbers of children from low-income families. To be sure, many of the problems faced by teachers in the classrooms we visited are common to all schools: a range of ability levels, students with problems outside the classroom, insufficient personnel, and so on. But these conditions tend to be exaggerated in high-poverty classrooms.

Despite often adverse conditions, the majority of the teachers we observed did amazingly well at creating constructive academic environments. This chapter examines their successes and failures, with a view toward isolating those strategies that are likely to be effective with this population of children.

DIFFERENCES AMONG ACADEMIC LEARNING ENVIRONMENTS

Success in the management of the learning environment is usually readily apparent to an observer: A class is busily engaged in academic tasks, there are few disruptions, and transitions between instructional segments occur smoothly. Teachers are often the first to admit when this is not the case; they are usually painfully aware when their agendas are not being followed.

Taking our cue from the amount and quality of student engagement in academic tasks, we separated classrooms into two groups. The first was characterized by an unresolved struggle over order; students spent considerable time disengaged from academic work and participated in various confrontations with the teacher. The second group most educators would describe as "orderly"; children spent most or all of their time engaged in academic work. The majority of the classrooms we studied fell into the latter category, but the important distinctions among them had profound implications for the kind of academic learning opportunities available to children.

Disorderly Learning Environments

Although there were relatively few among the classrooms we studied, the existence of disorderly learning environments poses an important contrast to those in which order prevailed. We distinguished two basic patterns: learning environments that were in some basic sense "dysfunctional" from the point of view of academic learning, and those in which an adequate minimum level of order existed but with a continuing, unresolved struggle between teacher and students over the way time should be spent.

Dysfunctional learning environments. The following example from a rural school typifies a truly dysfunctional classroom:

> *Ms. James's fifth- and sixth-grade class.* Although occasional bursts of enthusiasm are evident, the class is often filled with an air of tension and frustration. There seems to be a constant tug-of-war over discipline issues between Ms. James and the more than 30 students of various racial backgrounds in this combined fifth- and sixth-grade classroom. Although Ms. James is generally quite stern with the students, she often allows them to socialize. They are an unusually gregarious group: They take advantage of every opportunity to interact with one another — whispering, calling out, passing notes, moving around — especially during seatwork time. In cyclical fashion, the noise level slowly rises beyond what Ms. James will tolerate. She then angrily warns the class to quiet down, and after a couple of further warnings she signs individuals up for chore duty after school. If the whole class continues to be disruptive, Ms. James makes everyone "write lines" by filling several sheets of paper with a disciplinary statement or the school's mission statement. Things quiet down for a while, and the cycle begins again. Ms. James's students often seem eager to channel their energy into learning activities, and they happily

volunteer for group activities that involve reading aloud or writing on the board. But whenever they have to do anything at their desks, which is much of the time, they generally succeed in avoiding the tasks entirely.

In this case, a relatively inexperienced teacher was confronted with a curriculum mandate that required all students to be taught from the same level of material and not be grouped by ability. Having no specific training in this approach, Ms. James was overwhelmed by the complex management issues it created. Curiously, Ms. James's classroom was not a constant battle zone; this was true of many of the most poorly managed rooms. Although there were some nasty incidents, including a few serious fights, there were also occasional moments of laughter and warmth. In fact, we were surprised to notice that the students often seemed immune to the apparently tense, highly unpleasant situation. The students had developed coping mechanisms and in many cases managed to enjoy themselves. This energy, however, was not channeled into academic tasks; in this sense, what transpired in this room was clearly dysfunctional from the point of view of student learning.

In classrooms with dysfunctional learning environments, there was little evidence, other than the ubiquitous rules posted at the front of the room, that a systematic, sustained attempt had been made early in the year to establish a clearly understood basis for order. These classrooms had an apparently capricious system of cues for punishment; as in Ms. James's class, it might be a certain noise level — not always the same one — or some behavior that may have gone unnoticed the day before. Under such circumstances, students typically reacted and adapted to perceived personality or mood changes in the teacher rather than to established routines.

All the teachers in these classrooms were keenly aware of the problem. Some complained about a lack of training or their unfamiliarity with the type of student or the mandated curriculum; all expressed discontent with the administrative support for disciplinary matters. In all cases, the teachers perceived the principals as "too soft" on behavior problems (in fact, in the schools with dysfunctional learning environments, even the effective classroom managers echoed this sentiment). Poor managers were also less likely to have a close collegial relationship with other staff members and cited the lack of support from parents in developing students' social skills.

Adequate learning environments. Other classrooms with unresolved issues of order had begun the year with serious problems but managed to improve the situation to the point that many or most students were focusing on academics and completing assignments a large proportion of the time.

Often, however, order itself became the agenda, and enthusiasm was clearly lacking; in this context, disruptions continued to occur. Consider the following classroom serving a group of children comparable in size and background to those of Ms. James's room:

> *Ms. Durgin's first-grade class.* In this classroom, a definite routine was put in place early in the year and is followed without exception. For example, each day starts out with phonics instruction, followed by worksheets done independently on the "sound of the week." Further direct instruction in reading is followed by additional seatwork; the pattern continues in other subject areas. For the most part, students are comfortable in the room because the assignments are always manageable. They are eager to do well for the teacher and are virtually guaranteed success. Ms. Durgin has few severe disruptions to deal with. The overall atmosphere of the classroom is positive but not challenging. Students are given simple tasks and are not pushed to be creative or to grasp difficult concepts. When she does discipline students, however, Ms. Durgin is often inconsistent in her approach. She is generally more patient in the morning, when she gently calls students' names to refocus them on the task at hand. Usually by the afternoon her patience has worn thin, and she sometimes yells at the students for no greater infractions than had occurred in the morning. In addition, she often talks very loudly into the faces of individual students who do not attend or who are off task. She also occasionally singles students out in front of the classroom when they do not know an answer, which embarrasses them.

In other classrooms like this one, teachers appeared to achieve order, but often at the expense of meaningful academic content. The "feel" of these rooms was certainly less hostile and threatening than that of truly dysfunctional environments. They might be orderly to the point of being slightly oppressive, with little spontaneity evident, or they might be—depending on the population—quiet and passive. In such situations, the struggle over order was less overt (the observer, and probably the teacher as well, was less likely to fear that something would explode at any moment), but at regular intervals the teacher and several students, if not the whole class, would "lose focus" on what they were doing. This fact, in conjunction with the nature of the academic tasks themselves, contributed to a pattern of inconsistent engagement with academic work.

Generally, prior groundwork for successful management was much more apparent in classrooms with adequate learning environments than in those that were dysfunctional—as a result of the teacher's own efforts, socialization in previous years, or both. Because management issues were less of a problem, fewer teachers viewed these issues as insurmountable barriers. Typically, they described their students as unmotivated and uninterested in learning. Rather than administrative support, these teachers often lamented the lack of support from parents in academic matters.

Orderly Learning Environments

The majority of classrooms we observed resembled neither Ms. James's nor Ms. Durgin's rooms; in most of them, order was not a pressing issue. At first glance, this second set of classrooms exhibited learning environments with a high degree of student engagement in academic work. But on closer examination, there were distinct differences among them. Something other than the maintenance of order profoundly affected the way students engaged in learning. On this basis, we subdivided the orderly classrooms into two groups: those offering tightly controlled and in some sense "restricted" opportunities for learning, and those providing a wider range of opportunities that enabled students to expand their repertoires of routines and learning challenges.

Orderly, restrictive learning environments. In this group of classrooms, it was immediately apparent that students were engaged in the assigned tasks almost all the time. Clearly, achieving this state of affairs was a major accomplishment and had taken a lot of long, hard work on the part of the teachers. But even when assignments were completed and test scores showed that learning had occurred, some "spark" was missing from all or most students, as the following example implies:

> *Ms. Williams's fifth-grade class.* From the beginning, Ms. Williams takes firm control of the class, and the level of engagement is very high. Ms. Williams is an expert practitioner of the assertive discipline system, which is used districtwide. Basically, nothing is done without a cue, a system, or a specified procedure. Most of this constant reinforcement is woven into regular instruction, and disruptions are rare. Reinforcements come through marbles in the jar (which add up to goodies such as videos or popcorn), marks on students' desks, or simply the ever-present "Thank you, Curtis, I like the way you're sitting quietly." Ms. Williams smoothly inserts these management prompts into every aspect of instruction, but the system is always running (and the students are clearly aware of it). While weaving among the desks during a math lesson, she unobtrusively places marks on the permanent tallies on the students' desks if she notices appropriate behav-

ior. In general, Ms. Williams's approach results in a very orderly and mostly quiet classroom that does not feel as oppressive as it may sound. Although there is little spontaneity ("Think first, and don't raise your hand to answer until I say 'hands are OK'"), there is no time wasted during transitions, instructions are clear, and enforcement is consistent and fair. When disruptions occur (such as when an unmonitored group is doing seatwork), she handles them calmly, never letting herself get drawn into power struggles. Students get work done in this class, but they do so in large measure due to Ms. Williams's constant vigilance. By the end of the year, both class and teacher seem drained from the effort involved in holding it all together.

Not all the classrooms of this sort were as meticulously orchestrated. What they had in common was the fact that the instructional agenda was clearly followed: Students were involved, and academic outcomes were in line with goals and expectations. Nonetheless, management concerns were still driving many instructional decisions.

Many orderly, restrictive classrooms had a somewhat looser feel than the one just described. In many there was a cooperative spirit and more energy. In these cases, discipline still required hard work at times to prevent some students from counting themselves out entirely. In short, in classrooms of this sort, management worked either fairly well for all, as above, or well enough for moments of real creativity and bursts of enthusiasm — but not for everyone, and not unless dealing with interruptions was still an important part of the agenda. By comparison with classrooms having dysfunctional or adequate learning environments, it was clear that a great deal of time and energy had been invested from the beginning of the year in putting a tight management system in place in these classrooms. For most children, the system was running and nonnegotiable. In some cases, it left students out or inhibited spontaneity.

Having solved the major management problems, these teachers were more likely to notice that their instruction lacked a clear direction. They were often aware that many students were only going through the motions, and they welcomed the chance to find out about alternative approaches. Teachers in this group still thought of parents as a primary reason that students were compliant but unmotivated.

Orderly, enabling learning environments. Teachers' styles in this group of classrooms were varied. Some fit traditional images of strict, no-nonsense teachers; others were more effusive and affectionate. Through a combination of the "right" moves, they all succeeded in making their classrooms highly productive learning environments where students not only completed assigned tasks but also clearly enjoyed being and learning.

Ms. Olivetti's first-grade class. This first-grade class in a rural area has 28 children; half are white and half are Hispanic. In a word, the class "hums." It is a comfortable place where children enjoy being and doing schoolwork; the business of learning is central to everything that is done in the room. Children treat their classmates and the teacher with respect, as a result of her careful lessons in how to listen to one another, offer ideas verbally to the class, and respect what the others say. Ms. Olivetti's management style is calm and quiet. She is remarkably effective at maintaining order despite the fact that the classroom is one of four clustered together in a semiopen pod arrangement. She uses a combination of quiet reminders and pointing to each seating group (clusters of four desks), with individual praise for so-and-so, who is sitting nicely now. The result is that students do what she asks the first time she asks, with rare exceptions (which are quickly brought into line), and attention is not drawn to management issues very often. The principal remarked, "Ms. Olivetti is one of the most organized teachers in the school." Everything has a place and can be found. She has extensive training through a variety of professional development experiences in both language arts and mathematics teaching. The depth of her training is evident—she has picked up ideas from all these experiences and has developed a diverse repertoire of activities, many of which she uses on a regular basis.

With virtually no management issues demanding center stage, the academic focus was obvious in these classrooms. The teachers' energies were freed up (largely through their own efforts) to experiment with different instructional methods. Children felt successful, were respectful of one another, and willingly approached the tasks of the school day. A clear "system" was in place for this group of classrooms from the beginning of the year. Management concerns were seamlessly woven into the fabric of instruction.

None of the teachers in this group of classrooms was resting on his or her laurels. Indeed, they tended to take more responsibility than other teachers for their students' success and were somewhat less likely to blame other influences (e.g., parents). Many of the expert managers ascribed their success to the "niceness" of their groups this year. Most importantly, these teachers were often the most eager to learn from others and expand their already impressive repertoires of instructional strategies.

MANAGEMENT STRATEGIES THAT SHAPE THE
LEARNING ENVIRONMENT

The academic learning environments just described varied in the general atmosphere surrounding learning, the specific array of learning opportunities, and the depth of students' engagement in academic work. When we looked more closely, differences emerged in the management strategies teachers used to create the learning environment. In particular, teachers varied their ways of (1) dealing with disruptions, (2) ensuring consistency of routines, (3) providing student feedback and holding students accountable, (4) motivating students, and (5) pacing instruction. In addition, teachers (6) struck different degrees of balance between student and teacher talk and (7) developed different degrees of responsibility among students for their own learning. In approaching most of these management issues, teachers simultaneously made decisions about orderliness and subject matter.

Dealing with Disruptions

Although disruptions tended to happen less often in well-managed classrooms, every teacher we observed faced unanticipated outbursts from students that called attention away from academic work. In the least effectively managed classrooms, punishments for inappropriate behavior were typically arbitrary and unpredictable. Often, the teachers themselves created the major disruptions. It was not uncommon to see a reading group interrupted by a loud admonition from the teacher directed at someone on the other side of the room. Alternatively, teachers in these classrooms tried to ignore the disruptions entirely until they escalated to an unacceptable level. When this point was reached, all work generally ceased until order was restored. In the worst cases, the day's agenda was punctuated regularly by intervals of lights-out, heads down on desks, and so forth. During the course of one fifth-grade language arts lessons, we observed several students leaving the room without permission; the class rabbit getting loose and jumping around the room, causing the students to twitter and chatter; a pencil flying across the room; one student being stabbed with a pencil in his hand; several boys playing with a stencil kit rather than doing the reading lesson; several students yelling across the room; three boys popping paper with their pencils; several students kicking one another; and two boys giving a dance demonstration in the back. Behavior of this type occurred throughout the day until certain offenders were put into "time out." Several of the repeat offenders, however, did not seem to care about the consequences for inappropriate behavior, and they were rarely singled out for punishment.

Besides creating disruptions or attempting to ignore chaos, teachers in the less orderly classrooms often sought to cope with student disruptions by isolating the offenders. In extreme cases, this became a permanent situation, as in the case of Mr. Gates's mathematics classroom described earlier. In such instances, certain students (almost always boys) were relegated to the periphery of the classroom for all activities. In one room, a bookcase separated a potential troublemaker from the rest of the class, and although the teacher claimed that he was given individualized instruction, the site visitor never observed this. More commonly, single students were scattered around the edges of the room with no physical barriers, but they had no deskmates, were left out of groups, and often could not hear the teacher well or see the board.

When disruptions occurred in the more effectively managed classrooms, the teachers almost never dealt with them in an arbitrary fashion — enforcement and punishment were generally more consistent. Some of the expert managers did not treat all children equally, but the variation was based on individual circumstances rather than changes in the teacher's mood. Some of the better managers reacted to infractions differently, based on their personal knowledge of a student's current home situation. Unlike ineffective managers, teachers in orderly classrooms were much less likely to lose their tempers or be sharper with the students at certain times of the day; none of these teachers was an inveterate screamer, and disruptions were often dealt with quietly and privately.

A key to dealing with disruption in the most effectively managed classrooms was thoughtful prevention. In one first-grade classroom, the teacher built a series of routines from the beginning of the year that forestalled most forms of disruption. When the class as a whole began to grow noisy, he had students talk to other students to get their attention, and he also "counted eyes." From early in the year, the teacher kept a "think list" on the side blackboard of students who had been warned twice. For every check students got by their names they had to spend five minutes at a recess "meeting" with the teacher. The students responded immediately to the teacher's discipline strategies. During one observation, the class was sitting on the rug discussing the solar system and astronauts when the teacher told a student that he had to leave. With no discussion or comment, the student stood up and walked to the tables and sat down. He was later asked to rejoin the group. The class was never disrupted to discipline one or several students. These occasions were woven into the fabric of the lesson so smoothly that they could easily slip by unnoticed.

Effective managers occasionally used strategies that were prevalent in disorderly classrooms, such as ignoring behavior and isolating troublemakers. In classrooms with orderly learning environments, however, these strategies were used selectively; teachers chose when to intervene or when to overlook small infractions, mindful of the fact that an intervention is itself an interruption that might have further negative consequences for instruction. In some cases, this meant overlooking small incidents in the interest of keeping the flow of instruction going. In such classrooms, it was also necessary from time to time to pull a student or two away from the rest of the group to keep everyone from becoming distracted. In the hands of the most effective managers, however, this device was used sparingly and for relatively short periods. Putting a student into "time out" to keep him or her from dominating the class interaction was never allowed to become a de facto tracking mechanism.

Ensuring Consistency and Flexibility of Routines

Many of the teachers we studied talked about the need for *structure* in classrooms with students from low-income homes, which typically meant creating consistent routines throughout the day and year so that performance expectations were clear and little time was lost making transitions.

In the less orderly classrooms, routines existed, but they were generally dull and repetitive (e.g., 30 minutes of seatwork drill immediately following every math lesson) or were created with no clear expectations about behavior during each segment of the lesson or day. It was apparent that routines alone, without predictable consequences or challenges, became numbing for students, who soon learned that going through the motions was sufficient. Even in classrooms with adequate learning environments, where structures were clearer, the routinization of academic tasks without allowance for student differences (except with the occasional help of an aide) almost guaranteed that engagement would be low for part of the class.

The more successfully managed classrooms resisted the extremes of no consistency and too much consistency. These classrooms were characterized by a more flexible application of routines adapted to the needs of particular students or groups. There was very little of the "dead time" that can occur when a group of students waits for directions about what to do next, and this fact alone increased the amount of time focused on academics. In classrooms with orderly and enabling learning environments, structures and schedules were clearly in place, but the classrooms didn't suffer from the "overmanaged" feel of some of the orderly, restrictive classrooms.

The freedom that comes from having shaped a responsive and respectful group created flexibility to change routines when a fresh approach seemed appropriate.

Providing Feedback and Holding Students Accountable

Closely related to the predictability of consequences, teachers' attempts to provide feedback to students and hold them accountable for performance differentiated the more and less effectively managed classrooms. Indeed, teachers' monitoring activities ranged along a continuum from almost no (or extremely capricious) attention to what students were doing (in classrooms with dysfunctional learning environments), to occasional feedback for behavior and achievement (where order was adequately but not securely established), to careful record keeping with grades or points (in classrooms with orderly learning environments). Simply put, the best managers were vigilant monitors, and the least effective managers were inattentive to, or unaware of, student progress.

Thus, in classrooms with dysfunctional learning environments, monitoring and feedback were sporadic at best, and consequences were often random. In such classrooms, both disruptions and incomplete assignments often went unnoticed. For example, in one third-grade classroom, a point system for good behavior was used, along with checks and names on the board for bad behavior, but there was no pattern as to when this system was in operation. During instructional activities, the teacher's monitoring was equally inconsistent. When she asked "Is *book* a noun or a pronoun?" and half the class yelled out each answer, she would say "Right" and move on to the next prompt. When five students were at the board doing math problems, she might pay attention to only one — sometimes not even noticing whether the others had copied the problem correctly. In reading, accountability for workbook tasks was so haphazard in this classroom that completing assignments was generally understood to be voluntary.

In the classrooms with adequate learning environments, where more academic work was done, a more structured feedback system was typically in place. Predictable consequences were likely if assignments were not completed (e.g., 10 minutes of recess time lost if math homework was not done). In such instances, the systematic approach to accounting for assignments (done/not done) inspired students to complete their work, but it did little to inspire dedication to, or interest in, the task, since it gave the students no feedback about quality of effort. Although it may have helped maintain order and encourage task engagement in a behavioral sense, this type of feedback system was not particularly useful for academic learning.

In the classrooms with orderly learning environments, students were generally more closely monitored both for disciplinary infractions and for academic work. The teachers in these classrooms were more likely to be able to tell an observer exactly how any student was doing on a given task, and the students themselves received ongoing praise or correction. In some cases, the teachers actually used information from constant interaction with the students to adjust pace or tasks or to expand the review portion of the lesson. In less orderly classrooms, the use of feedback to inform instructional planning was extremely rare.

Monitoring in the most effectively managed classrooms was nearly constant, and the incentive system worked well because students knew that they would be judged on the quality of their efforts as well as task completion. These teachers were the legendary ones with "eyes in the back of their heads," and students were keenly aware of this. Moreover, even among those teachers who closely followed a mandated curriculum, pace and approach were modified according to an ongoing assessment of student need. Teachers used various devices for carrying out this kind of monitoring. In one third-grade classroom with an orderly, enabling learning environment, the teacher would meet with small ad hoc groups of students, selected at random, to assess student progress. During the approximately 10-minute sessions, she had students take turns reading a few sentences. She usually would not interrupt them as they read, but she sometimes explained the meanings of words in the text and occasionally asked some questions to see whether the students understood what they were reading.

Careful monitoring of learning does not necessarily imply constant evaluation for correctness. The expert managers used a wide range of evaluation criteria, and standards varied by instructional style. In reading instruction, teachers could pay close attention to the students' level of understanding, their grasp of reading mechanics, or both. The best monitors were not always the teachers with the strongest emphasis on the "right" answers.

Motivating Students

Teachers used a variety of approaches to motivate students, and many of these were closely connected to the feedback mechanisms in place. Predictably, in classrooms in which students and teacher struggled over order, the absence or mechanical nature of feedback was accompanied by a general inattention to motivational matters. Teachers seemed to assume that negative consequences themselves would be the primary motivators, and the results were generally disappointing.

Within orderly classrooms, teachers paid more attention to motivation and were more likely to have established some form of positive incentive system to encourage students to work. Some of these systems were based on extrinsic rewards, and others featured intrinsic rewards.

What distinguished classrooms with orderly, enabling learning environments from those with more restrictive environments was the balance of extrinsic and intrinsic rewards. Teachers in classrooms with orderly, restrictive learning environments tended to rely more heavily on extrinsic reward systems; those with more enabling environments were likely to emphasize intrinsic incentives. In the latter case, teachers monitored students' work constantly and gave extensive feedback, but they periodically refrained from attaching positive consequences to good work. In these rooms, teachers were consciously encouraging students to see learning as its own reward. In one inner-city sixth grade, we overheard an unusual amount of "free-time" conversation about books the students were reading and possible ways of solving the puzzles teachers had made and displayed in the cafeteria. At another inner-city school, a fourth-grade teacher constantly reminded students that the purpose of various activities was to learn, accept challenges, or have fun rather than simply to win the game or get the right answer. In another classroom, which included a number of students who had displayed significant behavior problems the previous year, the teacher—an expert manager—succeeded in getting the students' attention early on, and they quickly came to enjoy the challenging work they were required to do. The teacher used a variety of approaches to cultivate motivation to learn (rather than merely to complete tasks), including modeling of interests in ideas and designing challenging but carefully structured activities.

A few of the most successful managers were able to shift the locus of the reward system over the course of the year as students became more independently motivated. In one sixth-grade classroom, the teacher had established an elaborate system of rewards for both work habits and behavior. By midyear, all but one of these systems had disappeared. The one that remained was the class point reward system for everyone working hard or everyone handing in homework. Students had learned to be responsible for their own learning and could now exert pressure on one another for academic performance to attain group goals. In several other classrooms, this kind of internalized accountability system was evident; to the observer, a point system didn't seem to be necessary.

Pacing Instruction

The pace of the instructional agenda influenced the quality of the learning environment in several ways. At first glance, the most obvious difference among classrooms appeared to be the fast pace in some versus the slow pace in others. But on careful examination, a more important distinction emerged between those with a relatively fixed pace and those in which pacing was more variable and dependent on the needs of particular students.

In classrooms with dysfunctional learning environments, teachers were more likely to march through material to meet the requirements of the district's scope-and-sequence directives, unaware that the majority of students were being left behind. In such instances, many students became effectively "lost" for the year, although some were adept at mimicking appropriate behaviors. In one such classroom, the teacher felt that she needed to cover congruence in mathematics and decided to have the students make congruent shapes with manipulatives. After handing out the manipulative blocks and telling the children to trace them, the teacher and aide spent the next 20 minutes walking around telling students to sit down, be quiet, and draw their figures. Only 3 of the 21 students drew congruent figures; most just drew pictures or made bridges or other objects with the manipulatives. The teacher didn't bother students as long as they were "on task," although many students clearly had no idea what the task was. In this way, the classroom "got through" the concept of congruence; the next day, they moved on to the next topic.

In more competently managed classrooms, much of the off-task behavior stemmed from inappropriate pacing and the resulting inability to hold students' interest. In the best-managed classrooms, the pace of lessons varied according to student response and was rarely fixed, as was typical in classrooms with less orderly learning environments. In classrooms with orderly but restrictive learning environments, teachers were still very conscious of curriculum guidelines and often focused on "getting through" a specified amount of material in a given time period.

The pace of instruction in the most effectively managed classrooms tended to vary by task and degree of student understanding. When the pace was uniformly brisk, special arrangements were made for students who didn't catch on immediately, whether or not there was ability grouping. In such instances, all students might read the same material, with the slower readers getting extra practice on the same readings with an aide.

There was great variation in the amount of pressure teachers experienced to stay on track or, in some cases, to be on a particular chapter on a particular day. Furthermore, there were enormous differences in how teachers responded to this pressure. Some teachers, particularly inexperienced ones or ones new to a mandated curriculum, adhered exclusively to the scope-and-sequence guidelines provided by the teachers' manuals. Partly to give themselves a sense of structure and partly as a management technique, they were unwilling to provide their own embellishments to the recommended activities. With a relatively homogeneous group, a brisk, steady pace by the book can be a successful management tool. Too often, however, many students are left behind, eventually tuning out and frequently causing disruptions along the way.

More creative teachers (and those who were more confident in their management skills) were often more flexible in pacing. Some could keep up a steady beat but vary the rhythm for particular students; others used creative grouping arrangements to address student differences—sometimes even when these were proscribed by the district or school management.

The interrelationship between rate of instructional delivery and classroom management underscores the complexity of searching for explanations of teacher effectiveness. Although pacing can be used successfully as a management tool, it is affected by management concerns. Questions of appropriate pacing become more complex when choices about how fast to move, how much to review, and when to move on are constrained by decisions made outside the classroom.

Balancing Student and Teacher Talk

The amount and quality of student-teacher and student-student discourse are obviously determined by many factors besides management concerns—most importantly, the requirements of specific academic tasks. The relationship between classroom discourse and management is a complex one, since the quality of talk can be both a facilitator and an outcome of an environment conducive to academic learning.

In classrooms that were the least well managed, discussion of behavioral matters tended to dominate student-teacher interaction—the teacher scolds an offender, the student responds to the allegation. In the more extreme cases, evaluative comments by the teacher occurred throughout lessons, and variations of the admonition "Of course you don't know the answer—you were talking to your neighbor" punctuated all or most of the interaction. Because of the predominance of management concerns, little extended discourse about academic matters occurred in such cases. In one extreme example, a third-grade teacher stated that her foremost goal in reading was for the students to "learn to sit quietly and listen"; since they had not mastered this behavior by the last few months of the year, she did not allow them to read or do anything during the schoolwide sustained silent reading time.

Among teachers who were more competent managers of the learning environment, less talk time was devoted to procedural and behavioral matters. However, in classrooms with adequate learning environments, teachers were typically still uncomfortable with extended discourse on any topic, and direct instruction tended to occur in short segments with rapid-fire, closed-ended questioning sequences. Some of these teachers were trying partner and cooperative learning arrangements with varying degrees of success; without careful monitoring, these tasks seemed to engage students for only short periods of time.

In classrooms with orderly, restrictive learning environments, where management strategies effectively maintained order but were nonetheless uninspiring, student-teacher interaction was still highly structured and formulaic. Since an orderly classroom allows for more spontaneous activity on the part of both teacher and students, teachers had freedom to experiment with extended discussions and different forms of student-student interaction, including various cooperative learning arrangements. Teachers who created orderly, enabling environments took full advantage of the opportunity. Although interaction in these classrooms might still involve teacher-controlled question-and-answer sequences, these teachers were often more comfortable with — and more expert at managing — cooperative or peer learning activities. In these classrooms, students interacted extensively with one another and with the teacher throughout the day.

Developing Student Responsibility for Learning

The teachers' approach to classroom discourse mirrored the extent to which they sought to develop students' sense of responsibility for their own learning. Very few of the teachers with dysfunctional or adequate learning environments ever successfully ceded partial control of the learning process to their students. A number of teachers tried activities that required more active student participation, such as peer helping or cooperative learning, but they subsequently retreated from these approaches because they thought that the students did not do well without constant monitoring and structure. Classrooms with orderly, restrictive environments were almost entirely teacher directed; although well managed, these environments never allowed student input into the structuring of tasks, other than in brief intervals after assigned work was completed.

In classrooms with orderly, enabling environments, teachers allowed for more student discretion and responsibility, even though instructional agendas were still controlled predominantly by the teacher. The timetable for encouraging student discretion varied across classrooms: Some teachers moved into increasingly independent learning as the year progressed; others were able to orchestrate student-directed activities successfully from the first day by making expectations clear and carefully explaining ways of making choices. Teacher modeling of thinking strategies, steps in problem solving, or approaches to group work was evident in every classroom where students were actively engaged in independent work. One second-grade teacher, for example, frequently modeled "good help" (showing another student how you arrived at the solution) and "bad help" (just giving someone the answer) when students worked in pairs to solve a problem. Other teachers of this sort focused on strategies for independent learning throughout the school day on nongroup tasks as well. One fourth-grade teacher in a rural school emphasized the responsibility students had for their own learning by sticking to a simple rule: She never gave answers to student questions if they were capable of figuring it out by themselves, by asking a friend, or by consulting a reference.

Combining Management Strategies

As should be clear from the preceding discussion, teachers' strategies for handling disruptions, ensuring the consistency of routines, providing student feedback, motivating participation, pacing instruction, orchestrating classroom discourse, and developing student responsibility for learning complemented one another and formed an integrated management "style." Thus, teachers in the least orderly classrooms tended to manage disruptions in an inconsistent and explosive manner, have few established routines or excessively mechanical ones, do little monitoring of student work, and so on. At the other end of the continuum, teachers who managed orderly, enabling learning environments dealt with disruptions unobtrusively and consistently, had well-established yet flexible routines, and monitored student work continuously as part of their management strategies.

A brief glimpse of one classroom illustrates how management strategies might reinforce one another:

> *Ms. Liu's sixth-grade class.* Ms. Liu uses a social skills program that features frequent cooperative learning activities. Before students start their group activity, Ms. Liu sets the stage and makes expectations explicit. Sometimes she asks them, "What should I see when you're working together?" They respond with comments such as "Heads together," "Siamese," "Leaning on your chin and elbows." She then asks, "What might I hear if you're working together?" They answer, "Talking," "Compliments," "Oh, yeah!" and "Help me." Another time she tells the class, "The skill you're working on is involvement." Indeed, she often spends time talking with the students about the group process itself and how it works best. After one group activity, Ms. Liu asks the students to think about the kinds of participation

that went on in the group: "Look at how your group participated. Did people talk together? Were heads together? Was there eye contact? If not, talk about that in your group. How did you come to agreement? Looks like most did. Is it OK to disagree sometimes?" In her attempt to help the students understand how they learn, Ms. Liu asks each student who is assigned the role of group reporter to write down the thinking that goes on in the group. When she realizes that reporters are writing down only the steps that they used to get the right answer, she encourages them to describe what they tried that did not work as well.

Ms. Liu encouraged a great deal of student-student interaction and thereby gave her students considerable responsibility for guiding their own learning, but she structured the interaction carefully to ensure that students were meaningfully engaged. She monitored their work in groups continuously and gave periodic feedback that indicated how well they were doing and what they could do to improve. As she did so, she adjusted the pace of instruction, sometimes for a particular group and sometimes for the whole class, to suit the needs of the learners. Her group-work routines were consistent yet flexible throughout the year. Her use of group work was part of an overarching motivational strategy that relied on intrinsic rather than extrinsic rewards.

MANAGING THE LEARNING ENVIRONMENT
THROUGHOUT THE SCHOOL DAY

The discussion so far has considered management strategies as though they existed independently of instructional strategies, though we have noted the frequent overlaps between the two. But the fact that management and instructional strategies are intertwined begs the question of how teachers' management approaches might vary during the school day, as the class encounters lessons in different subject areas. In this final section, we first address similarities and differences in management styles across all subject areas covered during the school day. Doing so highlights the relationship between management of the academic learning environment and design and delivery of instruction in particular subject areas.

Theme and Variations Across Subject Areas

Not surprisingly, most teachers tended to be fairly consistent during the school day with regard to the first few management strategies discussed above. These strategies appeared to derive from personal style, and the resulting classroom climate was relatively constant. Other management strategies (regarding pacing, student interaction, and student responsibility for learning) were more closely tied to teachers' instructional decisions in particular subject areas. These approaches depended on the teachers' beliefs, backgrounds, knowledge of subject matter, and ability to translate that knowledge into engaging learning activities. As a result, many of the teachers we studied managed the learning environment somewhat differently depending on what was being taught.

Expert managers with great confidence in their abilities were able to alternate instructional patterns and create distinctly different learning environments suited to specific academic goals. In one second-grade classroom, when students were sitting in rows on the rug in front of the teacher, they were to attend to the teacher and refrain from talking to other students. During these segments, the teacher was usually giving information or asking questions to assess the students' understanding. When students worked on specific assignments, they were allowed to work wherever they chose within the room; they could talk with one another and move around freely. Because the teacher monitored the students continuously throughout the less structured segments, student engagement was high throughout the day.

Clearly the teachers' choices of academic tasks themselves had implications for management of the learning environment. Challenging and novel classroom activities, for example, were often noisy and might require a great deal of student movement. We found that teachers simply had different thresholds of sensitivity to the amount of disorder required by independent tasks or group work. A few of the most expert managers were able to retain a sense of control over their own agenda while allowing for a great deal of student participation. Those with less confidence in their abilities to keep the pattern of independent learning in place were likely to rein students in sooner. One second-grade teacher described her difficulty in giving control to students: When she had the students work with math manipulatives, engagement rates seemed intermittent; she preferred to lead them through the friendly, fast-paced competitions of math facts that kept 100 percent of the students on task.

Implications for Academic Instruction

In the final analysis, it is clear that management of the academic learning environment and the nature of what is taught or how it is taught are inextricably linked. Thus it is not surprising to find the association so clearly presented in Figure 1-1: Eighty-seven percent of the managers of orderly, enabling learning environments and 50 percent of those with orderly, restrictive environments approached the teaching of one or more

FIGURE 1–1. Relationship between academic learning environments and teaching for meaning

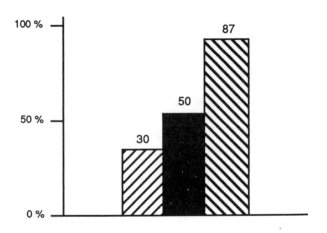

Among classrooms [a] with each type of learning environment,
the percentage of teachers emphasizing meaning
in mathematics, reading,
or writing instruction

a   Based on analysis of
     40 classrooms
     studied intensively
     during year 1

Legend

Type of academic learning environment:

 Dysfunctional or Adequate
(n=13)

 Orderly, restrictive
(n=12)

 Orderly, enabling
(n=15)

of the three subjects under study by emphasizing meaning-oriented activities, as described in Chapters 3, 4, and 5. Conversely, those teachers confronting a continuing problem of order in their rooms were unlikely to choose meaning-oriented instructional strategies; less than a third of the teachers with dysfunctional or adequate learning environments attempted this kind of instruction in one or more subject areas.

There is no simple way to disentangle the reciprocal relationship between management and instruction implied by such a finding. An orderly environment is thus both a prerequisite for academic instruction or learning and a consequence of the kinds of academic work students do. Nonetheless, the nature of the learning environment as we have defined it — some dimensions of which cut across the school day and others of which are unique to a particular lesson — is not synonymous with the approach to instruction in a particular subject area. Although they were likely to be actively pursuing meaning-oriented instruction in at least one subject area, few teachers with orderly, enabling environments did so in all three subjects, as discussed in greater detail in Chapter 8.

The problem of establishing classroom order confronts teachers in the kinds of schools we studied from the very first day of the year. At that time, laying a secure foundation for productive human interactions over the year is all-important; without a reasonable resolution of the ensuing struggle, not much academic learning of any kind will take place. The most effective managers described the process of laying this foundation in almost the same terms as they described any other aspect of their curriculum: It was a "curriculum" to be taught, and it had to be explicitly and systematically introduced to students, with associated rewards, sanctions, and reinforcement. Success with this curriculum early in the year might or might not be accompanied by immediate academic learning — that is, the teacher might not initially convey much about the content of reading, mathematics, or other subjects, but the children felt safe, respected, and attended to at the same time that they felt pushed and expected to perform. The importance of reaching this point cannot be overestimated in classrooms serving large numbers of children from low-income families.

Yet, in a paradoxical way, the resolution of management issues reflects children's response to the kind of work and work routines they experience. Typically, students in the kinds of classrooms we studied were not patient with work that was frustrating or mindless. In such situations, students often gave up because the tasks they faced appeared too difficult or incomprehensible or because the work demanded too little of them, as in the case of tasks that were simply repetitive. Thus, in classrooms in which there was a great deal of seatwork that was unconnected (in the students' minds) to anything important or interesting, teachers had a more difficult time establishing order. This is ironic, because some of these teachers emphasized seatwork precisely because they wanted to control the class. In contrast, classrooms with an interesting and varied diet of academic work were more likely to display a higher degree of order.

The resolution of many issues related to the achievement of an orderly learning environment cuts across subject areas. Although there were important connections between how their classrooms were managed and the way particular subjects were taught, each teacher we observed exhibited a basic management style that pervaded the school day. Thus, those who managed reading instruction well were, for the most part, likely to establish an orderly — but not necessarily enabling — environment during lessons in mathematics or other subject areas. Conversely, classrooms with dysfunctional learning environments tended to exhibit poor management in all subject areas.

Ultimately, choices about management approach affect the kinds of academic learning experiences available to children. Management issues tend to be resolved at a level that transcends the teaching and learning of particular subjects, and choices of management approach lead to those subjects being taught in certain ways, rule out other kinds of teaching, or both. For example, the "tight" and, from one perspective, "effective" management of classrooms with orderly, restrictive learning environments appeared to inhibit students' spontaneous responses to tasks, ideas, or discoveries they might be making as the school day unfolded. In such circumstances, extended discussion of the meaning of what had been read (a key dimension of meaning-oriented reading instruction, as described in Chapter 4) or student-student interaction while writing (an important dimension of meaning-oriented writing instruction, as described in Chapter 5) was unlikely to happen. Thus, the nature of the management system can interfere with, or enhance, the prospects for certain kinds of instructional activities.

Our overall conclusion is that the more orderly and enabling the learning environment, the more likely it is that academic considerations will guide or control what is taught and how it is taught, and the more evidence there is that such considerations have already been paramount in the teacher's instructional planning and execution. Many of the academic learning environments we studied were set by management choices made with little thought to academics. In the extreme case of the dysfunctional classroom, this fact is obvious; in many other classrooms, academic learning was happening, but it seemed to be driven more by generic management considerations than by academic learning goals. In classrooms with orderly, enabling learning environments, however, teachers seemed to feel — or create for themselves — the freedom to experiment with and enrich the academic curricula they were teaching.

CHAPTER 2

Engaging Children of Diverse Backgrounds

Patrick M. Shields

The children of poverty in the classrooms we studied, as in America in general, were *not* a monolithic group. Poverty comes in all shapes, sizes, and colors, and the student sample in our study reflected this diversity.

To begin with, the classrooms we studied were not populated exclusively by children from low-income backgrounds, though a majority of the children were growing up in impoverished circumstances: On average, 65 percent of the students received free or reduced-price lunches, a rough proxy for the poverty levels of their families. In some classrooms, however, nearly all the children lived in poverty; others served a mix of students from low- and middle-income families.

Reflecting the societal linkage between poverty and nonmainstream cultural backgrounds, the classrooms were filled with a broad range of ethnic and racial groups. Overall, 25 percent of the children in the classrooms we visited were white and 75 percent were from minority backgrounds. The largest proportion (42 percent of the total) were of African American heritage. Other groups included Hispanics (18 percent), Asian/ Pacific Islanders (9 percent), American Indians (1 percent), and other (5 percent). Yet even these categories masked important differences within groups. For example, depending on the classroom, the Asian/Pacific Islander group might include varying combinations of Filipino, Japanese, Chinese, Laotian, Cambodian, or Samoan students. Similarly, many of the classrooms we observed included students without a mastery of Standard English — including a small number of recent immigrants with no English proficiency, a significant number of students whose home language was other than English and who demonstrated various levels of limited English proficiency, and other students who spoke non-Standard English in their home communities.

Demographic markers such as poverty level, ethnicity, and language background are useful and necessary analytic tools for examining differences in populations. However, in schools—as in life—every individual's story is unique. That is the reality that teachers deal with every day. Children bring to the classroom complex combinations of circumstances and personal characteristics that are the starting point for learning. Consider Claude, an African American third grader whose father is incarcerated and whose mother is only intermittently engaged with his life. Yet Claude is lucky—he lives with supportive, loving grandparents who have bought him a computer and talk with his teacher regularly. Claude excels in school. Contrast Claude's story with Michelle's. She is a sixth grader, also African American, who has been retained twice and has physically, if not academically, outgrown elementary school. Michelle was fortunate to have a teacher who took a personal interest in all her students and believed that each could succeed. But Michelle's mother—a single parent—has an adversarial relationship with the school, which she does not hide. The messages that Michelle receives about the value of education, at least education in mainstream schools, are decidedly mixed.

Acknowledging that each story is unique and that the circumstance of being Hispanic or poor or immigrant tells us relatively little by itself, our work, as well as previous research (e.g., Heath, 1983), suggests that there are concrete aspects of students' backgrounds—often linked with ethnicity, poverty, and immigrant status—that affect how students respond to instruction and content. We know that students arrive at school with patterns of discourse, ways of interacting with adults and peers, and perceptions of the purpose of schooling and their own likelihood of scholastic success. These culturally generated characteristics help explain how children interpret and react to what takes place in the classroom. Differences in students' cultural backgrounds may also affect how teachers react and what opportunities they offer students.

The relationship between student background and what goes on in the classroom raises important questions about the way teachers respond to students from different backgrounds and the implications of their responses for student engagement in academic work. Previous research in the area suggests that teachers' responses can be important determinants of the way nonmainstream children function in school (Delpit, 1988; Tharp, 1989; Winfield, 1986). This and other research (see Shields, 1991, for a review) suggests the following working hypothesis: The more teachers acknowledge, demonstrate respect for, and build on the skills, knowledge, language, and behavior patterns that students bring to school, the more likely students will be to become engaged in academic learning and benefit from it.

In the remainder of this chapter, we address this hypothesis in light of what we learned. Although we were not engaged in a comprehensive examination of teachers' responses to students' backgrounds and did not collect systematic data on the cultural relevance of instructional materials, our study team was trained to consider how teachers took student differences into account in their interactions with students, in their design of lessons, and in their management of the academic learning environment.

HOW TEACHERS RESPOND TO DIFFERENCES IN STUDENT BACKGROUND

Two overlapping dimensions of response to diversity help characterize teachers' treatment of differences in students' backgrounds. The first of these combines teachers' perceptions of students' backgrounds (positive or negative) and teachers' actions (to provide appropriate learning opportunities or to exclude students from such opportunities). We use the terms *constructive* and *nonconstructive* to describe the two ends of this dimension. This distinction is similar to Winfield's (1986) differentiation between teachers who assume responsibility for student learning and those who shift that responsibility to others. Teachers who respond constructively believe that students can learn. Nonconstructive teachers begin with the assumption that students are inherently limited in their ability to learn because of their backgrounds. In short, we sought to distinguish teachers whose responses to culturally based differences were likely to make a more or less constructive contribution to academic learning.

Nested within the first, the second dimension involves the degree to which teachers take active, self-conscious steps to deal with student differences or, instead, proceed more passively. Teachers who respond passively either don't notice or choose to ignore such differences. In contrast, teachers who respond actively to students' backgrounds believe that they understand the important characteristics of the cultures and world experiences of the children they are teaching, and they use teaching strategies and curricular materials that reflect their convictions. Conceptually, we made no assumption that active responses would be intrinsically positive; conceivably, one could be actively nonconstructive in one's dealings with culturally different children.

The two dimensions can be arrayed together along a single continuum to describe different responses to students' backgrounds, from those that are actively nonconstructive to those that are actively constructive, with passive responses falling in between. With such a continuum in mind, we describe the principal differences in teachers' approaches to the diversity they faced.

Nonconstructive Responses

Among all the teachers we studied, only a small percentage treated students from nonmainstream backgrounds in ways that did not constructively support these children's learning. Among these teachers, most were simply unaware of, or chose to ignore, their students' backgrounds. A few, however, reacted to students from particular backgrounds in overtly negative ways.

Actively nonconstructive responses seemed to originate in negative stereotypes the teachers held about students from certain ethnic or socioeconomic backgrounds. In effect, they believed that all children from certain cultural or economic groups possess significant limitations that cannot be overcome (with rare exceptions). Teachers holding these beliefs were likely to take active steps in the classroom that restricted the academic opportunities of such students. In one first-grade room where half the students were Hispanic and the rest were white, the teacher rarely taught the children in the "low" reading group, all of whom were Hispanic, leaving their instruction to a bilingual aide. In an all-white third-grade classroom on the other side of the country, the teacher expressed very limited expectations for the members of her class who lived in a nearby public housing complex. Teachers in this category often rationalized their behavior by saying that they did not want to embarrass or frustrate these students with work that was too difficult or advanced. Therefore, the children did not get called on to answer questions or read aloud, even when their raised hands indicated their eagerness to participate.

The real tragedy with this group of teachers is the vicious circle that their beliefs and attitudes created. Negative beliefs about students' backgrounds led to lower expectations, which led to the provision of fewer or more impoverished learning opportunities. Then, when these children did not perform as well as their peers, the teachers felt justified in both their views and their practices.

A large contingent of teachers appeared to hold no overt prejudices against students because of their backgrounds, yet in subtle ways, their approach to certain groups of students placed limits on these children's learning horizons. Typically, these teachers knew little or nothing about the children's lives outside of school that might affect their participation in instruction. This ignorance led to missed opportunities, lessons that were often irrelevant to the children's lives, and misunderstandings of student behavior, resulting in misjudgments of students' needs. One school that we visited had, within the previous three years, changed from an all-white, middle-class student population to one that was primarily low-income African American as a result of court-ordered busing. In one third-grade classroom filled with the new arrivals, the teacher, a veteran with 25 years at the school, knew that the children in her classroom could and would learn. But her tried-and-true ways of explaining and illustrating new ideas and concepts often drew blank faces from the children because her examples and analogies were rooted in her experience (and perhaps the experiences of the children she used to teach) rather than that of the children she now faced.

Perhaps in an attempt to avoid controversy or overt discrimination, teachers who responded to student differences in passively nonconstructive ways often taught a "homogenized" curriculum in which all students were viewed and treated as middle class and "all-American." In politically charged and litigious times, this may seem to be a safe path to follow, but it does not help students make conscious connections between their own lives and the experiences of others. Introducing a lesson on Navajo Indians to her all-black class, one teacher talked about the Europeans taking the Indians' land and later returning some of it as reservations. She did not, however, explore parallels and differences in the New World relationships among Native Americans, African Americans, and Americans of European descent.

Constructive Responses

Other teachers approached the diversity facing them in ways that made more constructive contributions to student learning. These teachers brought to their teaching an awareness of who they were teaching, if not a clearly expressed respect. Teachers varied in how actively they built on their awareness and respect in approaching the task of teaching.

Passive, constructive responses. A number of teachers whose approach to student differences could be considered constructive responded to that diversity passively. At first glance, these teachers appeared to resemble their nonconstructive counterparts. They demonstrated no negative attitudes or dispositions toward student differences, nor did they adapt teaching and content to accommodate or reflect these differences in an overt way. The crucial difference, however, involved awareness and expectations. Unlike their nonconstructive colleagues, teachers who responded more constructively tended to possess a basic knowledge of their students' backgrounds (some were very familiar with their students' cultures). In addition, these teachers expressed uniformly high expectations of students, regardless of their backgrounds.

Perhaps most important, teachers who responded to student differences in a constructive, passive manner designed and implemented instruction so that students could bring their personal experiences into the classroom. For example, students might be asked to write about something important to them, and the teacher would be eager to gain insights from reading what they wrote. Yet the teacher would not design assignments that were based on specific aspects or dominant themes of the students' backgrounds and experiences (e.g., reading stories about leaving home or traveling to a strange country in a class with many immigrant students) and might not be quite comfortable with the unpleasant details of community or family life that some students brought from their own worlds. In one urban classroom, the teacher introduced a discussion of death and violence, but when a student commented that "a cop got beat up" in her neighborhood, this teacher's immediate response was to correct the student's use of language—"You mean a police officer?"—rather than to acknowledge or pursue the issue of police-community relations. In a similar vein, a first-grade teacher in a rural school fashioned writing assignments that elicited descriptions of life at home, but she confessed uneasiness at the descriptions of domestic violence that periodically emerged. Rather than address this issue in any way, she simply gave these children little "air time" in classroom discussions of what had been written.

For teachers who responded to students in constructive, passive ways, the development of academic skills was typically the overarching goal. Students were expected to master these skills in spite of their backgrounds. The teachers made forays into topics that were important and relevant to the experiences of the children they were teaching, but they shied away from fully acknowledging or exploring the meaning of these experiences for the topic at hand.

Active, constructive responses. Like their more passive counterparts, teachers who approached student differences in an actively constructive way tended to hold high expectations for student learning and believed that it was possible to overcome whatever disadvantages faced certain students at school (e.g., a lack of exposure to reading among some youngsters whose homes lacked most forms of printed material). Unlike their colleagues, however, these teachers believed that good teaching must build explicitly on students' backgrounds, especially on the children's cultural heritage. For these teachers, it was important to communicate explicitly to students that their cultural background was not a "problem" to be overcome but rather a strength to be acknowledged and exploited in schooling. An example of this emerged from one of the bilingual classrooms we studied:

Mr. Callio's first- and second-grade class. Mr. Callio teaches mathematics to a combined first- and second-grade bilingual class and language arts to English-dominant first graders. He is bilingual in Spanish and English and has taught a mixed population of Hispanic, African American, and white students for a dozen years, nine of them at this school, where a strong sense of community and a dedication to multiculturalism characterize the institutional ethos. Within this context, Mr. Callio holds high expectations for his students and demands strict accountability for the work assigned to them. He recognizes that his students do not arrive at school with all the skills he would like them to have and plans his instruction accordingly. At the same time, his approach builds in a respect for the strengths and backgrounds of the students in his class. For example, Mr. Callio's classroom is alive with pictures from different parts of the world, showing the different ethnic, racial, and cultural groups represented in his students. One display reads "Yo soy Latino y orgulloso" ("I am Latin and proud of it") in big letters surrounded by pictures of pyramids, indigenous Mesoamericans, and other Latino faces. Another reads "I am African American and proud" and displays pictures of African people, places, and artifacts. Mr. Callio argues that it is imperative to provide positive self-images and role models if a teacher expects students to be driven to succeed. Mr. Callio uses his Spanish extensively in the classroom — and not simply to help those students with limited English proficiency. Rather, he argues that Spanish is an important language to know and encourages his monolingual English speakers to try to learn it. One of the top students in the class, an African American male, regularly tries to piece together Spanish sentences.

Teachers like Mr. Callio did two important things that acknowledged student diversity. They tailored their instruction to overcome student background factors that could constrain student success in school *and* they made it clear that they recognized and valued the strengths and knowledge that all students brought to the classroom.

A relatively small number of teachers went even farther than Mr. Callio and others like him. These teachers' approaches to student differences could be more accurately characterized as *proactive*. Not only did they acknowledge differences, as Mr. Callio did, but they also initiated curricula explicitly designed to deal with student differences. Like Mr. Callio, those who responded proactively shared a commitment to seeing students succeed — often in rather traditional school environments — with their cultures intact and celebrated.

Beyond affirming each culture, however, teachers who responded proactively designed instruction to build explicitly on students' strengths and to address and ameliorate academic or social problems reflected in students' home lives. In addition to choosing specific curricular materials or exercises (e.g., a trade book about Africa or an essay on slavery) to maintain students' interest and communicate a respect for culture—things that teachers like Mr. Callio also did—proactive teachers altered their methods of teaching in response to students' cultural characteristics. These teachers not only used content and strategy to send signals of respect and to pique interest but also sought to take advantage of culturally generated ways of learning to teach students to acquire new skills. The efforts of a teacher who taught a fifth-grade class in which over half the students were of Asian descent provide a good example of this kind of response:

Ms. Tonouchi's fifth-grade class. Ms. Tonouchi is Japanese American and speaks "passable" Spanish, Japanese, and French. Her efforts to create opportunities for students to bring their cultures into the class-room and to communicate to students a respect for their cultures have entailed a good deal of personal time and commitment. She wrote a successful proposal to a local foundation for the purchase of multiple copies of novels and other books that would serve as the ba-sic reading material in her class. The books focused heavily on the lives of inner-city minority adolescents and their struggles growing up in big cities. She chose books that explicitly addressed issues rele-vant to Asian students, whom she thinks are often overlooked in dis-cussions about minority youngsters. In every subject area, she works hard to provide opportunities for students to direct their own learn-ing—allowing students to choose the topics they will analyze for graph-making exercises in math, for example. Beyond these activi-ties, Ms. Tonouchi also adapts instruction in response to students' strengths and weaknesses. She recognizes that her Asian students are typically able to work on their own with little structure from the teacher. She builds on this (and uses the students as role models for others) by providing many opportunities for students to direct their own learning in small groups. At the same time, she believes that the reticence of many Asians to speak up in class—a trait respected in cer-tain Asian cultures—places them at a disadvantage in school. Conse-quently, Ms. Tonouchi structures numerous learning opportunities re-quiring active student participation.

What differentiated Ms. Tonouchi and her proactive colleagues from other teachers was that they fashioned their instruction in relation to particular characteristics of their students' home cultures.

EFFECTS ON THE LEARNING ENVIRONMENT AND
STUDENT ENGAGEMENT

The way teachers approached student differences had direct implications for the classroom learning environment and, consequently, for students' engagement in academic tasks. Not surprisingly, those who were most likely to approach student differences in an actively constructive manner were also most likely to create the kind of orderly, enabling learning environment described in Chapter 1. In essence, these teachers were able to forge a positive and meaningful connection between students' lives outside of school and the world they experienced in the classroom. Their attempts to do so appeared to be linked with greater student engagement in academic learning.

Forging Personal Connections as a Management Strategy

Making instruction personally meaningful to students can increase student cooperation with the teacher's agenda, thereby reducing potential management problems. Teachers accomplished this in primarily three ways: by showing respect for and interest in students as individuals; by using personal experiences as a basis for teaching concepts and skills; and by explicitly building bridges that crossed the cultural gap that often existed between home and school.

Many teachers simply showed more consideration for their students as people; this was evident in the way they spoke, listened, and responded to them. In some cases, this meant that teachers also knew a great deal about their students' personal circumstances and family backgrounds. A few teachers worked or lived in the community (one had taught for years in the local YWCA) and had maintained relationships with the families over time. Others had less direct experience with the families but made efforts to understand their students' unique circumstances. This attention to students as individuals clearly contributed to the orderliness of the classroom, though it did not necessarily lead teachers to alter their approach to managing the learning environment. Teachers who created orderly, restrictive learning environments were just as likely as those whose learning environments were more enabling to develop this type of personal connection with students.

Many teachers used their knowledge of student backgrounds to elicit interest in and to explain academic tasks. Common examples of this approach, evident across management styles, included referring to the practical applications of learning new skills and linking reading and writing activities to students' own lives. In several cases in which teachers were not comfortable probing for students' feelings, they used anecdotes from their own lives to introduce or embellish material.

In classrooms with orderly, enabling learning environments, teachers were more likely to draw frequently on an experiential base for instructional purposes. A few teachers used students' personal experiences to integrate material across subject areas. One sixth-grade teacher, an enthusiastic proponent of integrated approaches to language arts instruction, told us, "Ultimately, everything that is taught should be tied to the real world." For her, all student learning consists of students' constructing meaning out of their own experiences, and her ideal curriculum would have all instruction revolve around themes that facilitate this process.

Either consciously or subconsciously, actively or passively, these teachers were making it possible for students to see connections between the world they knew outside of school and the world they experienced in the classroom. They thus found ways to treat students' backgrounds as a resource for learning rather than a limitation on it. Their constructive approaches to students' differences built a strong basis for managing the busy life of the classroom.

It would be misleading to suggest that most of the teachers we studied tried to forge these connections, much less succeeded. Among all the teachers we studied, the majority took few steps to explicitly connect instruction to students' backgrounds. For each subject area in each year, instruction in the majority of classrooms (ranging from 65 percent for year 2 writing to 88 percent for year 2 mathematics) had little or no overt connection to students' backgrounds. Stated another way, these classes were likely to be taught by teachers whose response to student differences was largely passive. In contrast, only a small percentage of teachers regularly connected instruction to students' backgrounds in two or more distinct ways—for example, by having students write about themselves or their experiences, highlighting students' backgrounds during prewriting activities, and focusing discussion on the personal or cultural implications of writing topics. Perhaps reflecting the nature of the subject matter and traditions for teaching it, connections to students' lives were more likely to be made in reading and writing than in mathematics.

Implications for Student Engagement

As the discussion of teacher response to student differences has implied, the act of connecting instruction to students' backgrounds is associated with students' engagement in their academic work. Quantitative data summarized in Figure 2-1 indicate that the more steps the teacher took to bring students' backgrounds into the classroom, the more consistently and

FIGURE 2–1. Relationship between student engagement and the extent to which teachers connect instruction to students' backgrounds

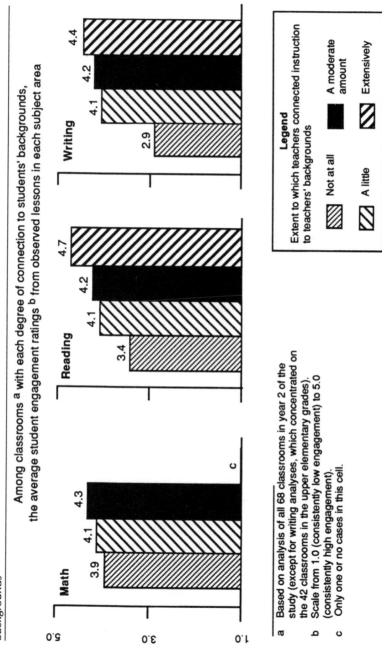

Among classrooms [a] with each degree of connection to students' backgrounds, the average student engagement ratings [b] from observed lessons in each subject area

Legend

Extent to which teachers connected instruction to teachers' backgrounds

Not at all | A moderate amount

A little | Extensively

[a] Based on analysis of all 68 classrooms in year 2 of the study (except for writing analyses, which concentrated on the 42 classrooms in the upper elementary grades).

[b] Scale from 1.0 (consistently low engagement) to 5.0 (consistently high engagement).

[c] Only one or no cases in this cell.

actively the students were involved in academic learning. For example, among math classrooms in which teachers made no connections with students' backgrounds, the average rating of student engagement was 3.9, as compared with 4.1 for those making a few connections and 4.3 for those making moderate connections.

To be sure, the indicators of engagement and connection on which the figure is based are crude at best, and the differences in engagement rates are small (reflecting the limited range of this variable across classrooms). But the pattern is unmistakable and especially clear when one compares extremes — classrooms in which teachers made no connections between instruction and children's backgrounds versus those in which extensive connections were made. What is more, the qualitative evidence from intensive observation confirms the pattern.

IMPLICATIONS FOR ACADEMIC INSTRUCTION

How teachers respond to students' backgrounds has important implications for teaching and learning in high-poverty classrooms. The potency of this factor emerges in upcoming chapters on instruction and achievement in reading, writing, and mathematics. Classrooms where teachers disparage students' backgrounds seem to be unlikely places for successful scholastic experiences and outcomes. In classrooms where teachers actively or proactively engineer constructive responses to student differences, students may have a better chance of success in both basic and higher-order skills.

As noted before, the sense of connection between home life and school is fundamental to our conception of "meaning" in teaching and learning. We consequently used indicators of the teachers' attempts to connect instruction with children's home lives as one of the components of our measures of teaching for meaning. Thus, in classrooms that emphasized meaning in mathematics, reading, and writing instruction, we expected teachers to make extra efforts to link instruction to students' lives. But other elements of these teachers' approaches to their work, which are described in the ensuing chapters, seemed to reinforce the expected linkage between responding constructively to student differences and teaching for meaning. The pattern is suggested in Figure 2-2, which shows for one year of the study the association between teaching for meaning and the degree of connection between instruction and students' backgrounds. For example, among math classrooms in which teachers made no connections to students' backgrounds, only 1 percent emphasized meaning in mathematics instruction, as compared with 33 percent of those making few connec-

FIGURE 2–2. Relationship between teaching for meaning and the extent to which teachers connect instruction to students' backgrounds

Among classrooms [a] with each degree of connection to students' backgrounds, the percentage emphasizing meaning in mathematics, reading, or writing instruction

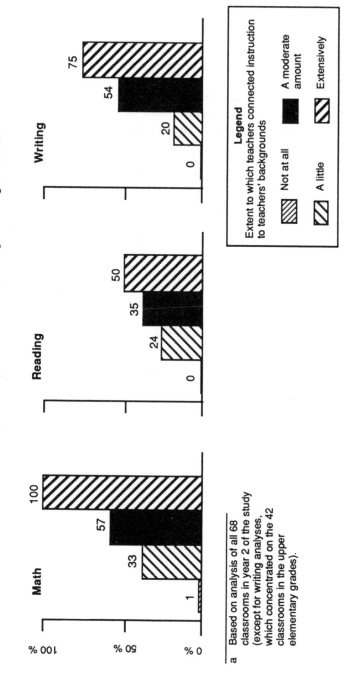

a Based on analysis of all 68 classrooms in year 2 of the study (except for writing analyses, which concentrated on the 42 classrooms in the upper elementary grades).

tions, 57 percent of those making moderate connections, and 100 percent of those making extensive connections.

Overall, what we observed in classrooms suggests that as teachers move along a continuum of responses—from those that exclude students from learning opportunities because of their backgrounds to those that ignore such differences to those that build on these differences as learning opportunities—student engagement in and excitement for learning seem to increase. The differences are more striking in reading and writing than in mathematics, perhaps reflecting the way teachers think about these subject areas. (It may be easier for many teachers to find ways for students to read or write about their lives out of school than to express the connections in the language and topics of mathematics.)

Teachers' responses to students' differing backgrounds are only one aspect of the complex way teachers manage instruction and learning in their classrooms. From this perspective, the fact that student engagement in learning (at least in reading and writing) is positively related to the extent to which teachers take students' backgrounds into account does not suggest that attempts to connect instruction to students' lives *by itself* leads to higher engagement. Caring about students is not enough. Although not caring is clearly destructive, the combination of understanding, caring, and adapting curriculum and instruction to diverse needs is necessary to create sound environments for learning.

CHAPTER 3

Emphasizing Conceptual Understanding and Breadth of Study in Mathematics Instruction

Andrew A. Zucker

The mathematics curriculum and instruction in the classrooms we studied are best understood in the light of national trends and directions advocated by members of the mathematics education reform community. Many prominent groups—for example, the National Council of Teachers of Mathematics and the National Academy of Sciences' National Research Council—suggest that major changes are needed in the way that elementary school mathematics is conceived and taught.

According to a wide variety of studies and analyses, the most common actual goal of elementary mathematics education is for children to achieve proficiency in rapid and accurate arithmetic computation. The reformers aim to reduce the time and energy spent on reaching this goal. Instead, they would have elementary school teachers place a greater emphasis on higher-order thinking skills (such as solving mathematics problems that are novel or more complex than those traditionally taught). In addition, reformers advocate an elementary mathematics curriculum that covers a far wider range of content than in the past, such as statistics, geometry, and data analysis.

There is, then, a vision of reform in mathematics education, and it has been quite widely disseminated. But vision is one thing and implementation quite another, especially within high-poverty classrooms. The reality is that the mathematics education provided in most elementary school classrooms today is little changed from that which has been provided for most of this century. In schools serving large numbers of children from low-income families, mathematics curriculum and instruction are even more likely to focus on computational "basics" to the exclusion of almost everything else (see, e.g., Oakes, 1990). Given that students in such schools appear to have many deficiencies in their grasp of basic mathematical knowledge, one might expect to find teachers redoubling their efforts to build the missing foundation, with little time to do anything else. Though this was true in many of the classrooms we observed, there were also many teachers who did otherwise.

Among the classrooms we studied, there were substantial differences in how teachers viewed mathematics, constructed learning activities, and guided the learning of the students for whom they were responsible. In fact, our classroom selection procedures (described in Appendix A) ensured variation in instructional approaches. On average, many teachers tended toward a "conventional" profile of mathematics curriculum and instruction; others departed in various degrees from conventional practice.

The purpose of this chapter is to highlight these departures from conventional practice, focusing on how teachers sought to build meaning into their teaching, and to compare them with more traditional approaches to mathematics instruction. We begin by discussing two broad strategies through which more challenging mathematics can be introduced into the classroom. These strategies form the basis of a typology by which we could distinguish fundamentally different patterns of mathematics teaching. We then describe and illustrate each pattern and finally show how they were distributed among the full set of classrooms we studied.

STRATEGIES FOR MAXIMIZING MEANING IN MATHEMATICS INSTRUCTION

Two overarching strategies for introducing and maintaining a focus on meaning in mathematics instruction help us characterize the different forms of teaching we observed. These strategies are: (1) orienting curriculum and instruction toward conceptual understanding of mathematical ideas and procedures, and (2) broadening the range of the mathematical content studied. We hypothesized that these two strategies would identify forms of mathematics instruction that would help children from low-income families (and, indeed, any children) gain greater understanding of mathematical concepts, expand their conceptions of what constituted mathematics, and increase their ability to reason mathematically when confronted with a variety of familiar and unfamiliar problems.

By focusing attention on these two strategies, we do not mean to imply that other dimensions of mathematics instruction (e.g., maximizing time on task, using educational technology) are unimportant. Quite the opposite is the case: Many features of mathematics instruction having important effects on student learning have been well documented. In addition, as we will describe, these overarching strategies subsume a great many more particular instructional approaches (e.g., creating multiple representations of mathematical ideas, engaging learners in discussions of mathematical problems and their possible solutions, deemphasizing the search for the one "correct" answer). These two strategies focus attention on the aspects of content and approach that are so often given short shrift in the schooling of children from low-income backgrounds (see Zucker, 1991).

Focusing on Conceptual Understanding

As we spent time in classrooms and reviewed weekly logs submitted by teachers, we paid attention to the relative emphasis they placed on developing skills or routine applications, on the one hand, and understanding of mathematical concepts or ideas, on the other. We noted that many teachers in the sample appeared to overemphasize the former at the expense of the latter. The nature of a math lesson in an elementary school classroom where discrete skills are emphasized is a familiar one, because this scenario is not limited to high-poverty classrooms. Because the math in these classrooms, if not most elementary classrooms, is almost always taught out of context and usually does not require students to make decisions about what mathematical process to use, teachers often offer students rote strategies for remembering procedures that will get them the right answer as they proceed with page after page of similar problems: "Remember, 'divide, multiply, subtract, bring down.' An easy way to remember this is 'daddy, mommy, sister, brother.'"

Contrast this familiar memory of fifth-grade math class with what we observed in a classroom where the teachers emphasized a conceptual approach and encouraged students to find multiple solutions to word problems:

Ms. Romero's fifth-grade math class. Ms. Romero's questions are posed to get her students to think and, when possible, to answer their own questions. On one occasion she asked a student to describe the process he used in arriving at the answer to an arithmetic-based word problem. Although the student's method (which he explained to the class) was correct, she asked the group if there was another way to solve the problem. A second student described a different approach, also correct. There was then a class discussion of the merits of solving the problem using the two techniques. During the course of the discussion, students in effect modeled for one another the process of understanding the problem and representing it in terms of arithmetic operations. Comparing the two approaches raised a number of interesting conceptual questions about the mathematical equivalence of what appeared superficially to be unrelated sequences of operations.

This example features a series of instructional strategies used by various teachers to enhance students' conceptual grasp of the mathematics they were learning. First, Ms. Romero constructed mathematical problems that could be solved in more than one way. Second, she focused students' attention on the process of solving problems as well as the answer(s) and explicitly acknowledged alternative ways of arriving at solutions. Third, by calling for alternative solutions and refraining from anointing an answer as "correct," she deemphasized rote "formula" solutions to mathematical problems. Fourth, she engaged students in discussion about the mathematical ideas or procedures involved. Fifth, she modeled ways to probe the meaning of mathematical problems or procedures.

Other strategies used by Ms. Romero and other teachers like her had a similar purpose. These teachers frequently created multiple representations of mathematical ideas (such as using pictures or physical objects as well as numerical symbols to represent an arithmetic operation). They also applied mathematical ideas or procedures to "real-life" situations and nonroutine problems, in particular, those that children might encounter in their lives outside of school.

Although they focused on conceptual understanding, Ms. Romero and other teachers did not ignore the need for their students to develop facility with mathematical skills and procedures. All mathematics classrooms that we observed, including Ms. Romero's, offered students a healthy dose of skill practice, including a good deal of rote work with "mindless" routine skills, such as memorizing multiplication tables or practicing sums. The real issue has to do with the balance between conceptual understanding and procedural skill and the relationship between the two in students' mathematical learning.

Expanding the Range of Mathematical Content

Of all the transitions currently under way in elementary mathematics education, one that seems especially important is the increasing variety being introduced into the curriculum. Slowly, the curriculum is moving away from a single-minded emphasis on arithmetic computation — a preoccupation that some observers (e.g., McKnight et al., 1987) claim is one of the central explanations for the poor performance of American students, especially those from low-income backgrounds. If it is important and desirable for students to be able to think mathematically and solve problems in domains beyond arithmetic, then they must be *exposed* to these domains, and their experience with these domains must go beyond the minimal exposure that often characterizes mathematics classrooms (e.g., a day spent on graphing as a "change of pace" after six weeks spent working on long division).

This strategy builds "meaning" into mathematics instruction in a way that is different from the focus on conceptual understanding. By giving students an introduction to geometry, statistics, estimation, measurement, graphing, logic, problem solving, and even preliminary forms of algebra, teachers convey a more expanded meaning of the concept of mathematics itself, at the same time that students are acquiring a broader repertoire of mathematical ideas and tools.

Among the classrooms we observed, the content of the mathematics curricula taught during the school year varied from a nearly exclusive focus on arithmetic computation to exposure to a much wider range of material. The third-grade curriculum designed by the teachers in one school offers a good example of how a school year of math instruction can cover far more than basic arithmetic:

Mathematics curriculum for third graders in the Washington St. School. This school's curriculum scope and sequence for third-grade mathematics is lengthy and detailed. The portion of the document covering "numbers and number systems," which includes arithmetic computation, is only one-third of the plan. That strand plus two others — geometry and measurement — are considered the core of the third-grade mathematics curriculum. In addition, four other strands are integrated into the year's work: problem solving, logical reasoning, statistics and probability, and patterns and sequences (which are also called functions in some documents). Despite the lengthy list of topics and skills to be covered, the class that we observed completed the third-grade curriculum by May and began working on some fourth-grade skills. The teacher's key strategies for covering a lot of material included presenting students with carefully sequenced problems that required more than routine skills and involved groups of students in the solutions.

As with a focus on computation, the breadth of study implied by this and similar math curricula does not preempt attention to arithmetic, although it may expand the time allocation to mathematics. Instead, the Washington St. School struck a *balance* between arithmetic and other mathematical topics that provided a healthy dose of both. As some teachers discovered, arithmetic can easily be taught in a much broader context than it normally is, so that as students encounter graphs, statistics, data analysis, geometry, and other subjects, they experience numerous opportunities to extend their mastery of basic arithmetic skills, not to mention their increasing grasp of the possible uses and meanings of numbers and number operations.

FOUR PATTERNS OF MATHEMATICS INSTRUCTION

The two overarching strategies for maximizing meaning in mathematics instruction are somewhat independent of each other. As we quickly found among the classrooms we studied, focusing on conceptual understanding did not necessarily imply a broadening of the array of mathematical topics to which students were exposed, and vice versa. Taken together as independent dimensions of mathematics instruction, the two strategies generate a simple typology by which we could identify four patterns of mathematics instruction, distinguished by the following foci:

- Focus on a broad array of topics, with emphasis on conceptual understanding
- Focus on a broad array of topics, with low emphasis on conceptual understanding
- Focus on arithmetic, with emphasis on conceptual understanding
- Focus on arithmetic, with little emphasis on conceptual understanding

As Figures 3-1 and 3-2 demonstrate, the four patterns of instruction differ in terms of the degree to which each of the two framing strategies is in evidence and in the allocation of time to mathematics instruction, the use of materials, and the role of educational technology in mathematics teaching. Classrooms with a broad topical focus in mathematics (especially those emphasizing conceptual understanding) averaged more time on mathematics per day and made greater use of calculators than arithmetic-only classrooms. Classrooms in which multiple topics were taught with an emphasis on conceptual understanding were most likely to use manipulatives as alternative representations of mathematical ideas. The more teachers departed from an exclusive focus on arithmetic computation, the more likely they were to bring calculators into instruction (after all, why spend endless days practicing long division when, in the real world, a hand-held calculator will do the job?). These indicators only begin to suggest the differences among the four instructional patterns. Classrooms in which these patterns predominated looked and felt different in various ways that are not easily represented by numbers.

FIGURE 3–1. Strategies that emphasize meaning in mathematics instruction

Among classrooms [a] with each pattern of mathematics instruction, the average value on an index indicating the presence of each strategy

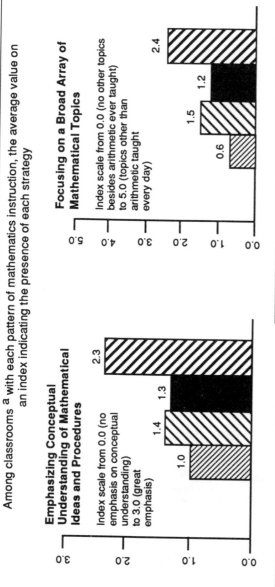

Emphasizing Conceptual Understanding of Mathematical Ideas and Procedures

Index scale from 0.0 (no emphasis on conceptual understanding) to 3.0 (great emphasis)

3.0   2.0   1.0   0.0

1.0   1.4   1.3   2.3

Focusing on a Broad Array of Mathematical Topics

Index scale from 0.0 (no other topics besides arithmetic ever taught) to 5.0 (topics other than arithmetic taught every day)

5.0   4.0   3.0   2.0   1.0   0.0

0.6   1.5   1.2   2.4

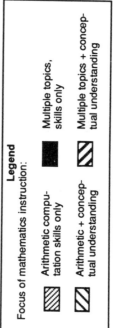

Legend

Focus of mathematics instruction:

Arithmetic computation skills only

Arithmetic + conceptual understanding

Multiple topics, skills only

Multiple topics + conceptual understanding

a - Based on analysis of all 69 classrooms in year 1 of the study.

FIGURE 3–2. Other features of mathematics instruction related to an emphasis on meaning

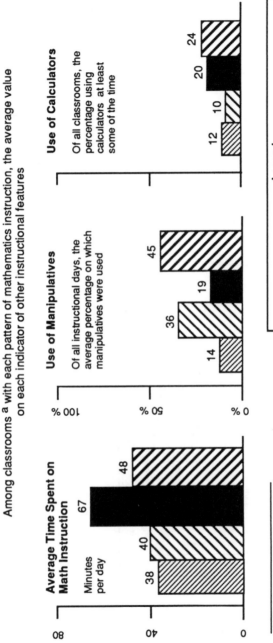

Among classrooms [a] with each pattern of mathematics instruction, the average value on each indicator of other instructional features

Use of Calculators

Of all classrooms, the percentage using calculators at least some of the time

12   10

24

20

Use of Manipulatives

Of all instructional days, the average percentage on which manipulatives were used

14

36   19   45

100 %

50 %

0 %

Average Time Spent on Math Instruction

Minutes per day

38   40   67   48

80

40

0

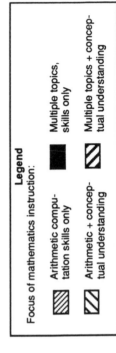

Legend

Focus of mathematics instruction:

▨ Arithmetic computation skills only

■ Multiple topics, skills only

▨ Arithmetic + conceptual understanding

▨ Multiple topics + conceptual understanding

a   Based on analysis of all 69 classrooms in year 1 of the study

Emphasizing Breadth of Study and Conceptual Understanding

The pattern of instruction emphasizing breadth of study and conceptual understanding comes closest to the vision for reform articulated by the National Council for Teachers of Mathematics curriculum standards. In classrooms displaying this pattern, teachers addressed the broad array of topics with a variety of instructional strategies resembling those already described as used by Ms. Romero: framing problems with more than one solution, inviting alternative solutions, discussing solutions, and so on. In addition, this pattern of instruction was generally accompanied by classroom organizational features and uses of instructional materials (in particular, various forms of manipulatives) that were different in kind and quality from what was typical in other classrooms. Two examples in inner-city settings located in different states provide a sense of what mathematics instruction in these classrooms can look like:

> *Ms. Ziegler's third-grade math class.* Ms. Ziegler teaches mathematics in a school that houses a science and mathematics magnet program. Students at the school receive about one and one-half hours of math instruction every day (far above the national average and among the classrooms we studied). Ms. Ziegler's room is rich with math-related materials and displays. Class usually begins with a "Mind Bender" problem. Calculators are used to solve a variety of "realistic" problems (such as spending up to $200 at a make-believe toy store), and computers are used for logic problems (as well as for skill practice). Each quarter, a schoolwide project in science or mathematics is incorporated into every classroom. The school uses the Developing Mathematical Processes (DMP) series, which teaches mathematics through measurement and a problem-solving approach and includes units on topics that are not frequently taught (such as statistics and probability). Ms. Ziegler routinely likes to aim for two or three different representations of key mathematics concepts and procedures (even more than the number used in the DMP text), so that if children do not understand one representation, they are likely to understand another.

Ms. Ziegler's situation was somewhat unusual since she taught in a school where mathematics instruction was a priority and high-quality mathematics instruction was valued. Further, she could focus on mathematics teaching because she was not responsible for her students' instruction in reading, writing, and the other subject areas that make up the total curriculum. Still, it is possible to offer children broad content and emphasize the understanding of math concepts in a more typical self-contained elementary school classroom as well:

Ms. Gray's third-grade math class. By the time we visited, Ms. Gray had made substantial adjustments to her teaching to reflect the intent of her state's new curriculum framework for mathematics. Although she emphasizes arithmetic computation skills throughout the year, she also integrates instructional strands relating to geometry, measurement, problem solving, logical reasoning, statistics and probability, and patterns and sequence. She frequently uses manipulatives to help teach concepts and assists students in making explicit connections between concepts (such as the relationship between the operations and properties of addition and multiplication). Perhaps most unusual of all, about one-third of the time devoted to math is in some sense "student directed" through the use of strategies such as cooperative learning.

In Ms. Ziegler's and Ms. Gray's classrooms, and in other classrooms displaying this pattern, there was a strong emphasis on learning concepts and learning to think, and there was a wide variety of mathematical content. However, although their classrooms displayed many of the features that reformers advocate, the full vision of mathematics teaching was not in place in most of these — at least not yet. For example, even though calculators were more in evidence in these classrooms than in those with other patterns of mathematics instruction, few made extensive use of calculators. Nor, as a group, did they make much use of computers for teaching advanced skills (as opposed to practicing arithmetic computation), emphasize the importance of problem formulation by students, or assign students complex project work in mathematics similar to what is often assigned in social studies.

Nonetheless, the classrooms displaying this pattern of instruction constitute a kind of "existence proof" of what is possible in classrooms serving large numbers of students from low-income backgrounds. Suggestions that a curriculum including a broad array of mathematics topics, combined with a strong emphasis on learning to think independently, cannot be sustained in high-poverty schools do not stand up in the face of the evidence from these classrooms.

Creating and sustaining these environments is not easy, and teachers are not routinely provided the kind of support they need to accomplish the task. The next pattern of instruction demonstrates what can happen when teachers do not get that support or do not fully understand either the mathematics itself or what is necessary to engage learners in understanding it.

Emphasizing Breadth of Study and Discrete Skills Learning

The pattern of instruction that emphasizes breadth of study and the learning of discrete skills might be characterized as failed attempts — or, at best, partial successes — in the reform of mathematics education along the lines advocated by the National Council of Teachers of Mathematics. It is unlikely that the teachers we studied would have attempted to expand the array of topics beyond arithmetic in the absence of the current reform thrust, so the fact that the attempt was being made in these classrooms can be considered one step toward the vision of the reformers. At the same time, providing instruction in these topics that focuses only on skills misses half or more of what the reform effort is all about. In one state we studied, the state framework aims to have elementary mathematics students formulating problems, pursuing conjectures, experimenting, and appreciating the beauty of mathematics. None of this is likely to occur unless the students are expected to master concepts and think for themselves about procedures — even to the point of inventing their own on occasion. Classrooms in which only skills are taught will not meet these expectations.

In a sense, the teachers displaying this pattern of instruction have learned the words but not the tune of reform. Their classrooms tended to be in settings where new approaches to mathematics instruction were actively advocated. More than half the instances of this pattern of instruction were in a state that is actively pushing reform. As an illustration of the conflicts that some teachers are experiencing around the reform of math education, we cite the following case:

Ms. Wong's third-grade math class. Ms. Wong is fairly uncomfortable teaching mathematics, and she freely admits it, devoting as little class time to this subject as she can. In response to the new state math framework, her district and school are making changes — a new textbook that takes a more conceptual approach and a centrally located mathematics laboratory that all students attend once a month. In the face of these changes, Ms. Wong feels that she *must* teach specific content (such as geometry) and *must* use particular approaches (such as manipulatives), but she is not happy about it. "I wanted to work on subtraction, but we are supposed to do whatever they are doing in math lab, so I'm doing geometry," she remarks. Her room is equipped with math manipulatives, and students are allowed to play with them, but these materials are not used meaningfully to help students learn concepts.

Ms. Wong was torn between what the district, the textbook, and the curriculum specialists represented as the "right" way to approach mathematics and her established way of treating a subject that she disliked teaching anyway. She illustrates an obvious dilemma for those who would reform mathematics education: how to create change in those classrooms in which the teachers are uncomfortable with mathematics and view an arithmetic-only approach focused on discrete skills as basically good and appropriate.

Emphasizing Arithmetic and Conceptual Understanding

The third pattern of instruction is characterized by a traditional focus on arithmetic computation, but the teachers who displayed this pattern also placed a substantial, often explicit emphasis on the importance of understanding the mathematical concepts underlying the skills. In short, these teachers introduced their students to a powerful, though limited, mathematics.

Teachers in this group tended to be impressive individuals. A number were recognized as exemplary or lead teachers (such as one third-grade teacher who was a lead science teacher in a regular elementary school before moving into a school with a mathematics and science magnet program). Many were described as having a "commanding presence." Students typically paid close attention to what was happening in these mathematics classrooms because the teachers insisted on it.

Nearly all the teachers in this group had established clear mathematical thinking as a prominent goal for their classes. One teacher with a combined fifth- and sixth-grade classroom stated that her general goals in mathematics were "to have the students think, problem solve, comprehend, and be creative." Such goals contrast sharply with those established by most teachers who displayed the preceding pattern, as well as those who focused on arithmetic computation skills only; both were more likely to emphasize mastery of discrete skills, doing well on tests, or covering the book.

The teachers in this group did not typically believe that there is a trade-off between teaching for mastery of skills and teaching for understanding (our typology does not imply an either-or dichotomy of this kind). Many of them included skill drills as well as activities (such as manipulatives) and other instruction aimed at developing an understanding of concepts. Ms. Smith's strategy is a good example of the combination of emphases in these classes:

Ms. Smith's first-grade math class. This young teacher, who works with impoverished children in an inner-city setting, sets two major mathematics goals for her students: development of an understanding of mathematics (primarily numbers, numeration, and arithmetic) and the ability to perform arithmetic computations accurately. Her routine includes drill-and-practice activities aimed at developing "automaticity" (e.g., chant-counting by fives and by tens, computer games). Yet almost every day, Ms. Smith also makes expert use of mathematics manipulatives and demonstrations to help children develop an understanding of arithmetic concepts. She was observed one day having students "act out" addition and subtraction problems and frequently asks students who are having trouble to "think about it" (e.g., "someone's taking it away from you . . . will you have less or more?").

Most often, classrooms like Ms. Smith's hum during math instruction; they have regular instructional segments that are well known to the children and are missed when they do not occur. Several other teachers in this group began each class with a "Mad Minute" — a timed test that focuses on rapidity and accuracy in solving basic arithmetic fact problems — before moving on to teacher-directed portions of the day's lesson.

This group of teachers tended to place a high value on children's thinking and on their understanding of the material. However, the way that the teachers approached this goal differed significantly from one classroom to the next. Several teachers followed the textbook quite faithfully; others used the textbook often but supplemented it with other materials and approaches; in still other classrooms, textbooks were hardly used at all. One of the teachers who gradually abandoned the textbook as the year went on commented, "There's not much in there for them" (her first-grade students); she was enrolled in a mathematics methods course at a local university and became adept at devising her own lessons. There was a similar diversity of approaches toward the use of calculators and computers. Several classrooms in this group made almost no use of these electronic tools, whereas they were regular features of instruction in others. One teacher hauled out the calculators on most Fridays and involved students in solving problems with "real-world" (messy) numbers. Still, we observed little application of computers to teaching advanced skills in any of the classrooms in any group.

Some of the differences among classrooms displaying this pattern of instruction were a function of grade level. The first- and second-grade teachers in this group made extensive use of manipulatives (Unifix cubes, beans or other counters, and so forth) to represent mathematical ideas and procedures, as in Ms. Smith's classroom; the third- and fourth-grade teachers made less frequent use of manipulatives; and in the fifth- and sixth-grade classes there was almost no use of these items.

Emphasizing Arithmetic and Discrete Skills Learning

The fourth pattern of mathematics instruction was characterized by an almost exclusive priority placed on the goal of mastering computation skills. Doing the procedures rapidly and accurately was more highly valued than understanding why the procedures work or learning how to apply the knowledge to new situations. Worksheets consisting of groups of similar numerical problems form a handy symbol of this approach to instruction (although they play a significant role in the other patterns of mathematics instruction as well).

Some teachers who focused on arithmetic without attention to conceptual understanding did very little actual instruction, relying instead on worksheets to accomplish their goals, as in this case:

Ms. Hayes's first-grade math class. The typical math lesson in this classroom consists of a few minutes of lecture or demonstration, combined with long periods of seatwork. The worksheets cover what is in the textbook. However, in part because there is so little real teaching, there is almost no way for students to grasp the meaning of the skills and procedures conveyed by the worksheets. Throughout the year, it appears as if the teacher is just carrying out the curriculum without a lot of attention to whether the children understand what is taught. Students are uncertain what addition really means and why or when one would want to do it. Ms. Hayes's main interest appears to be whether the children can produce the correct answer to $6 + 3 = ?$ It should come as no surprise that there is almost no student-student interaction in this classroom unless the children surreptitiously help one another.

Although Ms. Hayes's method represented an extreme in the amount of seatwork assigned, other teachers who used more varied instructional formats while focusing on arithmetic and discrete skills learning still conveyed to students a relatively impoverished form of mathematics: In these classrooms, mathematics meant little more than a task to be completed. The lack of student-student interaction that typified Ms. Hayes's room was all too common in other classrooms displaying this pattern of instruction, which further diminished the students' already low opportunity to ask questions, rehearse what they had learned, or learn from someone—another student — whose style was different from the teacher's. To be sure, some teachers focusing on the mastery of arithmetic computation used stimulating and sometimes imaginative devices to give their students practice, but neither more concrete materials nor game formats (in which students had at least minimal interaction) could change the restricted view of mathematics that pervaded the classrooms in this group. In one fifth-grade classroom, a 50-minute math class typically comprised five or six segments, including several review exercises, a game, the introduction of a new skill, and time to practice the skill. All activities, however, were focused on computation and getting the right answer. There was a lot of variety and relatively high student engagement, but in the end, mathematics was seen by the children as a series of discrete, skills-oriented tasks to be completed *for* the teacher.

Overall, the teachers in these classrooms were a diverse group. Some liked mathematics, and some did not; some were well liked by their students, and others were not. A few believed that they were aiming at higher-order thinking skills ("teaching the children to think"), even though the data suggest that they spent little time helping their students develop conceptual understanding. More often, however, teachers in this group expressed such opinions as, "These students need lots of drill and practice," or "The children cannot learn higher-order thinking skills if they don't have the basics," or "They cannot move on to division until they've mastered multiplication." These teachers adopted a linear view of curriculum, grounded in a rigidly hierarchical conception of their subject. These views were often coupled with limited expectations for their students.

Some teachers in this group did make use of manipulatives, but most did so only to motivate students. One teacher said as much: She used manipulatives simply because they captured students' interest and attention. By contrast, teachers focusing on conceptual understanding were much more likely to point to cognitive reasons for using manipulatives (e.g., a first-grade teacher who said, "The concepts just aren't there yet; going back to the concrete is the only thing to do"). Because they tended not to see manipulative objects as representations of mathematical ideas, few teachers whose sole goal was improving computation skills exploited the learning potential of these objects; they used them but didn't necessarily understand how or why they should be used.

The great majority of the teachers focusing on arithmetic computation without an emphasis on conceptual understanding stuck close to a traditional textbook. They tended not to supplement the textbook with puzzles, novel problems, or other types of print-based mathematics activities drawn from the vast storehouse of material that was generally available to them (e.g., through journals and specialized publications). In a few cases, the newer, less traditional textbooks were actually subverted by the teachers. One third-grade teacher (who appeared to teach other subject areas in a somewhat limited way) said that she preferred texts "with few words," and she was observed to use a lot of traditional worksheets to "supplement" the textbook.

Compared with the other groups, relatively few teachers displaying the fourth pattern of instruction made use of calculators. One teacher we interviewed suggested that she would be willing to buy one calculator out of each of her paychecks until she had a good supply, but she was the exception (the generally low level of calculator use among all the classrooms we studied seemed to be due, in part, to the fact that schools and classrooms did not have them in stock). Although few teachers across the entire sample indicated a strong desire to use calculators in their instruction on a regular basis, such a stance is most easily understood among teachers whose sole goal was the mastery of computation skills. These teachers generally believed that the use of a calculator would defeat the purpose of mathematics instruction, namely, learning to compute. One fifth-grade teacher in this group, frustrated with the poor performance of a student on a long division exercise, told her class, "This is the problem with calculators and parents who do homework and don't explain." Our data suggest that few, if any, of the students in her class ever used a calculator in school.

Limited use of computers as an electronic means of practicing arithmetic procedures was quite common in classrooms that focused on computation skills. Although only a few of the teachers in this group used computers extensively, it was not unusual to find that students went to a centralized computer lab once a week or every other week to practice arithmetic skills. Often, the software was in a game format of one kind or other, for example, rewarding students with laps around a simulated race track based on the number of arithmetic problems answered correctly.

HOW PATTERNS OF MATHEMATICS INSTRUCTION WERE DISTRIBUTED AMONG CLASSROOMS

As the preceding discussion might imply, these four patterns of mathematics instruction were not equally represented among the classrooms we studied. The actual numbers of classrooms conforming to each pattern appear in Table 3-1. As the table shows, the pattern of instruction that most exemplified discrete skills teaching — mathematics instruction focused solely on arithmetic, with primary attention to procedural skills — oc-

TABLE 3-1. How patterns of mathematics instruction were distributed among classrooms

	Number of Classrooms		
Patterns of Instruction	**Year 1**	**Year 2**	**Total**
Focus on arithmetic computation skills only	26	21	**47**
Focus on arithmetic, with emphasis on conceptual understanding	21	17	**38**
Focus on multiple mathematical topics, with emphasis on skills only	5	10	**15**
Focus on multiple mathematical topics, with emphasis on conceptual understanding	17	20	**37**
Total	**69**	**68**	**137**

curred in the largest number of classrooms (34 percent of all the classrooms we visited). However, we encountered the pattern of instruction that placed the greatest emphasis on meaning—a broad topical focus, with an emphasis on conceptual understanding—in a substantial number of classrooms (27 percent). In a similar number of classrooms (28 percent), the focus was solely on arithmetic, with an emphasis on conceptual understanding. Relatively few (11 percent) focused on a broad range of mathematical topics yet treated them as a matter of discrete skills teaching.

We also checked to see whether certain patterns of instruction were more likely at one grade level than another. Such was not the case: The two overarching strategies were as likely to be present (or absent) in first-grade classrooms as in those at the upper end of elementary school. Teachers who used meaning-oriented strategies saw the need to do so regardless of the age of the children they were teaching.

In later analyses attempting to link teaching for meaning with student outcomes (see Chapter 7), we concentrated on the two patterns (the first and last discussed in this chapter) that represented the sharpest contrast between an orientation toward discrete skills and an orientation toward meaning. The other two represented interesting hybrids, but, given the limit on outcome analyses, we believed that it would be less productive to explore the more subtle differences that might exist between these and either of the other two forms of mathematics teaching.

CHAPTER 4

Aiming Reading Instruction at Deeper Understanding

Nancy E. Adelman

As with mathematics, our study of reading instruction in high-poverty classrooms took place at a time when national concern about improving literacy skills was high and sweeping proposals for the reform of reading instruction—indeed, language arts instruction as a whole—were being given serious consideration in many quarters. Although reading experts are more often divided than mathematics educators on the nature of the problem and its solution, there is nonetheless widespread support for certain broad principles guiding a reformed approach to reading instruction.

Traditionally—and particularly for economically impoverished students, who are often considered language impoverished—reading instruction has been organized in a linear fashion leading from parts (letters, words) to increasingly larger wholes (sentences, paragraphs, whole stories). This approach sets the mastery of letter sounds, blends, vowel rules, and a basic sight-word vocabulary as a precondition for "real" reading. But thinking appears to be changing about the necessity of this precondition and about the ways learners acquire mastery over these features of reading. Many experts currently advocate a view of reading curriculum and instruction that (1) emphasizes meaning and deemphasizes discrete skills taught in isolation, (2) encourages wide exposure to appropriate and interesting text, and (3) focuses on material that connects with students' experiences and backgrounds (see Knapp, Turnbull, & Shields, 1990; Knapp & Needels, 1991).

A central issue has to do with the likelihood that children with apparent deficiencies in all of the presumably prerequisite skills will, in fact, attain higher-order reading comprehension skills. Our work was driven by a concern, increasingly voiced by reading experts, that the students in high-poverty classrooms may not be sufficiently exposed to instruction that helps them make sense of what they are reading, beyond a superficial or literal rendering of the printed words on the page. Correspondingly, these children may be receiving more instruction than is necessary or optimal in the "basic skills" of reading.

STRATEGIES THAT MAXIMIZE MEANING IN READING INSTRUCTION

Many of the teachers we studied had found various ways to get their students beyond mastery of discrete reading skills. Four instructional strategies distinguished the teachers in terms of their emphasis on understanding in reading: (1) maximizing the opportunity to read, (2) integrating reading with writing and other subjects, (3) focusing on meaning and the means for constructing meaning, and (4) providing opportunities to discuss what is read and extend knowledge.

Each of these strategies captures a different dimension of reading instruction. Teachers may use the strategies singly or in combination (including all at once) as they attempt to teach their students to read. As a preview to our discussion, Figures 4-1 and 4-2 summarize key indicators of each strategy. Each of the indicators in Figure 4-1 is broken out into a low, medium, and high range as a simple way of portraying when a strategy was given low (or no), moderate, or high priority in a teacher's approach to reading instruction. In Figure 4-2, the indicators of a focus on deeper understanding and the embeddedness of skill instruction are broken out by categories of third indicator (whether or not comprehension strategies were explicitly taught), which was closely linked with the first two. We refer back to these figures in the following discussion and make mention of variation across grade levels (not shown in the figures), where appropriate.

Maximizing the Opportunity to Read

This strategy is based on a simple premise: Students learn to read well by actually reading text on a regular basis. One indicator of this dimension is obviously the number of minutes spent reading. Although most children in this country spend approximately 6 hours a day, 5 days a week, in school, some children have much more opportunity than others to become immersed in actual reading of whole text. Some classrooms we observed offered students an abundance of opportunity to read all day, in all areas of the curriculum, with skilled teachers taking every occasion to directly or subtly increase student facility in understanding and interpreting text. Others severely restricted students' access to print, sometimes—but not always—for reasons that were largely beyond the control of the individual

FIGURE 4–1. Strategies that emphasize meaning in reading instruction

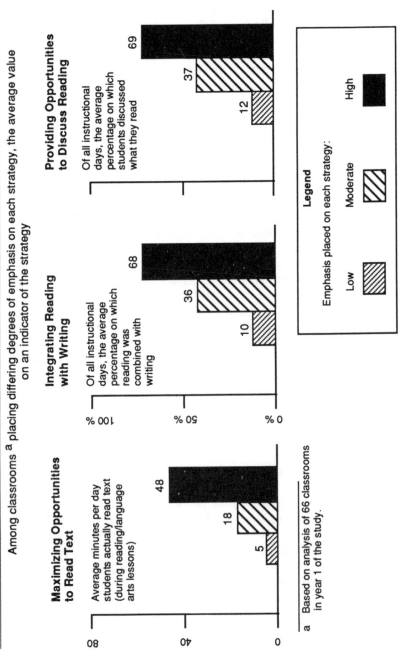

Among classrooms [a] placing differing degrees of emphasis on each strategy, the average value on an indicator of the strategy

Maximizing Opportunities to Read Text

Average minutes per day students actually read text (during reading/language arts lessons)

48
18
5

Integrating Reading with Writing

Of all instructional days, the average percentage on which reading was combined with writing

68
36
10

Providing Opportunities to Discuss Reading

Of all instructional days, the average percentage on which students discussed what they read

69
37
12

Legend

Emphasis placed on each strategy:

Low   Moderate   High

[a] Based on analysis of 66 classrooms in year 1 of the study.

FIGURE 4–2. Strategies linked to explicit teaching of ways to comprehend text

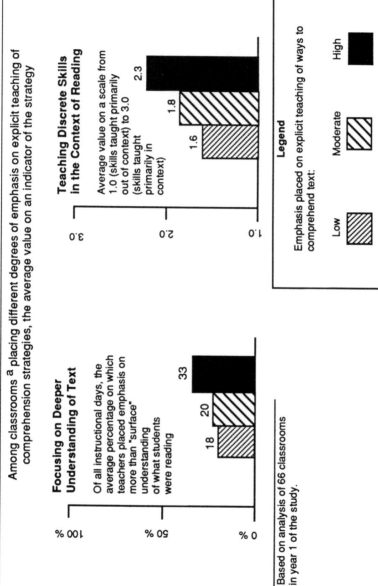

Among classrooms [a] placing different degrees of emphasis on explicit teaching of comprehension strategies, the average value on an indicator of the strategy

Focusing on Deeper Understanding of Text

Of all instructional days, the average percentage on which teachers placed emphasis on more than "surface" understanding of what students were reading

18 20 33

Teaching Discrete Skills in the Context of Reading

Average value on a scale from 1.0 (skills taught primarily out of context) to 3.0 (skills taught primarily in context)

1.6 1.8 2.3

Legend

Emphasis placed on explicit teaching of ways to comprehend text:

Low Moderate High

[a] Based on analysis of 66 classrooms in year 1 of the study.

classroom teacher, such as an overall organization of the school day or curriculum that broke up instructional time into numerous small units.

Students in the classrooms we observed spent, on average, about half an hour a day reading text during the reading/language arts block of time (this does not include reading that may have occurred during social studies, science, or other periods of the day). Grade level did not seem to have much impact on this estimate, but across the two years of the study, we noted an increase in average daily time that students were engaged with text—from about 30 minutes to closer to 40 minutes. We suspect that this increase in the time students spent directly engaged with text was more than a meaningless fluctuation and resulted directly from the fact that more teachers embraced instructional strategies promoted by literary basal readers, which were coming into use in most of the districts we studied. Teachers' manuals for these books tend to encourage both silent and oral reading of a selection; previously, teachers might have been expected to do only one or the other. The result was a net gain in minutes spent reading.

As usual, an average figure masks a great deal of variation. Surprisingly, in some classrooms (indicated by the "low" group in Figure 4-1), students read actual text for less than 5 minutes a day. Of course, the children in classes where text reading was minimal did read, but most of the reading they did was related to seatwork assignments—workbook or worksheet pages emphasizing discrete skills outside the context of reading for meaning. Students in the larger "moderate" group (44 percent of the observed classrooms) averaged 18 minutes, and the "high" group of classes in Figure 4-1 offered an average of 48 minutes a day of direct student engagement with text. Classrooms representing all grade levels were quite evenly distributed across the opportunity-to-read groupings; grade level thus cannot explain much of the variation.

In addition to differences in the time devoted to reading extended text, classrooms varied a good deal in the average total time allocated to reading instruction. This statistic (not shown in Figure 4-1) includes all reading instruction time, excluding transitions and time taken up with management issues at the beginning or end of a reading block. The range was from an hour of daily reading instruction for classrooms classified "high" in the figure to a little less than half an hour for those classified "low." Clearly, over a school year, some children spent a great deal more time in reading instruction than others.

Overall, the magnitude of the differences in time spent reading text among the three groups was striking. Common sense alone dictates that spending 48 minutes a day reading paragraphs, stories, and books will have a substantially different effect than spending 5 minutes a day reading in class, with little opportunity to interact directly with whole text. The differences become even more marked if we think about what this means over a full school year. On average, students in the "low" group of classrooms spent a total of about 15 hours (or about 3 instructional days) reading—assuming a 100 percent attendance rate (which is highly improbable). In contrast, students in the "high" group read for 144 hours (or about 29 instructional days). At a minimum, this disparity is bound to have an impact on what students think reading *is*. For some, it is a series of seatwork assignments involving short answers and unrelated words or sentences. For others, reading period is an opportunity to read another chapter in a novel or a selection in a basal reader.

The variability on this dimension is not simply a matter of minutes allocated to reading instruction. Many high-opportunity-to-read classrooms offered children an environment suffused with a literary richness. Regardless of their skill levels or personal backgrounds, students in these settings were surrounded by the written word, spent a great deal of time with books of all types in their hands, read or looked at picture books (sometimes when they should have been doing something else), and generally seemed to have assimilated the notion that reading is a desirable activity. Even some classrooms in the moderate range in terms of time measures successfully created a sense that reading was useful and important.

Based on our observations, the amount of time that children spent reading text also varied among students *within* each classroom, which may lead to differences in student outcomes. Individual children "catch on" to the concept of reading at different rates. Particularly in districts where whole-group instruction was emphasized, teachers worried about both the children who inevitably started to fall behind the pace and those who could go faster. The most typical responses to individual differences such as these were extra attention for the slower learners and enrichment for those who were ahead of the class. For example, in one first-grade room that fell within the high-opportunity-to-read category, the teacher arranged the daily schedule so that the lowest of her three reading groups received a "triple dose" of reading. Prior to participating in the day's lesson with the whole class, these children had the opportunity to go over what was to be read that day first with a teacher's aide and then with the school's reading specialist. (The trade-off was a little less time for these children on writing and other language arts activities.)

Of course, a teacher's need to cope with the different pacing needs of students does not always result in more reading time for the slowest children. We observed some classrooms where students who needed the most attention received the least. In one classroom, the teacher always worked with the top group first and gave them the most time. The middle and low groups bided their time with busy work that did not include reading text because "the material is too hard for them to do silent reading."

There is some evidence from our observations that students in split-grade classes (e.g., a room where half the children are third graders and half are fourth graders) tended to have fewer opportunities to read text. For example, in one combined first- and second-grade classroom, which also had some ESL (English as a second language) students at both grade levels, the teacher attempted to implement the whole-class instructional approach that her district preferred by creating four ability-based reading groups with very different needs and skill levels. Trying to ensure that each group had adequate opportunity to work with her and engage with text became an extremely frustrating experience for the teacher. In another combined classroom — this one at the fifth- and sixth-grade level — the teacher was not given enough of the literature-based textbooks and accompanying trade books to go around. As a rule, her 33 students were rarely able to have a book to themselves and were never allowed to take books home. Obviously, these children's opportunities to read were severely curtailed in comparison with those in other situations.

Integrating Reading with Writing and Other Subjects

Instructional strategies that encourage students to write about what they read represents a second strategy that reportedly enhances reading comprehension. The act of composing itself causes writers to review mentally what they know or understand about the story or passage. The approach also gives teachers a window on student misunderstandings or misinterpretations about the reading material.

Most of the classrooms we studied appeared to integrate reading and writing activities quite frequently (an average of one-third to one-half of all instructional days across all classrooms over the two-year period). This is certainly more often than we would have predicted at the outset of the study. Our initial hypothesis was that little writing of any kind would be found in the sample classrooms. In the majority of classrooms, that did not prove to be the case. Largely, we suspect, because of district adoption of the new literary readers or new curriculum guidelines emphasizing an integrated approach to language arts, many teachers routinely engaged children in activities that required them to write about what they had read.

Once again, we grouped the classrooms into high, moderate, and low groups in terms of their emphasis on integrating reading and writing. For the small number of classrooms designated "low," related reading and writing activities occurred an average of 1 day in 10, as shown in Figure 4-1. In the "high" group of classrooms, teachers integrated reading and writing on two-thirds (68 percent) of all instructional days during the year. The "moderate" group averaged approximately a third (36 percent) of all days with some form of integration of writing with reading lessons. There is thus the same wide discrepancy in the experiences of students on this score as there was in the opportunity to read whole text — and the same possibility that if the integration of writing and reading helps children develop reading comprehension skills, as some literacy experts claim, then students in the high-group classrooms might be gaining a significant edge on their peers who did less writing (see, e.g., Snow, Barnes, Chandler, Goodman, & Hemphill, 1991).

Classroom observations gave us some insights into how teachers used writing activities to reinforce or extend children's grasp of the material they were reading. In one third-grade classroom where half the students were Hispanic and half were white, the teacher devoted nearly three hours every morning to a fairly seamless block of time for reading, writing, and language arts. Her instructional units were thematically coordinated, usually around a book. When the class read *Charlotte's Web*, they wrote poems about the story as well as factual papers about farm animals. Elsewhere, a fifth-grade teacher had her students write frequently about the conceptually difficult novels they were reading. She firmly believed that writing facilitated reading comprehension and that her writing prompts encouraged the students to examine big ideas; in one lesson she asked the children whether their sense of justice was offended by what they had just read and requested that they write out their responses.

These teachers and some of the others we visited tended to create their own reading-related writing assignments. Most teachers who had children do substantial writing related to reading, however, relied on the prepared exercises or suggested activities that accompanied their literary reading series. As we noted earlier in the chapter, publishers of these texts have restructured workbooks and worksheets to include many more occasions when students are asked to respond to questions or ideas about a reading selection in sentence or paragraph form. The source of ideas for reading-related writing assignments was less important, however, than the fact that reading and writing were integrated as often as they were.

Focusing on Meaning and the Means for Making Sense of Text

In some sense, nearly all the teachers of reading we observed "focused on meaning." They wanted their students to become "good" readers, by which they meant independent readers who could use the printed word for their own pleasure and to obtain information. Whatever it took to achieve these ends, they were willing to do. In general, they were seeking some optimum but often not clearly defined mix of discrete skill instruction and teaching aimed at promoting comprehension. Nevertheless, among them, there were substantial differences in (1) how explicitly they taught children different strategies for making sense of text; (2) how much they attempted to promote children's ability to read for deeper-than-literal meaning; and (3) whether they "embedded" their teaching of discrete skills within, or closely linked it to, the act of reading text. What is more, these three aspects of approach to reading instruction appeared to be linked to one another, as suggested by the indicators displayed in Figure 4-2.

Explicit teaching of comprehension strategies. Students do not acquire the ability to search for deeper meaning by osmosis. Teachers must structure opportunities for children to learn how to analyze and think about what they have read. We therefore paid close attention to the ways in which teachers explicitly modeled or otherwise helped students develop comprehension skills, particularly the skills that lead to deeper understanding of text. Although cognitive psychologists continue to debate the efficacy and transferability of direct instruction in higher-order thinking skills, reading specialists suggest that classroom teachers can help children improve their comprehension by explicitly teaching or modeling the mental steps involved in particular aspects of reading comprehension, such as interpretation, prediction, or analysis of a situation (e.g., Garcia & Pearson, 1991).

Observers found that, on average across all grades, teachers did *something* related to explicit instruction in comprehension strategies in about two-thirds to three-fourths of the observed reading lessons. Some teachers taught children to use context clues — the pictures, title, chapter headings, and other features of the written work — to help them develop a richer set of tools for interpreting (or even grasping at a more literal level) the sentences and paragraphs they were reading. Others stopped children periodically during an episode of reading to have them make predictions about the direction a story might take and to indicate why they thought so. Still others talked aloud about their own mental processes for trying to make meaning from words on the page. A few teachers did all these things and more.

Attention to deeper-than-literal meanings. While students were reading each day (and all did for at least a few minutes a day, on average), teachers had at their disposal various means for drawing children's attention to different levels of meaning in the text they were reading. They did so primarily by asking questions as part of a preview to reading, during pauses in a session of read-aloud practice, or as part of a discussion about the text being read. The nature of their questioning (and the goal of the lesson) could focus on the literal, surface-level meaning of the words and sentences, or it could go deeper, probing for what was not directly said — inferences about causes and effects, hunches about the motivations of characters in a story, implications of an expository piece for other settings, and so on. By observing how teachers used questions during reading lessons and asking them to keep track of their own questioning patterns through the daily logs, we were able to track teachers' efforts in this aspect of their teaching.

As a crude indicator, the percentage of days teachers reported focusing on deeper understanding of text (as opposed to the surface meaning of words on the page) gave some indication of differences among teachers. As noted in Figure 4-2, teachers who were most likely to teach explicit comprehension strategies focused on deeper understanding nearly twice as often as those who were least likely to teach these strategies (33 percent of all instructional days in year 1 of the study versus 18 percent). Also, there was a general increase from the first to second year of the study among many teachers, who appeared to be making greater efforts to use probing questions in response to the adoption of new types of reading programs developed by commercial publishers.

Watching teachers pose questions, we could not always tell how focused on meaning they were or how fully they understood what they were doing. Many teachers relied on the questions formulated in teachers' editions of textbooks; some read them directly from the pages, and others paraphrased. There was some variety in the level of comprehension addressed by these questions. In addition to questions that drew attention to specific details of a reading passage, the publishers included items that encouraged teachers to have children predict what would happen next, put themselves in a character's shoes, analyze character traits, and so on. Drawing on these prompts, some teachers consciously and deliberately posed a range of questions and activities and could talk articulately about why they did so. But other teachers seemed to ask higher-order questions simply because these questions were in the teachers' manual; they were apparently unaware of any qualitative differences among the questions they posed. Similarly, some teachers did not seem to grasp that the strategies students used to answer predictive or analytic questions would be any different from the skills needed to locate a phrase in the text.

Embedding skills instruction in the reading of text. Figure 4-2 also indicates that teachers who did little explicit teaching of how to go about understanding a piece of text also tended to teach reading mechanics skills out of context. Conversely, teachers who emphasized comprehension strategies were more likely to find ways of embedding skill instruction in their actual reading activities. Some teachers even made it look easy. During a discussion of a chapter of a novel, one sixth-grade teacher read a sentence from the book and asked students to turn it into a direct quotation. When the students stumbled on this task, she reminded them of a previous activity in which they had rewritten a chapter of the book in the first person: "That's what we have to do here." Teachers who gave meaning a high priority in reading instruction resisted the obvious temptation in high-poverty classrooms to spend a great deal of time teaching discrete reading skills, particularly where tests indicated that these skills had not been mastered.

By embedding their teaching of skills in context, the meaning-oriented teachers we studied paid no less attention to discrete reading skills than their counterparts who taught these skills entirely out of the context of printed text. By the same token, no teacher we observed did all of his or her skills teaching in relation to text; there was still time set aside for isolated drills of one kind or another. The real distinction between meaning-oriented teachers and their more skills-oriented colleagues had to do with the *relationship* they forged between the learning of skills and the act of reading text. In the hands of meaning-oriented reading teachers, skills were taught as tools to be used immediately (or very soon) in the work of making sense of the printed page, not to be mastered for their own sake without clear applications to the act of reading.

Teachers' approaches to teaching discrete reading skills also varied somewhat by grade level. Phonics played a very minor role in the fifth-grade classrooms and occupied relatively little time at the third-grade level, although teachers at both these levels continued to instruct or remind students about word attack skills, the meaning of prefixes and suffixes, and homonyms or homophones (in addition, some third and fifth graders in these classrooms continued to receive some phonics review in supplemental instruction classes, as described in Chapter 6). But in the first-grade classrooms, the teaching of phonics and other beginning reading skills was a high priority. The great majority of first-grade teachers we studied said that the introduction to reading must combine and balance skills instruction with reading of real and meaningful material. One first-grade teacher articulated a four-pronged philosophy of teaching literacy skills to young children that emphasized motivation to read, exposure to written material, teaching of basic decoding, and the opportunity to manipulate words through writing. This teacher spent about equal amounts of time on skill building and reading comprehension, but the skills were taught mainly out of context; in other first-grade classrooms studied, much of the skill teaching was accomplished as part of reading text.

Providing Opportunities to Discuss Reading and Extend Knowledge

Under this heading we cluster instructional strategies and activities that allow teacher-student or student-student verbal interactions about topics related to reading. Some observers of elementary school education speculate that talking — like writing — may be an important ingredient in any formula to improve the reading capabilities of children from low-income families (see, e.g., Snow et al., 1991).

The basic indicator by which we estimated the relative emphasis on class discussion as a part of reading instruction was drawn from the teacher logs. This indicator represents the frequency of group or class discussions to explore the meaning of what had been read. On average, in the first year of the study, students discussed reading selections with some or all of their classmates and their teacher on about one-third of all school days — or somewhat less often than they wrote about what they read. By the second year, discussion appeared to have acquired more importance as an ingredient in reading instruction, once again reflecting the nature of curricular changes in the districts we were studying.

In the best of all possible worlds, we might envision many classrooms where teachers and students read good literature together and pursue extended discussions of meaning and interpretation of text. In fact, among the lessons we observed, we encountered relatively few examples of highly stimulating and extended student-teacher discussions about reading selections — either to set the context before reading began or to analyze what had been read. Overall discussion seemed to be a low priority in a large number of classrooms. As shown in Figure 4-1, in 25 classrooms — over a third of those for whom we had usable data on these variables — students discussed what they were reading an average of only 12 percent of the days that they attended school — about once every two weeks. Others, in the "high" category on this indicator, discussed what they had read an average of two out of every three days (69 percent of all instructional days).

According to our observations, teachers did slightly better in providing children with a context for reading. Usually this meant offering some background information related to the setting or situation the students would meet in a story. Sometimes, but not as often, it also meant questioning children to ascertain any previous knowledge they might have about the topic or simply talking open-endedly about the topic of an upcoming reading selection. Our observations indicated that teachers engaged students in this type of preparation for reading about one-third (in the "low" group of classrooms) to one-half (in the "high" group) of the time.

Our discussion of teachers' responses to cultural backgrounds, reported in Chapter 2, raises another possible dimension in teacher-student discussion: greater personalization of instruction by explicitly drawing attention to the parallels between real lives and literary lives. This was not a frequently used strategy among the total set of classrooms, although in classrooms with a high degree of discussion, connections between reading and students' lives were made nearly 40 percent of the time, or two days a week on average. In theory, increased discussion time would allow teachers to build on students' background knowledge and experiences. We observed a number of occasions when teachers explicitly drew students' attention to aspects of a story that might relate to real events or experiences in their lives, but we saw relatively few instances in which a teacher capitalized on students' cultural backgrounds to enhance learning. Student-student discussion was somewhat more common than teacher-student discussion.

The crude indicators shown in Figure 4-1 may oversimplify the nature of and variation in classroom discussions about reading: Discourse versus no discourse is conceptually too restrictive a framework to be of much use in describing what happens in high-poverty classrooms, or in any classroom for that matter. Much of what we observed during teacher-student interactions in reading was in a rapid-fire question-and-answer format that anyone would be hard-pressed to define as "discourse." Yet children seemed to enjoy it, and it allowed teachers to form some judgments about how well students were understanding what they read—at least on a literal level. In fact, even in classrooms where virtually no real discussion went on, any type of teacher-pupil interaction—even direct instruction on rather tedious skills—seemed to engender high student engagement.

We observed several classrooms where teachers believed in the importance of class discussions and thus had a sense of the possible power of this tool for helping children augment their understanding of an author's meaning. The context for such discussions was usually as a prereading or a postreading activity—or both. Use of discussion was not necessarily related to whether a teacher's basic approach to reading instruction was traditional or innovative in some way. For example, in a classroom where reading instruction was organized by ability-based groups and the materials of instruction were a traditional basal reader and lots of worksheets, the teacher nevertheless talked a great deal with her students. Her particular technique for engaging students' interest in reading and helping them understand what they read was through analogies that had particular meaning for them. Over the course of the school year, the observer in her room noted reading-related instruction that drew on films such as *Do the Right Thing* and *Star Wars* as well as on television wrestling.

In our observations, we paid special attention to instances of "extended discussion," but in interpreting what we observed, we did not attempt to attach any specific time limits to the term. Some meaningful interactions between teachers and students were very brief. For instance, in a first-grade class in which all the children were bilingual, the teacher prepared the students for a picture book by asking what they knew about the season of the year (autumn). When it became clear that their background knowledge was limited (leaves fall off the trees, the birds fly to Mexico), she moved directly into sharing with them the beautifully illustrated pages of a picture book, talking about each page in depth. This teacher realized that there was little point in pursuing the originally intended discussion in the absence of information. At the end of the session, the students were able to generate a list of 18 words related to autumn. Later, each dictated an autumn story to a fifth-grade "buddy."

When the activity was well managed, the give-and-take of discussion could teach students (and their teachers) many things. For example, in addition to developing their own powers of analysis, reasoning, and interpretation, students could learn to entertain and evaluate the ideas of others. Discussion also gave teachers insights about the experiences and perspectives that students brought to a reading assignment or that colored their understandings of the material read. However, as any skilled group facilitator knows, there are techniques that enhance the value of group interactions for all participants as well as behaviors that inhibit a genuine interchange of ideas.

For some teachers, facilitating student discussion seemed to be an inherent talent. For many others, it was clearly an instructional skill that had to be learned and practiced. In the hands of a teacher who was not terribly comfortable with the relatively unstructured give-and-take between instructor and student, a discussion segment of a lesson could easily backfire. One teacher we observed was trying hard to follow the approach described in the teacher's manual of her new literature-based reading series. As it directed, she read some phrases and asked the class to discuss the images evoked by the words: "Girl looking out window; cat dreaming; Christmas tree." One child said, " I saw some homeless people sitting on a mattress and the snow was falling down and keeping them warm." For him, the words elicited the winter season and something from his own experience—seemingly an appropriate response to an open-ended type of activity. The teacher, however, chastised the student for not listening well and admonished him to "form a picture based on what I say; do not add anything." This response, of course, squelched both the individual child and the spontaneity of the overall interaction.

In this instance, the teacher treated the response to an interpretive activity as if she had asked a literal question — the approach with which she was most familiar. Without some type of training or opportunity to observe other approaches, she was unlikely to have allowed the discussion to unfold in the ways envisioned by the authors of the textbook she was using.

THREE PATTERNS OF READING INSTRUCTION

Although the four strategies for maximizing meaning in reading instruction can be described separately, they are not independent of one another. Unlike the two strategies discussed in Chapter 3, they are interrelated. Although the strategies could be and were blended by the teachers in various ways, depending on each teacher's belief system and style, they had a tendency to cluster so that students in some classrooms were exposed to instruction featuring several of the strategies at once, while their counterparts in other classrooms had little or no exposure to any of the strategies. In short, the clustering of strategies indicated that a broader pattern of reading instruction was operating in the classrooms we were studying.

To explore more effectively the cumulative effect of these strategies, we created an index combining them and divided the classrooms into three groups based on their index values: those placing little or no emphasis on strategies aimed at maximizing understanding, those with a moderate emphasis, and those with high emphasis on these strategies. Thus, the procedures for creating the index (described in more detail in Appendix A) ensured that classrooms in the "high" category on all or most of the strategies described earlier in this chapter would fall in the "high emphasis" group, those in the "low" category for all or most strategies would be judged in the "little or no emphasis" group, and the others would fall in between.

It is important to keep in mind that the three patterns do not reflect an overall evaluation of instructional quality. Rather, they were created to help us distinguish qualitatively *different* approaches to the teaching of reading in high-poverty classrooms. Among the teachers who put each pattern into practice were expert practitioners — teachers who would widely be viewed as good at their craft — as well as those who were less expert, including some who would generally be viewed as ineffective teachers. Acknowledging this range of expertise among the teachers within each group, we ultimately wished to find out whether, on average, one pattern appeared to do a better job of teaching reading in the setting of the high-poverty classroom (see Chapter 7).

High Emphasis on Meaning-Oriented Reading Strategies

In the high-emphasis pattern of reading instruction, all or most of the strategies were in place. Their presence together in the same room, and the connections among them, are natural, when one thinks about it. Spending more time reading actual stories, poems, or nonfictional works exposes children to more text from which to extract or puzzle over meaning; focusing on the deeper meaning of texts naturally creates the opportunity and even the desire to discuss what is being read; discussions as well as the reading itself provide topics for writing; and so on. The clustering of these strategies, then, was in part a reflection of the teacher's awareness of, and discoveries about, the interconnections among these strategies. An example illustrates the point:

Ms. Abernathy's fifth-grade reading class. In her multiracial fifth-grade classroom, Ms. Abernathy has shifted from basal readers to a literature-based curriculum that she and a colleague designed. During reading instruction, she pushes her students to expand not only their vocabularies and knowledge of the world but also their ability to interpret what they read. For example, while reading two stories that center on the experiences of African Americans during the Revolutionary War, the class is assigned to write about fairness in the stories. Later, the students share the results of their efforts with one another. As the teacher guides the students in the presentation of their thoughts to peers, she teaches them how to compliment and support one another in a group setting. As the children read what they have written, the teacher finds something encouraging to say to each before offering constructive criticism and suggestions for expansion or rewriting. This teacher finds that having students write about what they read facilitates comprehension. In addition, she reads aloud to her class extensively and regularly; she also types and distributes song lyrics as a music-related activity.

This example hints at how the different reading strategies can be integrated and how they reinforce one another. The teaching of discrete skills — at this level, developing vocabulary — was interwoven with the interpretive act of reading. Ms. Abernathy pushed her students to get deeply into the tough issues raised by the stories they read, and she used writing about the stories as a principal device for doing so. Not only did the students write, as a way of crystallizing their thoughts individually, they also talked with one another in groups and as a whole class about what they thought. Recognizing that this form of discourse was not familiar to her students, Ms. Abernathy taught them how to discuss such ideas productively.

This is only one of the ways that a high emphasis on meaning-oriented strategies manifested itself in reading instruction. Not all teachers devoted as much time to deep interpretive work as Ms. Abernathy. Not all teachers connected reading with writing as extensively as she did, and several did not draw on reading material at all for the topics of written work, preferring to assign compositions that grew out of their students' direct experience. Some teachers displaying a high emphasis on meaning-oriented reading instruction were much more didactic in teaching comprehension strategies than she was. The form that reading lessons took in Ms. Abernathy's classroom was also a natural reflection of the level of the students she was teaching. Teachers in the primary grades found their own ways of integrating these strategies that were especially suited to the age and developmental level of their students; first-grade teachers, for example, were more likely to weave together reading work and various forms of decoding practice in a way that was unnecessary in Ms. Abernathy's classroom. Nonetheless, across all these classrooms, irrespective of grade level, the fundamental connections between a number of the meaning-oriented strategies were clearly in place.

Moderate Emphasis on Meaning-Oriented Reading Strategies

The moderate-emphasis pattern of instruction was more prevalent among teachers who, for one reason or another, found less room in their repertoire of teaching techniques for extended discussions, the integration of reading with writing, a focus on deeper understanding, and so on. Typically, these teachers attempted some of these strategies, but by comparison with their colleagues described above, they tended to fill the instructional time with a heavier diet of discrete skills teaching and practice (though nearly all the reading teachers we observed spent a lot of time on decoding and related skills).

Many of the teachers who displayed this pattern of instruction resembled those described in Chapter 3 who focused on a broad array of mathematical topics but failed to emphasize conceptual understanding—teachers who got part of the reform message but missed other ingredients. The following example from among the teachers whose reading instruction had a moderate emphasis on meaning-oriented strategies illustrates the point for reading instruction:

Ms. Ferguson's reading class. Ms. Ferguson, a primary grades teacher, is in her second year of using a literary reader. One morning, her students complete a story in the basal reader. She then breaks the class into six groups, each of which is assigned a question related to the story. After 10 minutes of small-group discussion about the answer they will offer, each group reports back to the whole class. Table Two, reporting on setting and characters, asserts that it was noontime when the story took place— an inferential response, since the text did not directly state a time. Rather than probe the group to see how the children arrived at that conclusion, the teacher accepts the answer and moves on, thus missing an opportunity to learn something about the reasoning skills employed at Table Two (Were they just guessing? On what did they base their inference?) and demonstrate the reasoning process to the whole class. After spending several days in this classroom at different times during the school year, the observer notes that the teacher "consistently implements potentially enriching activities, only to have them not realize their potential because the objectives are not vigorously considered or pursued."

In all likelihood, reading instruction in Ms. Ferguson's room took this form due to her inexperience with the new reading program being encouraged in her school and the lack of professional support that would have helped her recognize the possibilities and purposes of the activities she was using. But there were other reasons that teachers placed only moderate emphasis on meaning-oriented strategies, among them, ambivalence about the value of one or more strategy, philosophical commitments to a more skills-oriented approach, or experienced-based beliefs about what would work best for the kinds of students in the classroom.

Little or No Emphasis on Meaning-Oriented Reading Strategies

In a third set of classrooms, the predominant mode of teaching reading involved few or none of the strategies described earlier in the chapter. Children were nonetheless busily engaged in learning activities, and in the most effectively managed of these rooms, they were on task nearly all the time, and generally happily so. The teacher's approach typically combined a great deal of discrete skill practice (e.g., phonic decoding and word-letter recognition in the younger grades, syllabification and vocabulary development in the older grades), with oral reading practice aimed at developing fluency (e.g., in ability-based groupings). The following example, which describes how reading instruction was handled in a well-managed classroom described in Chapter 1, was not atypical of what children encountered when taught this way:

> *Ms. Williams's fifth-grade reading class.* Ms. Williams keeps a tight rein on instruction in reading, as she does in every other aspect of her classroom. Her students, all African American, respond well to what they experience in her room. Ms. Williams's approach to reading instruction follows the district-prescribed curriculum closely. Instruction relies exclusively on basals in reading, accompanied by texts and worksheets in language arts. Academic tasks tend to be distinct from one another and of short duration, with few visible connections made between one assignment and another. The 45-minute reading group time, for example, is often broken up into three or four activities that come from the reading mechanics workbook and the basal reader. Ms. Williams keeps careful track of progress on each activity. She records grades for each piece of work each day. During the teacher-directed portions of instruction, students are eager to contribute. Ms. Williams slows down the pace for students who aren't getting it, and other students don't complain: They are clearly used to this. This is a well-managed and busy classroom, but there is rarely any visible enthusiasm or evidence that students are curious enough to pursue any academic task beyond what is required of them.

This vignette highlights an overarching characteristic of the reading instruction in classrooms such as this: Though carefully organized and masterfully orchestrated, it is in some sense *fragmented*, a series of parts without a clear sense of the whole. In this sense, the pattern gives meaning a lower priority than in classrooms displaying the other two patterns of instruction, even though comprehension of what is read is one goal of reading instruction. To be sure, students do a lot of work in classes such as Ms. Williams's, and their test scores at the end of the year are likely to reflect that fact, particularly if the tests measure the disaggregated form of skill exposure that typifies this approach to reading instruction. But the ultimate test, which is addressed in Chapter 7, is how well this approach teaches children to understand what they are reading.

HOW THE PATTERNS OF READING INSTRUCTION WERE DISTRIBUTED AMONG CLASSROOMS

The three patterns of reading instruction were created in a different way from those related to mathematics instruction: by combining a single index value rather than looking at the intersection of two independent index values. It was still possible, in principle, for classrooms to exhibit the different patterns of reading instruction somewhat unevenly. As it turned out, approximately a third (31 percent) of all the classrooms exhibited the pattern most associated with discrete-skills reading instruction, approximately a quarter (23 percent) offered students the most meaning-oriented form of instruction, and the remainder (46 percent) fell in between. The resulting numbers are as shown in Table 4-1.

As with mathematics, we checked to see whether the patterns were more closely associated with particular grade levels than others. There is no doubt that there were some inherent differences in instructional emphasis as children moved through the grades, acquiring and solidifying reading skills. Whether or not they had adopted new materials and alternative instruction strategies, primary grade teachers generally spent more time on teaching discrete reading skills than did teachers in the middle grades. This fact did not, however, artificially push them into a pattern of instruction that placed low or moderate emphasis on meaning-oriented teaching. The underlying principles were clearly as applicable in grade 6 as in grade 1, though their particular expression might take a form that was more age-appropriate.

TABLE 4–1. How patterns of reading instruction were distributed among classrooms

	Number of Classrooms		
Patterns of Instruction	**Year 1**	**Year 2**	**Total**
High emphasis on meaning-oriented reading strategies	15	16	31
Moderate emphasis on meaning-oriented reading instruction	29	32	61
Little or no emphasis on meaning-oriented reading instruction	22	18	40
Total	**66**	**66**	**132**

CHAPTER 5

Focusing Writing Instruction on Meaningful Communication

Margaret C. Needels

The teaching of writing at the elementary school level once received scant attention, but over the past decade, a movement has begun to expand the role of writing instruction in the elementary language arts curriculum. Heeding the findings of the National Assessment of Educational Progress on the poor quality of writing instruction and consequent poor performance of the nation's fourth and eighth graders, the National Council of Teachers of English has advocated not only placing greater importance on writing instruction but also integrating reading and writing. Other activities such as the National Writing Project, which has touched many schools and individual classrooms, have given momentum to the movement.

The deficiencies that have prompted national concern over writing instruction are especially apparent in schools that serve children from low-income families. In such schools, writing is often (perhaps typically) considered less important than reading, too difficult for children who lack "basic" language skills, or both. As a consequence, in the early grades especially, writing tends to be given less time and attention.

The preceding chapter on reading made it clear that in the classrooms we studied, a fair amount of writing was going on and, on average, much of it involved the composing of extended or elaborated text. But the descriptive averages obscure enormous variation among teachers in their approaches to writing instruction—for example, in the kinds of writing tasks they created, their attention to writing processes, or their approaches to the discrete skills of writing and the "correctness" of written products.

In this chapter we turn to these matters by concentrating on teachers' use of instructional strategies intended to maximize meaning in writing instruction, chiefly by providing students with the opportunities and tools to communicate with valued audiences through the written word. The strategies are similar to those discussed in the chapter on reading, and these two facets of literacy instruction are related and can be integrated

84

(indeed, we have identified this as one of the key strategies in both areas). There are, nonetheless, differences in the meaning-oriented instructional strategies for reading and writing that relate to the unique nature of each subject area.

STRATEGIES THAT MAXIMIZE MEANING IN WRITING INSTRUCTION

In parallel with the analyses of mathematics and reading, we identified a series of instructional strategies that collectively increased the emphasis on meaning in the teaching of writing. Each strategy reflects a key underlying dimension of writing instruction and serves as a useful tool for distinguishing differences among the classrooms we studied. Our analysis concentrates on six strategies that, based on the research literature and our own fieldwork, appear to have special relevance to high-poverty classrooms: (1) maximizing opportunities for students to write extended text, (2) integrating writing with other areas of the curriculum, (3) deemphasizing the mastery of discrete language mechanics skills and the mechanical correctness of written text, (4) teaching the processes of writing, (5) connecting writing to children's backgrounds or base of experience, and (6) changing the social context of the writing task.

Although independent of one another in one sense, these strategies are interrelated in many ways, as subsequent analyses will show. First, however, we discuss each strategy and the dimensions that underlie it. A few simple indicators, displayed in Figure 5-1, help summarize how the strategies varied. Because the first strategy (maximizing opportunities for writing extended text) turned out to be closely linked to all the others, we used a simplified version of it in Figure 5-1 — that is, low, moderate, and high amounts of opportunities — as a way of displaying the range on each of the other indicators. Later in the chapter, the same three-part division underlies the basic patterns of writing instruction we identified.

Maximizing Opportunities for Extended Text Writing

The first strategy rests on a simple premise that parallels the assumption underlying teachers' attempts to maximize students' opportunities to read text: Given more chances to compose text requiring some complex thought, students are more likely to become proficient writers. To classify the complexity of the writing tasks assigned in the study classrooms, we use three categories of text: (1) noncomposed, (2) composed-restricted, and (3) composed-extended. The three differ chiefly in terms of the com-

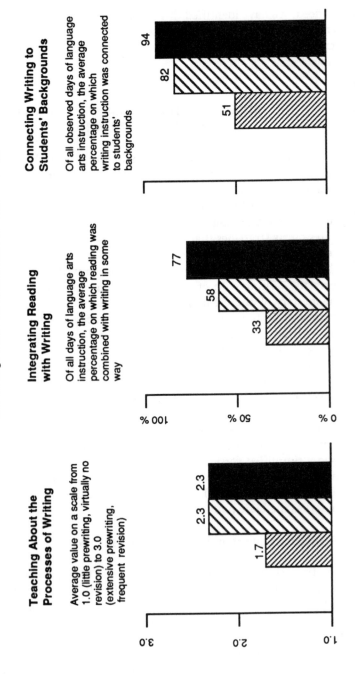

FIGURE 5–1. Strategies that emphasize meaning in writing instruction

Among classrooms [a] offering differing degrees of opportunity for extended text writing, the average value on an indicator of each strategy

Teaching About the Processes of Writing

Average value on a scale from 1.0 (little prewriting, virtually no revision) to 3.0 (extensive prewriting, frequent revision)

Integrating Reading with Writing

Of all days of language arts instruction, the average percentage on which reading was combined with writing in some way

Connecting Writing to Students' Backgrounds

Of all observed days of language arts instruction, the average percentage on which writing instruction was connected to students' backgrounds

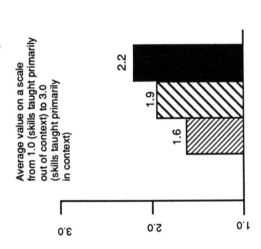

Teaching Discrete Skills in the Context of Writing

Average value on a scale from 1.0 (skills taught primarily out of context) to 3.0 (skills taught primarily in context)

1.6   1.9   2.2

3.0   2.0   1.0

Legend

Extent of opportunities for writing extended text:

Low   Moderate   High

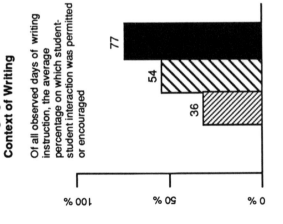

Changing the Social Context of Writing

Of all observed days of writing instruction, the average percentage on which student-student interaction was permitted or encouraged

77   54   36

100 %   50 %   0 %

a   Based on analysis of 64 classrooms in year 2 of the study.

plexity of written expression demanded of the child. Noncomposed text refers to writing requiring no thought about the process of composing. Activities such as copying, writing text dictated by the teacher, and single-word exercises are classified as noncomposed text. Composed-restricted text requires the student to compose a short piece of writing that has a well-defined length, such as assignments requiring the student to write a phrase or sentence containing one of the week's spelling words. Composed-extended text requires the writer to create text that does not have a well-defined or predetermined length (although the teacher may require a certain number of words, sentences, or pages) and that elicits an elaborated thought in written form. Book reports, journal writing, a story, a letter, and a poem would all be classified as composed-extended text.

Teachers varied greatly in the priority they placed on the writing of extended text. At one extreme, even though a significant amount of time might be devoted to writing instruction, very little of it involved writing extended text (in a few classrooms, no pretense at teaching writing was made whatsoever). In these classrooms, students wrote answers on exercise sheets, spelling words, or sentences dictated by the teacher. Classrooms at the other end of the continuum provided many opportunities for students to write extended text. Writing often occurred throughout the day — during reading, social studies, and science, as well as during periods of time designated for writing or, more broadly, language arts. Daily journal writing and assignments such as book reports were also frequent in these classrooms.

Although the great majority of classrooms offered some form of writing instruction, several simple numbers from the first year of the study help pinpoint the substantial differences among classrooms. In classrooms with low opportunities for writing extended text, for example, students drafted text on only 15 percent of all instructional days across the year, compared with 60 percent of all days for their counterparts in high-opportunity classrooms and 38 percent in classrooms offering moderate opportunities. When they did write, the students in low-opportunity classrooms spent much less time at it — 14 minutes a day on average versus 31 and 18 minutes, respectively, for students offered high or moderate opportunities for writing. The differences were equally obvious to the observer: During the two-week and one-week observation periods, learners in the high-opportunity classrooms tackled three times as many extended writing tasks as their low-opportunity counterparts.

Integrating Writing with Other Areas of the Curriculum

A second strategy promotes writing as a useful communicative tool by integrating writing into the instruction of other subject areas, in particular, reading (as noted in Chapter 4), but also social studies, science, and mathematics. We encountered many classrooms where writing and reading were integrated—students wrote about what they had read and read what they had written. In a few classrooms, writing was an important part of social studies and science instruction, but we found virtually no cases in which writing was used during mathematics instruction, though this has been advocated by some reformers. In other classrooms, writing was taught as a separate subject, and no extended composing occurred in the other subject areas.

Integration with reading instruction, the most common form of integration, provides a useful point of comparison among classrooms. For example, as noted in Figure 5-1, students in high-opportunity classrooms received writing instruction that was in some way related to reading lessons on approximately three-quarters (77 percent) of all instructional days during the year, on average, as compared with an average of one-third (33 percent) of all days for students in low-opportunity classrooms.

In one sense, integration of writing was logically linked to the previous strategy (maximizing the amount of extended text writing). When writing becomes a part of more than one subject area (e.g., science or social studies), the frequency of writing is likely to increase. In some classrooms, reading and writing were completely integrated, with little distinction made between these two elements of literacy.

This strategy is especially important for students from low-income backgrounds because of its focus on meaningful communication in Standard English. When writing was taught as a separate subject and for its own sake, the assignments usually involved self-expression or description. Although these are important reasons for knowing how to write, they are by no means the only ones. When writing was included in the instruction for other subject areas, it conveyed to the students the multiple uses of writing and its importance in a literate society. When writing was integrated across the curriculum, it was presented not as an isolated skill but as a vehicle for learning, persuading, reporting, and presenting points of view.

Deemphasizing Discrete Language Mechanics Skills and Mechanical Correctness

The essence of this strategy was to reduce, but not eliminate, the emphasis placed on discrete language skills (e.g., punctuation, sentence structure, spelling) and the mechanical correctness of written text. Like its counterpart in the preceding chapter on reading, this strategy reflects a concern about teaching in high-poverty classrooms that cuts across subject areas: the relative importance of discrete skills taught in isolation from the activity (in this case, writing) to which the skills apply. Counter to research suggesting that students tend not to benefit from such instruction (Hillocks, 1986), many educators assume that students from low-income backgrounds will develop greater writing competence if they are taught the mechanical skills of writing first and if their writing opportunities are designed to ensure that these skills are applied correctly. But to do so risks disconnecting the skills from their meaningful application to the act of communicating with others. Closely related is the priority placed on correcting mechanical errors in written text, which is a great temptation in classrooms populated by students without full mastery of Standard English. But focusing learners' attention too much on mechanical errors risks losing the point of writing as communication — losing sight of the whole for the parts.

Among the classrooms we studied, teachers can be sorted into those who (1) placed minimal emphasis on correctness and devoted little time to teaching language mechanics skills; (2) emphasized correctness and language mechanics skills, but as they were encountered in students' written text; and (3) concentrated on teaching these skills out of context of the students' writing.

In classrooms where a high degree of emphasis was placed on correctness and language mechanics skills taught out of context, students tended to have less opportunity to write extended text, as Figure 5-1 suggests (the differences across groups of classrooms on these crude indicators are smaller than our qualitative observations suggested). In one third-grade classroom that fell within the low-opportunity-for-writing group, for example, the teacher believed that the language arts textbook was too difficult for her students. For this reason, she refrained from using the textbook, which contained various extended writing assignments, and assigned virtually no extended writing. Because the teacher believed that her students needed training in language mechanics, writing assignments consisted of grammar exercises and spelling for about 20 minutes each day. Contrast this with another third-grade classroom in which the teacher taught a grammar lesson (on adjectives) in the context of a poem by Edna St. Vincent Millay.

Teaching the Processes of Writing

A fourth strategy aims at giving students better communicative tools by teaching the different phases of the writing process — prewriting, drafting, editing, and revising — and by helping students see writing as a multiphase process in which one evolves what one has to say, progressively extending and clarifying its meaning for intended audiences.

Classrooms varied, principally in the extent to which the teacher formally introduced students to the notions of prewriting and revision (and offered students opportunities for engaging in both). As can be seen in Figure 5-1, classrooms offering extensive opportunities for extended text writing were also more likely to feature extensive prewriting and revision than low-opportunity-for-writing classrooms.

An emphasis on prewriting—that is, activities to prepare students for the actual writing of text—seemed to offer numerous ways for teachers to draw on students' backgrounds and experiences (an important strategy in its own right, which is discussed later in this chapter). Prewriting also provided students with new information or experiences that they were unlikely to encounter outside of school, which they could then use in their writing assignments. When one teacher assigned her students to write about life on another planet, the actual writing task was preceded by extensive reading on the solar system, a visit to the local science museum, and discussions of imaginary trips to each planet. To prepare her fourth graders for writing about a story called "The Garden," another teacher had the children plant their own seeds, instructing them to touch the soil, think about where she might have gotten it, smell it, and look at it. This led to a class-generated list of descriptive words for the soil that students could use in their writing.

The quantity and quality of students' opportunities for revisions enabled them to extend the communicative power and meaning of their written work. In one fifth-grade classroom, for example, students worked with partners and gave each other suggestions for revising a particular piece of writing. By midyear, this activity was an established routine in the classroom, and students knew that for all extended writing assignments, their partners would help them with their assignments before they were given to the teacher. In another classroom of second graders, the teacher taught her students to edit their writing by circling words they thought they had misspelled and then asking the teacher to help with corrections. These kinds of routines differed greatly from those that were typical in classrooms where less attention was paid to teaching and supporting the writing process. In those classes, students generally turned in their writing assignments for evaluation by the teacher with little or no opportunity for revisions.

Connecting Writing to Students' Backgrounds

As noted in the discussion of prewriting above (and in the discussion of teachers' responses to student differences in Chapter 2), writing instruction can offer students the chance to connect their base of experience to the academic learning they are asked to do in school. For the students in high-poverty classrooms, these connections are neither obvious (to the children or the teachers) nor easily made, because of the differences between the children's and the teachers' backgrounds. But as a matter of instructional strategy, teachers can foster or illuminate these connections in a variety of ways.

Teachers across the study sample were not reluctant to make some form of connection between writing assignments and children's personal lives. Certain forms of writing instruction, such as the widely used journal writing, invited "personal" writing. Nonetheless, there were substantial differences on this score between classrooms offering limited opportunities for extended text writing and those with the most extensive opportunities. As Figure 5-1 indicates, in the second year of the study, teachers in the latter case made such connections on nearly all days of writing instruction (94 percent of all days), as compared with only half (51 percent) of all days in the case of their colleagues in low-opportunity classrooms.

Across both years of the study, many teachers sought in varying degrees to allow or encourage children to draw on what they knew from their lives outside of school as a source of material for writing assignments, as a basis for interpreting what others had written, or as a kind of "expertise" that could help students reflect on the meaning of what they and others wrote. In doing so, writing teachers were simply capitalizing on what is a natural impulse for children, who use what is familiar in making sense out of the world. But the key factor was the degree to which teachers communicated to students that their home lives—however different those lives might be—were a respected, welcome, and valuable part of classroom discourse, both written and otherwise. Not all teachers felt comfortable sending this message to students, because of either ignorance of the world the children came from or fear that drawing on their backgrounds might open up a Pandora's box of experiences that the teacher wouldn't be able to manage in the classroom.

Changing the Social Context of the Writing Task

A final strategy involves the attempt to construct a social context for writing that motivates and encourages communication with others. The relationships between writers and their peers, the teacher, or other audiences are crucial elements of this social context. Accordingly, in an effort to understand how the social environment might facilitate or inhibit students' writing, we paid attention to various aspects of the social context during writing instruction—in particular, peer interaction during writing, the degree of student self-direction in learning activities, and the degree to which students wrote for audiences other than the teacher as evaluator.

One scholarly view (Dyson, 1983) argues that children write for one another and that interactions among them during the writing task are crucial to the development of literacy. As a consequence, we observed not only whether children were encouraged or permitted to talk to one another during their writing but also what they talked about. For example, did they read their writing to one another? Did they communicate ideas and help one another elaborate on their ideas? Did they ask one another technical kinds of questions? In general, we hoped to understand how much, and how, children worked together on their writing tasks. As a rough indicator of differences among classrooms, Figure 5-1 shows that classrooms differed considerably in the frequency with which students were permitted or encouraged to interact with one another during writing instruction. Teachers in high-opportunity classrooms were more than twice as likely to do so as those offering few opportunities for extended text writing.

Related to the social environment created for the children is the degree of control maintained by the teacher over the writing task. Approaches to writing instruction that depart from conventional practices encourage more choice by the student and a greater degree of student direction in doing writing assignments. Traditional classrooms, in which instruction is highly teacher controlled, allow little room for students to choose or shape their writing tasks, such as when the writing task requires students to follow a pattern. After reading the story "Just Like Daddy," one first-grade teacher instructed the students to write a sentence using the following pattern, "I _____ just like _____ ." This kind of task contrasts with those that allow more room for students to determine the content and even the form of expression. For example, in another first-grade classroom, the teacher devoted considerable time to a prewriting activity that stimulated students to think about what kinds of things they see in springtime, followed by an activity in which students drew pictures of spring and then wrote about their pictures. Between these two extremes lies a range of environments that surround the students' efforts with varying degrees of "scaffolding" — support by the teacher that structures and simplifies or guides the writing. We encountered a wide range of scaffolding that provided varying degrees of structure to the students' writing efforts.

The audience for students' written work may also have a key role in encouraging writing as meaningful communication. We define *audience* as the person(s) to whom the product of a writing task is addressed, either explicitly (as in a letter, memo, or other form of targeted writing) or implicitly. The concept of audience is of concern because so much of the writing that occurs in school has the same audience — the teacher, who also serves as evaluator. Writing text for an audience that will also serve as an evaluator can add to children's anxiety about writing and impede the development of their writing competence, especially among students who are not particularly secure about their ability to write. Meaning-oriented approaches to writing instruction encourage writing for a variety of audiences, none of which acts in an evaluative capacity.

This dimension is especially important when looking at the writing opportunities provided to the student population on which this study focuses. As in the teaching of language mechanics, conventional wisdom argues that such students need a high degree of structure — that is, clear rules about the task, a structure for carrying out the assignment, and clearly specified criteria for evaluation. When teachers structure their writing lessons in accordance with this view, they tend to create a social environment for writing that precludes student-student interaction and student choice and deprives students of some responsibility for communication. This kind of environment may work against the acquisition of writing competence within this segment of the student population.

THREE PATTERNS OF WRITING INSTRUCTION

The first of the six strategies — maximizing opportunities for extended text writing — provides a convenient basis for describing distinct patterns of writing instruction. As the discussion so far has hinted, and as we will subsequently demonstrate, other strategies for maximizing meaning in writing instruction cluster in such a way that each pattern exhibits a characteristic combination of the remaining strategies. Thus, we found that in those classrooms where students had frequent opportunities to compose extended text, teachers also tended to integrate writing into the curriculum, place a high degree of emphasis on the writing process, and place less emphasis on the mechanical correctness of text. Although we label the three patterns by the emphasis placed on extended text writing, much more is involved in each pattern than just this feature of writing instruction.

High Emphasis on Extended Text Writing

As the label implies, this pattern is characterized first of all by the kind and quantity of extended text writing that was likely to take place. At least two different kinds of opportunities existed for students to write extended text on almost a daily basis — typically, journal writing and some sort of writing assignment related to classroom activities, out-of-school experiences, or the content of the academic curriculum. A first-grade classroom from an inner-city school serving a multiracial population illustrates one way in which this pattern manifested itself at an early stage in children's progression through school:

> *Ms. Carrera's first-grade writing class.* A visit to this classroom at any time during the year reveals the importance given to written text. The walls of the classroom are filled with word lists, poems, the class daily newspaper, and stories dictated to the teacher early in the year and later written by the students themselves. Shortly before Christmas break, for example, three large word-list posters of 20 words each are seen, one listing Christmas words, one listing "s" words, and a third listing different kinds of forest animals (the "s" words reflect the phonetic sound the children are working on). Each morning, the students dictate to Ms. Carrera five or six sentences that make up the day's newspaper, which is posted throughout the day and taken home by a different student each day. Not only the newspaper but also other kinds of text come from the students and are drawn from their experiences outside of school. Approximately 90 minutes of each morning is devoted to students' dictating different kinds of text to the teacher and subsequently reading this material. There is additional time for journal writing each day. In the early weeks of the school year, when students have yet to acquire facility with written language, they draw story pictures and label these pictures, using words from the lists displayed around the room. Later in the school year, the students write three- and four-sentence stories. They take turns reading their stories to Ms. Carrera, who types the stories onto a computer file and prints them. These stories are related to a current theme integrated across the curriculum. The children write their stories only after several days have been devoted to reading and discussing the theme.

It is clear that more strategies are at work in Ms. Carrera's classroom than simply the number and variety of opportunities to write extended text. She integrates writing with reading and other subjects. She engages in extensive prewriting and, in ways that are appropriate for her students, introduces them to various features of the writing process. The manner of creating text (extensive use of dictation) deemphasizes students' initial attention to mechanical writing errors; much of their learning of discrete skills is directly connected to what they are writing. Furthermore, there is a close connection between what children are doing in writing (or other aspects of the curriculum) and their home lives.

Other teachers developed their own versions of this pattern, weaving the different strategies together in a variety of ways. Virtually all integrated reading with writing. For example, one fifth-grade teacher systematically had her students write chapter summaries on what they had read each day. She also assigned essays related to the themes of their reading stories — themes such as justice and villainy. In a third-grade classroom, after the students had read a story about imagination, the teacher assigned a writing task asking the students to write about a problem in their lives that had been solved by using their imagination. Among first-grade teachers, writing was integrated with reading in various creative ways that took account of the children's early limitations in both writing and reading. Some teachers chose a variation on Ms. Carrera's approach by having children "write" stories through dictation; the stories were then available for reading by the author and other children as well. Others experimented with inventive spelling: One such teacher asked her students early in the year to write about something that they remembered from reading the story *Corduroy the Bear*. One student in the class wrote, "Corduroy had a bntn bot he ctin fiod ti" (translation: "Corduroy had a button but he couldn't find it").

However they forged the connections between writing and reading, teachers placing high emphasis on extended text writing typically did so by making no overt distinction between the two facets of literacy. Both were treated as part of long, multifaceted language arts lesson. While stories were being read, themes, meaning, and language were discussed. The reading time was rich, and ideas were presented and exchanged. Thus, writing was a natural accompaniment to reading and class discussions. Breaking down the traditional barriers between reading and writing seemed to facilitate students' enthusiasm for the writing task.

Several, but not all, of the high-emphasis teachers integrated writing with other aspects of the curriculum, usually in the form of reports or letters in social studies or science. Students wrote letters to persons such as the principal, baseball players on a local team, and officials at the local public broadcasting station about events that were happening in their lives. One exceptional fifth-grade teacher attempted to facilitate the development of her students' metacognitive skills by systematically giving her students science problems and requiring them to write their thoughts as they went through the process of solving the problem.

As a group, teachers placing high emphasis on extended text writing tended not to allocate a lot of class time to introducing their students to discrete writing skills. Nonetheless, some time was devoted to teaching these skills, typically within the context of the students' writing. One fifth-grade teacher taught her students correct usage of quotation marks as part of a story-writing assignment that contained dialogue. Other teachers used examples from students' writing to discuss certain grammatical concepts.

Teachers' approaches to the mechanical correctness of their students' writing were more varied. Nearly all the upper elementary teachers who placed high emphasis on extended text writing were concerned about the correctness of their students' compositions. Some used peer editing sessions, thus removing the teacher from the role of evaluating correctness. Others noted needed corrections on written work and gave the students an opportunity to revise their work before they submitted the final draft. But however they approached this issue, the primary concern of these teachers was to establish an environment conducive to students' generation of text and to avoid hindering students' fluency by overemphasizing the mechanical correctness of the text.

The attention given to the writing process varied considerably among teachers placing high emphasis on extended text. In their own ways, the teachers devoted substantial time to prewriting activities. Because writing in these classrooms was so often integrated with reading, much of the prewriting involved reading and discussion, as in the example of Ms. Carrera's classroom. Prewriting was sometimes the entire lesson for a given day, or even several days. During this time, the teachers attempted to develop motivation, provide information, and build scaffolded structures that would facilitate their students' writing of extended text. Fewer than half of the classrooms with extensive writing opportunities, however, devoted much time to revising and editing. Some teachers simply ignored the revising and editing phase, believing that it was not important or necessary. In several classes, peer response groups were used (although apparently not with any kind of formal response sheets). For the most part, these response groups did one of two things: edit the writing for mechanics, or identify areas where the writer might provide further description or more information.

Regarding the social context of the writing task—as it manifested itself either in student-student interaction or in the relationship between the students and the audience for their writing—student-student interaction was often permitted (as implied by the indicators in Figure 5-1), but generally this did not happen during the actual composing process. Most exchanges of ideas were led by the teacher and occurred before the actual composing began. In some of the upper elementary classes, student-student interaction took place as part of peer editing as students helped one another (usually with mechanics) in their final editing. Students wrote to various audiences besides their teachers — to themselves (because they did a great deal of journal writing) and to individuals or groups outside the classroom (because they did a great deal of letter writing). Letters were typically about local topical events or issues and were, for the most part, actually sent to the person or group in question.

Moderate Emphasis on Extended Text Writing

In classrooms in which a more modest emphasis was placed on extended text writing, students encountered similar opportunities to those described above, except that the opportunities were generally less frequent, less varied, and less challenging. Students typically wrote some kind of extended text regularly (e.g., two or three times a week or more), often through regular journal writing. In addition, on special occasions (e.g., holidays or community events), the students might write extended text related to that event, but such assignments were not consistently included in the daily schedule.

The pattern of meaning-oriented strategies used by teachers in classrooms with a moderate amount of extended text writing looked somewhat different from that of the high-emphasis group. Typically, writing was integrated with reading or other subjects less often or not at all. In part, this reflects the fact that because less extended writing was done, there was less to integrate. But teachers also tended to assign writing tasks that were not designed to connect with the learning taking place in reading, social studies, or other areas. Thus, in journal writing in these classrooms, either students would select their topics or the teacher would assign a topic unrelated to other subject areas. In addition, broad, generic writing assignments, such as "write what you do when you get bored," were common among these classrooms.

It appeared that this pattern of writing instruction reflected less thinking on the teachers' part about how writing could be related to other aspects of the curriculum. To be sure, some teachers gave students opportunities for writing extended text that related to other subject areas, for example, by asking students to write in the same genre as what they were reading — a poem, a letter, a story, or whatever. One third-grade teacher in this group gave her students the following instruction for writing: "Think of a name for your story. Think of something your character has done. It might be a trip you went on or a real story like *The Lost Key*. Think of a story. It might be a strange or funny story." In a rare writing assignment, another teacher in the moderate-opportunity group assigned the following writing task: "Write about one of your favorite stories; it doesn't matter which one, as long as we've read it." These instructions reveal a lack of scaffolding, a characteristic of many classrooms placing only moderate emphasis on extended text writing. These teachers provided little framework for the writing activity that would help students move from reading to writing. In all these examples, the writing was simply a "tag-on" to the reading, not an integral part of a unified activity.

Teachers in the moderate-emphasis group focused heavily on discrete language mechanics and correctness. Their view of writing development tended to place importance on the early acquisition of discrete skills, which could later be applied to extended text. In comparison with teachers displaying the first instructional pattern, these teachers were more likely to focus on correctness because they believed that students needed to acquire the rules of writing before they could write meaningful text. Accordingly, language arts lessons in these classrooms were often devoted to exercises from a textbook — mainly requiring seatwork. The teacher might talk briefly about the concept to be covered, such as past tense and present tense, and then students would be asked to complete the exercises from the book. In such instances, the time used for teaching mechanics took away from the time that could have been used for writing extended text. In contrast, teachers who placed a high priority on extended text writing organized instruction so that students were too busy composing elaborated text to devote a great deal of time to learning discrete skills out of context.

Regarding the attention they gave to the writing process, teachers in the moderate-emphasis classrooms generally paid less attention to writing as a process than did teachers who concentrated on extended text writing. There were some exceptions, such as one teacher who had her room decorated with posters describing the various phases of the writing process and examples of each. Unlike in high-opportunity classrooms, however, this teacher and others like her did not invest large amounts of time in prewriting, preferring to spend equal time on all aspects of the process. The key difference across the sample probably had less to do with *whether* teachers taught about the writing process than with *how* they taught it. Along with their lower emphasis on prewriting altogether, teachers in moderate-emphasis classrooms used prewriting time differently. Rather than bringing students' cultural backgrounds or out-of-school experiences into the prewriting activity, as many teachers displaying the first instructional pattern did, teachers in the moderate-emphasis group tended to use the activity as a way to provide the students with new information. The reason may have been that teachers preferred all students to have a common experience for a given writing assignment or that they were fearful of the kinds of experiences their students might report.

Little Emphasis on Extended Text Writing

The remaining classrooms displayed a pattern of writing instruction characterized by few opportunities for extended text writing. Most of the "writing" in such classrooms consisted of worksheets or exercises that involved limited composing at best. If journal writing was used at all, its use was inconsistent during the school year. An illustration captures more concretely what such a pattern meant for students and teacher in a case that contrasts sharply with the first instructional pattern:

> *Ms. Polacek's first-grade writing class.* Writing mechanics are the centerpiece of Ms. Polacek's writing curriculum. Her objectives for the year are to help her students write a simple sentence, recognize a sentence, know punctuation and mechanics, and spell common words. Writing instruction occurs about once a week, including work on spelling, based on a list provided in the basal reading series. During this time, students usually complete worksheets focusing on some sort of writing mechanics skill. Occasionally, students write in journals by copying sentences such as the following from the chalkboard: "Today is Monday, December 4, 1989. It is a sunny day. It is a beautiful day." The students illustrate their writing after they finish copying it. Later in the year, Ms. Polacek encourages the students to add their own sentences after they have copied the sentences written on the chalkboard. Most of the writing done in this classroom is related to spelling assignments. Students have to write sentences using their spelling words, and the teacher corrects these sentences for spelling, punctuation, capitalization, and neatness. Ms. Polacek places great emphasis on correctness, so much so that when students are given the freedom to express themselves through writing, they are greatly concerned about their spelling. Because they have not been taught to spell phonetically and very few word lists are displayed around the room, they depend on the adults in the room for the correct spelling. Thus, it is common to see much movement and waiting in lines during the infrequent writing activities.

Although this example is in some ways an extreme case, it is instructive because of its sharp contrast with the vignette of Ms. Carrera earlier in the chapter. The two teachers made profoundly different strategic decisions about how they would approach the teaching of writing; indeed, they viewed the nature of writing itself in different ways. The result in Ms. Polacek's case was a wholly different configuration of the strategies aimed at meaning-oriented instruction: In brief, none of them had an important place in her instruction, and their absence made sense, given her goals and assumptions about what she was doing. Because writing at the first-grade level was, to her, primarily a matter of mastering discrete skills, extended text writing was not a particularly useful activity. The skills of language mechanics are separate from those of reading, so there was little reason to integrate writing instruction with reading. A great deal of emphasis was placed, for obvious reasons, on discrete skills teaching, and once the students were able to produce whole sentences, it made equally good sense from her perspective to keep an eagle eye out for their mechanical errors. Given that her students did very little composing (which she did not feel they were ready for), lessons on the stages of the writing process would have been a waste of time. Although she might concede that some connections to the children's world outside of school would have been motivationally sound, there was not much opportunity to make such links, given that the principal business of the lessons was to encounter and practice the next skill in the sequence.

Ms. Polacek's pattern of writing instruction was conceived with early learners in mind—children who were entering formal school for the first time and who could read or write little, let alone recognize all the letters of the alphabet. But there were counterparts to her in the higher grades, teachers whose goal was, in essence, to teach children to produce mechanically correct and appropriately structured paragraphs (or even whole essays) rather than sentences. Their rationale for doing so was often strikingly similar to hers. Not surprisingly, the pattern of instruction in those classrooms displayed a similar lack of meaning-oriented strategies.

It is tempting to dismiss this pattern of instruction as unsound—that is, unlikely to produce good writers—but to do so ignores the fact that it rests on a clear rationale. In competent hands, such a pattern can theoretically produce young writers who are confident of their ability to put down on the page correct Standard English—not a small achievement. The analyses described in Chapter 7 summarize our attempt to understand whether such writers were in fact able to do so, and how they compared to students exposed to other patterns, especially those in classrooms offering extensive opportunities for extended text writing.

HOW THE PATTERNS OF WRITING INSTRUCTION WERE DISTRIBUTED AMONG CLASSROOMS

As Table 5-1 shows, three patterns of writing instruction were found among classrooms and grades in numbers that paralleled what we found with reading in Chapter 4. To be sure that the patterns were not somehow

TABLE 5–1. How patterns of writing instruction were distributed among class-rooms

	Number of Classrooms		
Patterns of Instruction	Year 1	Year 2	**Total**
High emphasis on meaning-oriented writing instruction	18	19	37
Moderate emphasis on meaning-oriented writing instruction	25	26	51
Little or no emphasis on meaning-oriented writing instruction	21	19	40
Total	**64**	**64**	**128**

associated with a particular grade level or range, we checked the distribution across grades and found it to be relatively even. Across both years of data collection, 18 classrooms from the first three elementary grades were classified as offering extensive opportunities for extended text writing; 21 classrooms in grades 4, 5, and 6 did so. We checked further by each individual strategy but found that, in general, there were few major differences in the use of these strategies across grades within our sample. However, there were some exceptions. Younger students were more likely than their counterparts in higher grades to be allowed to interact with one another during writing lessons. Older students in the sample wrote longer, on average, although they typically had fewer tasks involving extended writing (these assignments were generally more substantial than what first graders were asked to do). Otherwise, the approaches to teaching writing were reasonably well distributed across the elementary school grades.

The differences across grades had more to do with the nature of activities, content, and other features of learning and schooling linked to students' developmental age than with meaning-oriented writing strategies per se. What Ms. Carrera and other first-grade teachers did fit the needs and current stage of their first graders. In classrooms at the upper end of the elementary school grades, a different diet of writing opportunities was more appropriate, as in the case of a fifth-grade teacher who found occasion for many extended writing assignments that fit naturally with other classroom plans and activities. Before taking field trips, students wrote about their expectations for the event; afterwards, they wrote thank-you letters to their hosts and reports on what they had learned. Over the school year, the students in this room prepared several creative writing assignments, wrote numerous personal and business letters, and kept journals about their feelings on any topic of their choice.

CHAPTER 6

Supplementing Classroom Instruction: Implications for Meaning-Oriented Instruction

Brenda J. Turnbull

The regular classroom teacher, on whom the preceding chapters have focused, is not the only one who teaches mathematics, reading, and writing to many children in high-poverty schools. Nor is the regular classroom the only venue for such instruction. The schools that we studied—as do most schools with high concentrations of children from low-income families—house a variety of special-purpose programs designed to supplement regular classroom instruction for some or all students. Depending on how these programs operate in any given school, the services they offer may complement and support the regular classroom teacher's philosophy, goals, and approach, or they may undermine or even contradict the regular classroom instruction. Whatever the interaction between them and regular classroom instruction, supplemental programs are likely to be a significant factor in the instructional experience of many children, especially those at the low-achieving end of the student spectrum and those with particular identifiable learning needs stemming from their linguistic backgrounds, disabilities, or other characteristics.

We learned about supplemental instruction in much the same way we studied regular classroom instruction, though there were limits on our sources of information. Concentrating on programs in which children from the study classrooms participated, we observed supplemental lessons (fewer than in the regular classrooms, however), examined instructional materials, talked informally with children in these classes, interviewed the teachers, and had periodic conversations with program administrators or coordinators.

This chapter summarizes what we learned from these sources and highlights some issues raised by the presence of these programs. We pay particular attention to the implications of such programs for regular classroom teachers' attempts to emphasize meaning in their instruction.

SOURCES OF SUPPLEMENTAL INSTRUCTION

Each of the schools we visited had its own unique mix of federal, state, and local support for supplemental programs and services. Among these services, the federal Title I (formerly Chapter 1) program[1] was the most ubiquitous. This program offers extra dollars to high-poverty schools, with the requirement that the money support "compensatory education" services for students who are performing poorly in academic subjects. Chapter 1 programs most commonly target the improvement of reading skills, but mathematics may also be emphasized; a focus on writing is relatively unusual.

In its most recent legislative overhaul, Chapter 1 acquired a stronger focus on bringing participants' performance up to that expected for their grade levels, including performance in more advanced skills. This change was intended to discourage schools from focusing their Chapter 1 programs on low-level drills in basic reading and math skills. In addition, the law emphasizes the need to coordinate Chapter 1 instruction with the regular classroom program. Within these mandates, districts and schools are free to design and staff their Chapter 1 programs as they choose, using reading specialists, math specialists, and instructional aides either inside or outside the regular classroom. In theory, at least, the supplemental assistance available to schools and classrooms through the Chapter 1 program can mesh well with efforts to offer children in high-poverty classrooms a more interesting and challenging education.

Other supplemental programs present in the schools included "special-education" services offered under the federal Education for All Handicapped Children Act and various services for students with limited English proficiency, which had either federal or state support. For students in the classrooms we observed, participation in special-education services generally consisted of spending part of the school day in a resource room with a special-education teacher. For students with limited English proficiency, supplemental programs were generally designed to ensure that students made a transition, at an educationally appropriate pace, to participation in English language instruction. The services offered by these programs might take the form of supplemental classes in language development or in-class assistance from someone proficient in the students' home language. These services might be combined with, or even replaced by, more ambitious bilingual education arrangements, as in several

---

1. The change in name from Chapter 1 to Title I happened as this book goes to press and the program will be known as Chapter 1 throughout.

schools we studied, whereby the regular classroom was taught in both English and the children's home language.

Other than compensatory education, special education, and language-related programs supported by federal and state programs (as well as local budgets, in some instances), more specialized circumstances make other sources of supplemental support available to high-poverty schools. For example, two districts we studied offered special services as a result of desegregation proceedings. Schools in these districts that were racially imbalanced received extra resources, which were used to lower student-staff ratios and pay for specialists to help with reading, mathematics, or instruction in English as a second language (ESL).

THE ORGANIZATION AND DELIVERY OF SUPPLEMENTAL INSTRUCTION

The classrooms we visited varied tremendously in the array and extent of services available to the students. Consider the pattern of supplemental instruction we found in the following classroom:

> *Supplemental instruction serving Ms. Jones's sixth-grade class.* Ms. Jones's 30 sixth graders are served by a Chapter 1 program in reading and a locally funded program in mathematics. Every day, twenty-two students receive remedial reading help in a room down the hall, where two teachers instruct them in phonics, the use of new vocabulary words, and comprehension strategies (e.g., finding the main idea and distinguishing general statements from statements of detail). Meanwhile, the other eight students read and discuss novels with the regular teacher. In mathematics, an instructional assistant takes five to eight students into the coatroom to work with a skill until they master it.

In some other classrooms, students did not leave their regular classrooms to work with specialists, as the students in Ms. Jones's room did. Students designated in need of extra help might find themselves working with various adults in the regular classroom itself, as in the following case:

> *Supplemental instruction in Mr. Day's third-grade class.* Mr. Day has been given a smaller than average group of students as a "language development class" — 22 students, only eight of whom are native English speakers. The class size is small because of the district's desegre-

gation consent decree. Three aides each spend 40 minutes a day in the room. One works with a reading group that Mr. Day does not teach; another sits at a table in the back of the room and offers extra help to students identified by the teacher; the third works with students having limited English proficiency who need ESL instruction or support in language arts and math. Some students get help from individuals outside the classroom. The assistant principal works with lower-achieving math students, starting with five students at the beginning of the year; three are sent back to the classroom in January, and the others return in the ensuing months. Students also go to a computer lab periodically; this lab is taught by another specialist, who plans computer instruction with the classroom teacher.

These examples only begin to suggest the variability in supplemental instruction arrangements among the classrooms we observed. Across all schools, we found the same kinds of students eligible for different programs, depending on the classroom and the school; the same program staffed differently from school to school; a wide range of individual staff capabilities; and an equally diverse set of working relationships between special staff and classroom teachers. Thus, the set of services a child could receive and the way these did or did not connect to regular instruction were unique from classroom to classroom.

Amid the variety of arrangements, one can distinguish several broad patterns in the way supplemental instruction was organized and delivered, defined by its location (outside or inside the regular classroom) and staffing (with aides or certified teachers). A school or district did not typically restrict itself to one of these patterns; most classrooms experienced more than one organizational mode, and many students did as well. The examples illustrate how the forms of supplemental instruction worked and highlight the ways they might contribute to both teaching and learning in the regular classroom.

Supplemental Instruction Outside the Regular Classroom

Supplemental instruction outside the regular classroom is generally intended to supply students with specialized remediation in the skills they lack. In the schools we studied, the instructors in such "pullout" settings were almost always certified specialist teachers; rarely did students leave their classrooms to receive supplemental instruction from an instructional aide, unless a specialist teacher was also present in the pullout room. This way of organizing and delivering supplemental instruction typically relies on a relatively formal diagnosis of children's needs, either individually (e.g., in special education) or as a group (e.g., ESL instruction for Spanish-dominant children).

We encountered four main forms of pullout instruction, most with a targeted subgroup of the classroom population: (1) compensatory or remedial services offered in pullout rooms, targeted to low-achieving youngsters; (2) instruction in special-education resource rooms, targeted to children with identified disabilities; (3) various forms of small-group pullout instruction offering English language assistance, targeted to individuals with limited or no English proficiency; and (4) computer laboratories, a special case of pullout instruction serving all the children in the regular classroom. In addition to these four, a few schools experimented with other forms of out-of-class assistance involving instruction after school hours or during the break between school terms.

Compensatory and remedial pullout services. Remedial services provided by Chapter 1 and state or locally funded special services commonly followed the form of pullout instruction exemplified in Ms. Jones's room. In the schools served by this kind of remedial program, services offered outside the regular classroom often — but not always — focused on improving students' performance in discrete skills. The connection to the regular classroom program tended to be fairly weak, especially when the regular program offered an integrated or academically advanced curriculum. In one school, five second graders received all their language arts instruction in a separate Chapter 1 classroom. Although they used the same basal reader as the rest of their class, the pace was slower and the emphasis on phonics, decoding, spelling, and vocabulary was much greater. Over the course of the year, they did much less writing than the rest of their class and virtually no extended text writing.

This scenario can also play in reverse. In another school, fourth-grade mathematics in the Chapter 1 room focused on conceptual understanding and made extensive use of manipulatives, in contrast to the regular teacher's program, which followed the text closely and included a great deal of drill. In another district, where serious efforts were being made to restructure curriculum and instruction in all classrooms, one school structured a pullout program, partially funded through Chapter 1, to enrich regular classroom instruction. Students from several grades participated in a modified version of the Higher Order Thinking Skills (HOTS) program, a software package that focused on the development of generic thinking skills.

The provision of remedial or compensatory services outside of the regular classroom can stir strong feelings among teachers. When specialized remediation had its own instructional agenda that differed from that of the teacher, the teacher tended to ignore it or dislike it. In other cases, however, teachers respected the specialists' expertise and considered the supplemental instruction a useful way to shore up students' skills. As we discuss later in this chapter, these differing perceptions appeared to have an important influence on the amount of communication between regular and special teachers.

Special-education resource rooms. A number of classrooms we studied were served by special-education resource rooms, a classic example of pullout instruction, where a specialist teacher works to remedy the educational deficits identified in each "disabled" child's individualized education program. Special education was not a prominent part of the instructional scene for any of our classrooms, since at most only two or three children from each classroom participated in it. In general, the resource room represented a kind of Bermuda Triangle for the instructional program: The classroom teachers tended to know little or nothing about the instruction that took place there. One fifth-grade teacher complained that she had asked the special-education teacher for a written report on what she was doing with the children but had never received one. In another school, a student assigned to the resource room for three hours a day simply didn't go there, with the result that he effectively had no academic instruction all year (since his regular classroom instruction was far over his head). Although these examples are extreme ones, they illustrate the disconnection between special education and most classrooms we studied.

ESL instruction outside the regular classroom. The ESL instruction offered in separate settings in these schools typically proceeded along a track that was independent of regular classroom instruction. A group of students left one first-grade classroom for 40 minutes every afternoon to participate in language development activities such as singing songs and learning rhymes. During this time, their English-dominant classmates were reading and discussing stories. In another case, four fifth graders who left their classrooms every day during reading time were experiencing many opportunities to write in the ESL lab.

The special case of computer labs. Instruction in computer labs differed from many other kinds of pullout supplemental instruction in two respects: It was not funded from outside sources, and it was not targeted to particular students. However, it is worth including here because it supplemented regular classroom instruction and because it presented a remarkably homogeneous story among the schools we visited: Once a week, either half the class or the full class spent 30 to 45 minutes in the computer lab, where students worked on software selected by the computer specialist in consultation with the classroom teacher. A primary aim of this work was to provide drill and practice on isolated skills through a medium that the children enjoyed more than workbooks. There was often an attempt to match the skills to those being taught in the regular classroom, especially in mathematics but sometimes in language arts as well. However, the success of these attempts was limited by the availability of appropriate software.

Other forms of supplemental instruction outside the regular classroom. In a few schools, supplemental instruction outside the regular classroom was provided in ways that do not fit any of the forms just discussed. A relatively rare mode of organizing and delivering supplemental programs sought to increase the amount of instructional time available to students by working with them outside the regular hours of the school day or year. We found just two examples of using outside funding in this way. One was a Chapter 1 program offered during intersession (the four-week period between regular school sessions) in a year-round school, which featured a relatively challenging curriculum. The other was an after-school tutoring program funded by Chapter 1. A few schools and individual teachers also used local funding sources to offer opportunities for extended instruction time, such as after-school tutoring or extra help at lunchtime.

Supplemental Instruction in the Regular Classroom

Over the years, many educators and scholars have expressed reservations about supplemental instruction offered outside the regular classroom, charging that it may foster a fragmented instructional experience for students. Thus, a number of schools — and most of the ones we visited — have organized supplemental programs so that this instruction is delivered inside the regular classroom. At least in the schools we were studying, in-class supplemental instruction was typically staffed by paraprofessional aides, sometimes in conjunction with specialist teachers of some kind. We observed three principal variations on the theme: (1) aides whose role in the classroom was to help with seatwork and clerical chores, (2) aides or teachers who provided "pull-aside" teaching or specialized group work, and (3) specialist teachers who team-taught with the regular classroom teacher or gave demonstration lessons.

Help with seatwork and clerical chores. Help with seatwork was an especially common mode of supplemental instruction in this sample of schools and classrooms. Almost always provided by an instructional aide, this help was often available on an ad hoc basis for any child who asked. Sometimes, though, it was restricted to certain children. When funded by Chapter 1, it was restricted to low-achieving children eligible for these services (as diagnosed by a placement test at the beginning of the year). In other cases, the help came from a bilingual aide and was offered only to those students who spoke a language other than English.

Help with seatwork served three main functions in the classroom. First, by providing extra adult supervision for seatwork, it freed the teacher to concentrate on a small group of students while the others were productively occupied. This was especially common in reading instruction, when the teachers often worked with small groups. Second, it gave some reinforcement for the skills that the students were practicing in their seatwork; this was true in both reading and mathematics instruction. Third, it reduced students' frustration and apparently contributed to their productivity by enabling them to receive answers to their questions more quickly. (However, in at least some cases, the students might have derived more long-term benefit from puzzling out the answers themselves rather than relying on an adult to help.)

Sometimes the seatwork helper stationed herself or himself at a table in the classroom, where students knew that they could bring their questions. In other cases (or at other times) the helper circulated around the room, pausing to help individuals. In a typical example from a first-grade classroom, a Chapter 1 aide came regularly into the room at the beginning of the math period and unobtrusively worked with individual Chapter 1 students at their desks on the day's assignments. Occasionally, she pulled one or more children aside for drill on math facts or to play a game. Bilingual aides sometimes sat right next to particular children for extensive periods of time. Children in need of this kind of attention were usually new to the country, and such intensive assistance was generally of relatively short duration. In these situations, the aide translated and provided assistance with assigned tasks.

Help with seatwork was available for only part of the school day in these classrooms, but it could be available for as much as four hours a day. The most complicated arrangement we encountered was in one classroom where three or four different aides were present for about 40 minutes each at different times during the day.

Although there seemed to be a general feeling that help with seatwork was a good thing for students, one first-grade teacher pointed out a drawback—that students could become too dependent on adult help. She commented that she watched for signs of dependency and asked the aide to "pull back" if it seemed to be developing. Although this was a potential problem in other classrooms as well, teachers did not seem to worry about it.

Using an aide to provide help with seatwork may reflect an underlying problem of the aide's unpredictable availability or limited instructional skills. Some teachers might have planned a more structured supplemental learning opportunity for their students if they could have counted
on the aide both being there and having the needed skills. But when the
aide "usually appears at math time," as in one classroom we studied, the
teacher had little choice but to use the aide's time in less structured, more
peripheral ways. Another teacher who used her Chapter 1 math aide for
help with seatwork was concerned that the aide would do things that
might confuse the children. Although these teachers did not explicitly say
so, there is good reason to believe that using aides to help with seatwork
was a way of making the best use of a poor resource.

Some aides served largely in a clerical capacity due to their limited
skills, their unpredictable availability, or the availability of other sources
of help with academic instruction (e.g., in one classroom a student teacher
took over the role of seatwork helper that an aide had previously filled).
We encountered more than one situation in which an aide was in great
demand as a translator for the whole school, including the main office.
In one instance, an aide who had been a teacher in Hong Kong before
immigrating to the United States obviously had the skills to assist in the
classroom, but she was constantly being pulled away from her regular
schedule to help in ad hoc situations requiring her language facility.

Pull-aside instruction or special grouping. In several classrooms, the supplemental instruction that took place inside the classroom was no different
from that which might take place elsewhere in the building. This instruction includes what could be called "pull-aside" teaching, in which a specialist teacher or an aide pulls a small group to the back of the room for
special instruction or practice in skills that the students are judged to need.
It also includes grouping arrangements that provide different experiences
for subgroups within a class.

In these cases, a major function of supplemental instruction was to
provide students with extra, or more differentiated, work in small groups.
In one first grade with traditional reading groups, the lowest group received pull-aside instruction twice a day—once with an aide and once
with a state-funded reading resource teacher. In another classroom,
whole-class instruction was interspersed with small-group work in which
the regular teacher, regular aide, Chapter 1 teacher, and Chapter 1 aide
each took one group. The teacher characterized the Chapter 1 groups as
providing "remediation for students with deficits in several skills areas."

An important part of the story in both of the above examples was that
these classrooms were under a mandate to provide whole-class instruction.

As the teacher in the second example put it, her less able students "have to struggle along with the smartest in the whole [class]." Concerned that these students would be unable to keep up, these teachers (and others who were reluctantly adopting whole-class instruction) welcomed a special small-group intervention as a supplement to their whole-class technique.

We saw other classrooms where supplemental grouping arrangements represented a division of labor between the teacher and the aide for reading instruction, and sometimes this structure seemed problematic. For example, one bilingual aide worked with individuals or small groups at the back of the classroom. At first, she followed lesson plans provided by the teacher. However, as the year wore on, the aide's program became more and more independent of the teacher's and less congruent with the overall instructional approach in that classroom. In another situation, the teacher allowed the aide to choose a reading group to work with. The aide usually chose the lower group because she considered that group easier to prepare for. Clearly, the lower reading group in this classroom was placed at a disadvantage by this arrangement, since those children rarely had an opportunity to work with the certified teacher during reading instruction. However, the strengths and weaknesses of the other special grouping arrangements we observed were less clear-cut.

Team teaching or demonstration lessons. In some cases, specialist teachers entered the regular classrooms on a regular basis to do more than provide pull-aside instruction to an identified group of children. We observed several cases in which specialists taught the whole class (with or without the regular classroom teacher) and often worked with the teacher on instructional improvement. In one school, this model had an especially important impact on students. A mathematics specialist, funded under a desegregation consent decree, conducted the mathematics instruction for a fourth-grade class once each week. His instruction, which emphasized concepts and modeled the thinking process for students, was strong. Even more important, however, was the fact that as the only male African American teacher in a school where almost all the students were African American, he provided an important presence for the boys and brought a cultural dimension to the instruction through his selection of problems and examples.

Elsewhere, districts capitalized on the special expertise of certain supplemental program staff and used them as a professional development resource for the regular classroom teachers. One district revamped its Chapter 1 program during the course of our study and used the resources during the study's second year to support itinerant teams of staff developers, who spent two to five weeks at each school. The teams conducted in-service sessions on topics related to the district's new integrated approach to language arts instruction, and they demonstrated mathematics and language arts lessons in the regular classrooms at the request of individual teachers.

CONTRIBUTIONS OF SUPPLEMENTAL INSTRUCTION TO HIGH-POVERTY CLASSROOMS

The purposes and designs of supplemental programs differed in many ways among the classrooms we studied, but a fundamental distinction in the scope of these programs helps pinpoint what they were able to contribute to instruction in high-poverty classrooms: In some programs, funding was targeted to specific students (as in special education, ESL, and most Chapter 1 programs in the schools we observed), in others, it was intended to support or alter instruction for the classroom (or school) as a whole. In the latter category were local funds provided under desegregation orders as well as a small portion of Chapter 1 funding (in situations in which federal regulations permitted these funds to benefit the entire school); these funds typically supported classroom aides who could work with any student or do clerical tasks.

Bearing in mind these differences in program design, four issues are crucial to understanding what these programs contributed to academic instruction in high-poverty classrooms: the content and methods of supplemental instruction, the philosophies that guided the targeting of supplemental services, communication among supplemental and regular staff, and supplemental staff expertise.

Content and Methods of Supplemental Instruction

The instructional content and methods we observed in supplemental programs varied enormously, as did the congruence between supplemental instruction and the regular classroom program. Some of this variation—as well as the most common themes—is captured by data summarized in Figures 6-1 and 6-2, which display the principal focus of observed supplemental instruction in mathematics and language arts.

As can be seen in the figures, three-quarters or more of the supplemental instruction we observed—inside or outside the regular classroom—focused on discrete skills, regardless of subject area. The percentage was greatest in pullout math instruction. A focus on discrete skills was especially common in services targeted to low-achieving students, as in the following case:

FIGURE 6–1. What is taught in supplemental mathematics instruction

Among classrooms [a] served by supplemental mathematics programs, the percentage in which supplemental instruction had each focus, when offered:

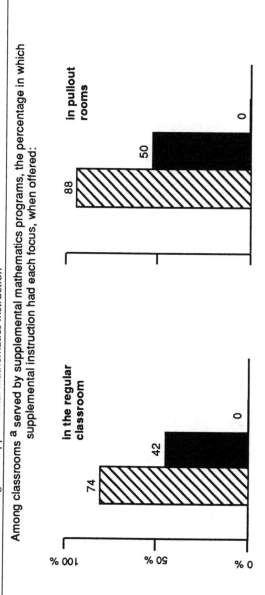

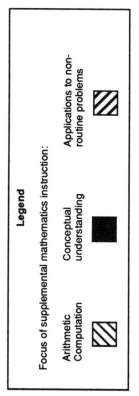

Legend

Focus of supplemental mathematics instruction:

Arithmetic Computation

Conceptual understanding

Applications to non-routine problems

a   Based on an analysis of all 56 classrooms served by supplemental programs in year 2 of the study.

FIGURE 6–2. What is taught in supplemental language arts instruction

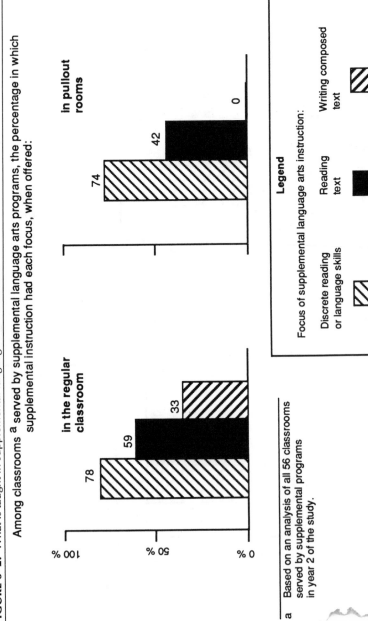

Among classrooms [a] served by supplemental language arts programs, the percentage in which supplemental instruction had each focus, when offered:

In pullout rooms

74

42

0

In the regular classroom

78

59

33

100 %

50 %

0 %

Legend

Focus of supplemental language arts instruction:

Discrete reading or language skills

Reading text

Writing composed text

a   Based on an analysis of all 56 classrooms served by supplemental programs in year 2 of the study.

Pullout instruction for students from Ms. McManus's class. Fifteen first graders from Ms. McManus's classroom go to the Chapter 1 reading room for 45 minutes each day, where they split into groups that work with two teachers and two aides. The activities observed on a typical day include a drill on vowel sounds (featuring flash cards, exaggerated sounding out, and answers in unison from the children), a word-recognition game, a workbook several levels below the regular class work, and an aide reading from a trade book. Ms. McManus notes the heavy skill focus of this program and the limited demands it makes on the children; she says that the children just come back from the reading room "with another 'sh' ditto when they learned 'sh' months ago . . . they never do any writing up there."

Not all teachers expressed displeasure with the discrete skills practice their students received from supplemental program teachers. Many relied on aides or specialists to reinforce and solidify the skills that their "slower" students were unable to master during regular classroom instruction.

The supplemental instruction we observed was not exclusively focused on discrete skills. In various cases, students were engaged in activities through supplemental instruction that may have brought them closer to the meaning-oriented instruction described in earlier chapters. This includes much of the supplemental instruction that was not targeted to low achievers (e.g., that supported by funding associated with desegregation). As Figure 6-2 indicates, in more than half of all instances of supplemental language arts instruction in the regular classroom, students *were* reading text; in almost half of the instances of observed supplemental mathematics instruction, as shown in Figure 6-1, there was some attempt to enhance students' conceptual understanding of mathematical material. Although writing generally receives scant attention in supplemental instruction settings, in a third of all the classrooms with in-class supplemental programs, this assistance involved writing some form of composed text.

The limitations on our data about supplemental instruction prohibit us from characterizing this instructional assistance further. We cannot say how systematically supplemental teachers or aides implemented the various meaning-oriented strategies discussed in earlier chapters, though we can make some reasonable inferences about the likely presence or absence of these strategies.

On balance, the content and methods of most supplemental instruction seemed to be in line with patterns of mathematics, reading, and writing instruction oriented toward discrete skills rather than meaning-oriented instruction as we have described it. There were many forces and conditions that contributed to this pattern, including the traditions of the more established supplemental programs (such as Chapter 1, which has a long tradition of diagnostic-prescriptive teaching aimed at basic skills in language arts and mathematics); the capabilities of the supplemental program staff, which are discussed in greater detail below; and the organization of the supplemental program (which often allowed supplemental teachers or aides to work with students for only short periods, perhaps 10 to 20 minutes in many cases).

Regular classroom teachers, including many who favored meaning-oriented approaches, may well have been another voice encouraging supplemental programs to continue operating along the lines of conventional practice. Having supplemental program staff assist students with the basics that they had not yet mastered may have appeared to be a reasonable way of covering all the bases. A curious example of this pattern occurred in a number of schools in which teachers were struggling with a state- or district-mandated shift to whole-class instruction. Particularly in reading instruction, a number of teachers were not sure that this new policy would work. In several of these situations, teachers appeared to use supplemental instruction as a kind of buffer against a complete transition to the whole-class approach. When the schedule included help from supplemental staff, teachers felt justified in (and looked forward to) breaking the class into small, achievement-based groups, just as they had before the mandated change.

Unfortunately, these arrangements may not have been optimal for the children served by supplemental programs. Isolation of the lower-achieving children — either in a pullout room or in separate groups within the same classroom — seemed to free up the regular teacher to place more emphasis on meaning with the remaining students. The students who were pulled out or aside missed this enriched activity and too often endured tedious drills on discrete skills taken entirely out of context.

Philosophies That Guide the Targeting of Supplemental Instruction

The contribution of supplemental instruction to the classroom also depends on the nature of program targeting: Who is served, and for how long? What are the consequences for these children's relationships to others in the classroom? Reflecting the two distinct purposes for supplemental programs, two philosophies were apparent across the many supplemental programs we encountered.

On the one hand, many children were served by supplemental programs in a temporary and flexible fashion, on an "as-needed" basis as something arose in their learning. In one busy sixth-grade classroom, many "helpers" appeared on a regular basis, including drop-in visitors from two teachers colleges, a student teacher, a volunteer from a local company, a volunteer on leave from college, and a Chapter 1 aide. In this room, most students asked for and received individual help from someone. Chapter 1 students were therefore not singled out as the only students in need of assistance.

On the other hand, children served by other supplemental programs were typically identified for services because they were not succeeding, with the expectation that they would need sustained attention over a long period. This more common approach assumes that children will be served in an instructional group (or individual tutoring assignment) that remains stable over time. This is the approach usually favored for supplemental services funded through Chapter 1 and special education because of their more formal mandates for fiscal or programmatic accountability.

Underlying these two approaches is a difficult philosophical issue about targeting supplemental instruction: Is it ad hoc assistance, geared toward helping students keep up with the class, or is it a separate and relatively permanent track? Although our limited observations do not allow us to resolve the matter, we can indicate the likely consequences for students in the classrooms we observed. First, it was clear that many students did indeed stay with an assigned supplemental program over a long period—in some cases, two years or more—and the individuals in question were generally referred to by program label as a "Chapter kid," "a special-ed student," or so on. Second, it was clear that these permanent targeted arrangements often resulted in a more differentiated array of learning experiences than would otherwise have been the case—higher-order questioning from the regular classroom teacher, discrete skills practice from the Chapter 1 aide; one textbook in the regular classroom, another in the pullout room; and so on.

In short, in response to federal and state programs that emphasize serving particular students and not others, the school districts and schools we studied had become adept at sorting students and arranging differentiated services for them, whether inside or outside the regular classroom. The question is whether this enhances or limits these students' learning opportunities. The fact that some students remained in supplemental programs for years, coupled with our other findings about these programs' pervasive focus on discrete skills, suggests that supplemental instruction may unnecessarily limit these children's learning while helping them master some particular parts of a complex whole.

Communication Between Supplemental and Regular Staff

The contribution of supplemental instruction to the regular classroom program rests, in part, on the communication between their respective staffs. As long as supplemental services are distinct from the regular classroom program (whether or not they take place in the same room), there will be an issue about the connection between regular and supplemental instruction. In the schools we observed, we found a continuum from close connection between supplemental and regular instruction to total isolation from each other. We saw some effective partnerships between teachers and aides or between pairs of teachers. We also saw teachers who supervised their aides closely because they thought they had to, and a few others who had given up on supervising aides with whom they disagreed. We saw many supplemental programs that operated in isolation from the regular classroom — with educational effects that we were often unable to judge, although there were a few cases of special instruction that clearly mired students in isolated, low-level skills drills.

We were able to learn about the working relationships among staff and, in particular, the classroom teacher's degree of control over the instruction offered by supplemental staff, which appeared to depend on the type of supplemental staff hired. Teachers customarily told aides what to do, particularly when the aides worked in the regular classroom; they did not tell other teachers what to do. Thus, although there were some exceptions, most of the in-class instruction provided by aides was relatively closely connected to the regular classroom program. The teacher often wrote a set of instructions for the aide or presented the aide with materials to use.

By contrast, when classroom teachers and supplemental teachers worked together, they often engaged in planning or collaborative sessions. Doing so was more time-consuming than giving instructions to an aide, and both parties contributed to the discussion. Such planning and collaboration happened when it was administratively feasible (that is, when time was specifically set aside for it) and when the teachers wanted it to happen (that is, when they liked and respected each other enough to feel that collaboration was worthwhile).

Teachers who perceived specialized remedial instruction as valuable tended to have more communication with the supplemental program specialists, but it is probably not accurate to say that better communication improved the perceived contribution of the program. Instead, it seems at least as likely that teachers were inclined to communicate more with the specialists whose skills and programs they respected.

Scheduling had a big influence on the extent of joint planning. An aide who helped with seatwork might be available in the classroom for only an hour or two, which might not coincide with any of the teacher's planning time. Thus, the district and school could increase or decrease teachers' and aides' opportunities to plan; the unpredictable schedules of some supplemental staff seriously detracted from their ability to plan with teachers. The other side of the story was found in those districts and schools that were deliberately working to increase the opportunities for collaborative planning. The Chapter 1 director in one district orchestrated a schedule by which each teacher who served Chapter 1 children had a weekly three-way planning session with the assigned Chapter 1 aide and the building's reading resource teacher. This was not easy to do, and it took some time to work out the glitches, but it was a start.

Another important determinant of working relationships among staff members was the stability of supplemental instructional arrangements from year to year or even within a school year. From the perspective of the classroom teacher, supplemental services and staff members often seemed to come and go in mysterious ways. It was rare for a teacher to face a stable configuration of programs and supplemental staff from year to year. In one district, it became necessary to use virtually all staff members who were not regular classroom teachers as substitutes. Reductions in force and other types of fiscal crises could create havoc with supplemental programs as well.

Instructional Expertise of Supplemental Program Staff

In ways that were both obvious and subtle, the teaching capabilities of supplemental staff greatly influenced what their teaching offered to classroom instruction. In general, aides were at the low end of the instructional skills continuum and specialist teachers were at the high end, although there were many individual exceptions to this pattern. At the same time, many aides shared a cultural background with the racial or linguistic minority students in the class, which could help establish the all-important sense of connection between home and school discussed in Chapter 2.

The background and expertise of supplemental program staff clearly predisposed them toward teaching certain kinds of content (if they taught at all) and even toward certain methods of teaching. Thus, at one extreme, the aides with the least training in reading or math were likely to teach discrete skills in a highly traditional way, whether or not the regular classroom teacher emphasized different things. Such staff members were typically not equipped to help teach comprehension strategies or to probe students' reading comprehension at other than a literal or recall level of understanding. At the other extreme, specialists were often at least as prepared as regular classroom teachers to handle more challenging teaching approaches. Supplemental program teachers even offered professional leadership in several of the schools: In some cases, the specialist teachers supported by supplemental funds offered demonstration lessons, staff development, and materials to help teachers who were trying alternative approaches to instruction. (Contrary to many local educators' beliefs, this can be a legal use of Chapter 1 funds when the assistance is carefully designed to strengthen classroom teachers' capacity to work with participating Chapter 1 students.)

Classroom teachers varied in the way they handled the issue of supplemental staff expertise. Some teachers kept a close watch when their aides helped with seatwork because they did not have a high opinion of the aides' skills; others assigned clerical tasks to aides for the same reason. However, classroom teachers who had reservations about the skills of specialist teachers were often unable to do anything about this problem.

Similarly, teachers varied in their responses to supplemental staff members who had wide repertoires of instructional skills. Some were eager to learn from these staff members and arranged opportunities to do so (e.g., by remaining in the room while the supplemental teacher worked with the whole class). Others were either unable or unwilling to watch their colleagues at work and thus did not know what these staff members brought to the overall instructional resources of the school.

Implications for Meaning-Oriented Instruction

The dominant purpose of supplemental programs in the schools we studied was to provide targeted services for selected students. This often meant that instruction focused on the discrete skills in which these students had shown deficiencies. The targeting might be relatively flexible or relatively permanent; the services might involve seatwork practice with an aide that built directly on the day's classroom lesson, or they might involve a virtually separate curriculum with a specialist. In a small number of schools, targeting was not a main feature of program design; instead, supplemental programs were designed to upgrade instruction for whole classes or whole buildings. This was a feasible use of local desegregation funding, and it could sometimes be accommodated in a Chapter 1 program design as well.

In schools that took the latter approach — where supplemental staff taught demonstration lessons, offered other forms of professional development, and generally brought ideas about teaching for meaning — the contribution of supplemental funding could clearly be in line with the instructional strategies discussed in this book. There are, of course, pitfalls in this endeavor: Specialist teachers vary in their skill as staff developers, and this way of organizing supplemental services may neglect the needs of low-achieving students. However, we saw examples that convinced us of the promise of this approach.

The analysis of outcomes associated with each pattern of instruction takes us one step toward understanding how supplemental instruction might contribute to the learning of targeted children. In analyzing outcomes, we subdivided our total pool into those at the lower-achieving end of the student spectrum—the majority of whom were served by some supplemental program—and those at the higher end—few of whom worked on a regular basis with a supplemental program teacher or aide. The results, described in detail in Chapter 7, point to various benefits of meaning-oriented approaches for low-achieving students. Our analyses cannot, however, disentangle all the sources contributing to students' learning outcomes.

Ultimately, the question of what specific contributions supplemental instruction makes to the academic learning of *individual* children cannot be answered by studies such as ours that focus on curriculum and instruction at the classroom level. Only research that follows individual children can properly assess the impact of supplemental services on their learning. Our investigation makes it clear that, in principle, supplemental instruction has a lot to offer and can accomplish much. Many barriers exist, however, that diminish the contributions supplemental instruction is likely to make to students' acquisition of the advanced skills on which this book focuses.

CHAPTER 7

The Outcomes of Teaching for Meaning in High-Poverty Classrooms

Michael S. Knapp
Camille Marder
Andrew A. Zucker
Nancy E. Adelman
Margaret C. Needels

The instructional practices in mathematics, reading, and writing described in the previous chapters beg three important questions. First, what implications were there for student learning? In particular, did students who received the most meaning-oriented instruction learn the "advanced skills" of reasoning, problem solving, comprehension, and composition—which are the ostensible focus of teaching for meaning—better than their counterparts in skills-oriented classrooms? Second, did these approaches to instruction work as well for students at the low end of the achievement continuum as for the brightest? Third, what about students' mastery of discrete basic skills in literacy and numeracy—that is, were students who were heavily exposed to teaching for meaning able to learn to decode, compute, spell, and punctuate as well as students whose instruction focused primarily on these discrete skills?

This chapter describes in broad, summary terms what we found in answer to these questions. Space precludes us from a complete, technical presentation of the analyses and findings on which our conclusions are based; readers wishing that kind of detail may find it in the full study report (Knapp et al., 1992).

HOW WE INVESTIGATED EFFECTS ON STUDENT LEARNING

To investigate the degree and kind of student learning that can be attributed to meaning-oriented or skills-oriented instruction, one needs appro-

124

priate measures of student learning. In this regard, teaching for meaning poses a significant challenge to the investigator, because such measures are in some instances not available or are prohibitively costly for large-scale studies.

Outcome Measures

We resolved the matter by settling for a mixture of outcome measures that would offer a crude picture of the range of effects such instruction might have. Thus, to get at conceptual understanding and problem-solving ability in mathematics, we concentrated on:

- *Conceptual understanding of mathematical ideas*, as measured by a widely used standardized instrument, the Comprehensive Test of Basic Skills (CTBS)/Level 4, Mathematical Concepts and Applications subtest. This outcome was measured for students in all elementary grades. For analyses, we converted the raw score into normal curve equivalents (NCEs).
- *Mathematical problem-solving ability*, as measured by a test consisting of "mathematical problem solving superitems" developed and validated by the Center for Research on Mathematics Education at the University of Wisconsin (Romberg, 1982). These items pose nonroutine problems to students and then ask questions at varying levels of difficulty about the problems in an open-ended rather than multiple-choice format. The superitems tests were used with students in the third through sixth grades. For analyses, we used the percentage of correct items, because there is no way to create a norm-based score comparable to NCEs.

In addition, we gathered data on the students' proficiency in arithmetic computation, using the corresponding CTBS/4 subtest.

In selecting these measures, we were well aware of their shortcomings, but given the constraints on the study design and the number of data-collection tasks, it was not feasible to gather data on mathematical outcomes more intensively (e.g., through individual measures or with instruments that required more administration time). Nor did we use additional instruments to get at students' attitudes or beliefs about mathematics, which are arguably an extremely important outcome of instruction. In addition, our measures did not directly tap the extent to which students' metacognitive abilities were affected by mathematics instruction.

In reading, we used a more limited set of measures, only one of which captured advanced skills:

- *Reading comprehension,* for which we used the Reading Comprehension subtest of the Comprehensive Test of Basic Skills (CTBS)/ Version 4 as a measure of students' ability to read with understanding.

To get at mastery of reading mechanics skills, we used the "Word Attack" and "Word-letter Identification" subscores of the Woodcock Language Proficiency Battery, an individualized measure thought to be especially useful with young students. Because of resource limitations, the test was given only to first through third graders (for whom the learning of discrete skills is often a major preoccupation of literacy instruction). In addition, the tests could not be given to all students; consequently, a subset of six students representing the range of abilities in each classroom took the test, and their scores were aggregated to form a classroom measure. In addition, the Woodcock was administered only in the spring of each data-collection year (fall pretest scores on the CTBS Reading Comprehension subtest were used as covariates for analyses).

This outcome measurement procedure had significant limitations. Chief among them, the test of reading comprehension does not pose for children the task of reading "authentic" material — a whole book, story, letter, memo, article, or whatever — and attempting to make sense of it, using all the means at their disposal. Although this complaint can be raised about many testing procedures, it is especially pertinent in the case of reading. Although experts generally agree that tests such as the CTBS capture some aspects of comprehension, there is a widespread feeling in the reading-assessment community that these kinds of measures miss important aspects of comprehension. Nonetheless, the measure does indicate whether children can extract meaning from several forms of written text, and to that extent it serves the purpose of distinguishing in a rough way between more or less effective instructional approaches. In addition, certain items on the CTBS attempt to capture other dimensions of comprehension that cannot be assessed by conventional short-passage items, for example, the students' ability to predict and make appropriate inferences from brief situations in text.

With regard to writing, we drew our measures from writing samples generated by students in response to one of two writing prompts (because of limited resources and the difficulties in assessing the writing of young children, writing samples were used with grades 3 through 6 only, as described in Appendix A). To get at the students' capacity to communicate meaningfully in writing, we developed the following measure:

- *Competence in written composition,* as judged by a panel of raters who assessed writing samples holistically. This measure focused on the quality of written expression without attention to the mechanical correctness of writing, which was captured by a second measure.

To provide a parallel measure of students' mastery of discrete writing skills, the same holistic scoring process was used to create a separate score for the mechanical correctness of students' writing (see Appendix A).

Although it is generally accepted that writing samples provide the most direct way to assess writing competence, the procedure has important weaknesses. The brief (approximately 20-minute) time for writing in response to the prompt gave students a chance to create only a first, rough draft; there was no time to edit or revise in ways that they may well have been taught. Nonetheless, the writing samples employed for this study offered a reasonable approximation of the writing proficiency of the students.

Linking Outcomes to Instructional Practices

The variation in approach to mathematics, reading, and writing instruction among the 140 classrooms we studied enabled us to examine through correlational techniques the relative effectiveness of meaning-oriented and skills-oriented instruction, while controlling statistically for other differences among classrooms that might influence outcomes. For simplicity, we summarize here the principal findings by contrasting classrooms placing the least emphasis on meaning (approximately a third of the classrooms for most analyses) with those that placed the most emphasis on meaning (between a quarter and a third for most analyses).

The study results answer questions of instructional effectiveness in three ways. First, for each school year and over 12-month periods (e.g., from one fall to the next), we assessed the associations between each type of instruction and measures of mathematical understanding, problem-solving ability, reading comprehension, and competence at written expression. Second, measures of mathematical computation, reading mechanics skills, and the mechanical correctness of written text provided a way of assessing the relative contribution of each classroom type to students' mastery of basic skills. Third, by comparing results for students in the lowest third of the overall achievement distribution with those in the highest third, it was possible to determine whether the associations between outcomes and instructional approaches depended on the students' initial levels of achievement.

In analyzing outcomes, we concentrated on the absolute level of students' scores at the end of the school year or after the 12-month period, controlling for the students' pretest scores and poverty levels. We chose this indicator, rather than gain scores, because we did not have fall pretest measures for several outcomes. In addition, by controlling for student pretest level (using a related measure as a proxy for the missing outcome measures), we could mathematically approximate what would have been learned from gain-score analyses.

Analyses of mathematics, reading, and writing outcomes were performed at the classroom and student levels (by attaching to each student's record the corresponding variables for the student's teacher or instructional approach). The latter mode of analysis provided a reasonable approximation of effects on students, although it was limited by the assumption that all students are independently — and equally — affected by instructional variables.

CAPACITY TO UNDERSTAND, REASON, AND COMPOSE

Armed with these measures, we tried to identify the extent to which teaching for meaning might be linked to student learning over the short term (fall to spring) and over a twelve-month period (fall to fall or spring to spring).

Short-Term Results (Fall to Spring)

Our analyses yielded clear evidence that students exposed to instruction that emphasized meaning in each subject area were likely to demonstrate a greater grasp of advanced skills at the end of the school year. As displayed in Figure 7-1, children receiving instruction focused on multiple mathematical topics and conceptual understanding performed significantly higher in advanced mathematical skills (e.g., in year 1, between 6 and 7 NCEs higher on a standardized test of mathematical understanding) than their counterparts in classrooms that focused on arithmetic skills only. Similar differences appeared with regard to results on a test of mathematical problem-solving ability. The evidence was not so strong in the second year, though also in a positive direction. We found comparable results for reading comprehension and competence in written composition, as summarized in Figures 7-2 and 7-3. For example, the students in

FIGURE 7-1. Mastery of advanced skills in mathematics: Comparing outcomes of meaning-oriented and skills-oriented instruction

Differences in scores (in normal curve equivalents) at the end of the school
year, on the CTBS/4 Concepts & Applications Test, controlling for initial
differences in achievement and poverty level

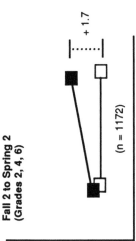

Fall 1 to Spring 1
(Grades 1, 3, 5)

+ 6.4*

(n = 1061)

Fall 2 to Spring 2
(Grades 2, 4, 6)

+ 1.7

(n = 1172)

Legend

Students exposed to:

■ Meaning-oriented mathematics instruction (emphasis on
multiple topics and conceptual understanding)

□ Skills-oriented mathematics instruction (emphasis on
computation skills in arithmetic only)

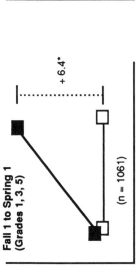

* Statistically significant at p < .05

Figure reads: "By comparison with their counterparts
exposed to arithmetic skills only, students exposed to
meaning-oriented mathematics instruction performed an
average of 6.4 NCEs higher at the end of year 1 (taking into
account initial differences in poverty level and achievement).
The result is statistically different from zero at the
.05 level . . . ."

FIGURE 7–2. Mastery of advanced skills in reading: Comparing outcomes of meaning-oriented and skills-oriented instruction

Differences in scores (in normal curve equivalents) at the end of the school year, on the CTBS/4 Reading Comprehension Test, controlling for initial differences in achievement and poverty level

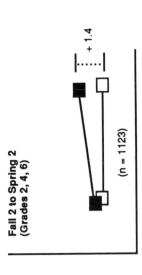

Fall 1 to Spring 1
(Grades 1, 3, 5)

+ 5.6*

(n = 1068)

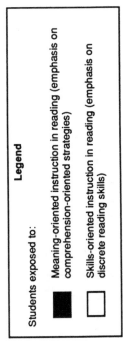

Fall 2 to Spring 2
(Grades 2, 4, 6)

+ 1.4

(n = 1123)

Legend

Students exposed to:

■ Meaning-oriented instruction in reading (emphasis on comprehension-oriented strategies)

□ Skills-oriented instruction in reading (emphasis on discrete reading skills)

* Statistically significant at p < .05

Figure reads: "By comparison with their counterparts in classrooms with skills-oriented approaches to reading instruction, students exposed to meaning-oriented reading instruction performed an average of 5.6 NCEs higher at the end of year 1 (taking into account initial differences in poverty level and achievement). The result is statistically different from zero at the .05 level . . . ."

FIGURE 7–3. Mastery of advanced skills in writing: Comparing outcomes of meaning-oriented and skills-oriented instruction

Differences in scores (in z-score units [a]) at the end of the school year, on a measure of competence in written composition (based on a writing sample), controlling for initial differences in achievement and poverty level [b]

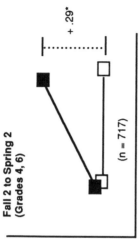

Fall 1 to Spring 1 (Grades 3, 5)

+ .27*

(n = 704)

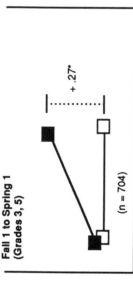

a See Appendix A for description of measures.
b Based on grades 3-6 only.
* Statistically significant at P < .05.

Figure reads: "By comparison with their counterparts exposed to skills-oriented writing instruction, students exposed to meaning-oriented writing instruction performed an average of .27 z-score units higher at the end of year 1 (taking into account initial differences in poverty level and achievement). The result is statistically different from zero at the .05 level . . . ."

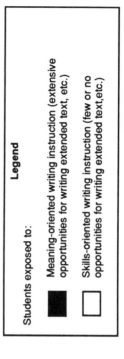

Fall 2 to Spring 2 (Grades 4, 6)

+ .29*

(n = 717)

Students exposed to: **Legend**

■ Meaning-oriented writing instruction (extensive opportunities for writing extended text, etc.)

□ Skills-oriented writing instruction (few or no opportunities for writing extended text, etc.)

reading classrooms with the most teaching for meaning ended the year between 1 and 6 NCEs higher than their counterparts in skills-oriented reading classrooms.

These results represent the difference in learning outcomes at the end of each school year, controlling for initial differences in students' levels of poverty and achievement. Put another way, the analysis identifies the increment of students' performance that can be attributed to the instructional approach, once initial differences among students are taken into account. Readers should bear in mind that this study is not reporting average NCE *gains* from pretest to posttest, as is typically done in many studies of instructional programs. Instead, our NCE figures represent the differences between the posttest scores of students receiving contrasting forms of instruction, controlling for differences in pretests and poverty levels at the beginning of the year.

The results in writing are replicated in both years of the study, whereas in mathematics and reading the effects are not as strong in the second year. There are various possible explanations for this fact, among them the uneven implementation of alternative forms of instruction and the possibility that less ambitious attempts to implement meaning-oriented instruction may have been more effective in the second year. For example, when one controls statistically for differences in teachers' backgrounds or general proficiency at managing instruction, the end-of-the-year difference in mathematics outcomes increases and reaches statistical significance. Also, when one considers the comparison (not shown in the figure) between classrooms with a *moderate* emphasis on meaning-oriented reading instruction and those aimed primarily at discrete skills, the former group scores consistently higher than the latter, and the differences are statistically significant in both years (3.9 and 4.4 NCEs, respectively).

Our findings mask some important differences between grade levels (although given the relatively small number of classrooms per grade, our ability to identify clear grade-by-grade differences was somewhat constrained). In mathematics, for example, effects of meaning-oriented instruction on the mastery of advanced skills appeared to be less pronounced in the upper elementary grades.

Longer-Term Results (Fall to Fall, Spring to Spring)

The evidence regarding the retention of learning over a 12-month period (thus including the summer months) tells a similar story, although the results are slightly more mixed. Over the 12 months from fall to fall, students exposed to instruction aimed at meaning and understanding performed significantly better than their counterparts exposed to conventional instruction in two of the three subject areas (mathematics and writing), as can be seen in Figure 7-4. Parallel analyses over the 12 months from the spring of the first year to the following spring reveal, in all three subject areas, positive differences that favor students exposed to instruction aimed at meaning and understanding—in one instance (writing) the difference is statistically significant, and in another (reading) it narrowly misses being significant. These analyses must be viewed as somewhat inconclusive, however; findings over both 12-month periods are seriously hampered by the loss of more than half the year 1 students from the year 2 sample.

The 12-month findings leave open the possibility that the results of meaning-oriented instruction are in various degrees susceptible to "summer fall-off," as are the results of other instructional approaches. This fact does not negate the positive effects of such instruction over the school year, but it raises questions about the importance of additional educational support over the summer months and also about the value of continued exposure to alternative instructional practices from year to year. We were unable to explore the impact of sustained exposure to meaning-oriented instruction, because so few of the students from year 1 who had experienced this kind of instruction ended up in classes the following year with comparable instructional experiences.

Because the size of effects is modest for most outcome analyses, it is worth asking whether the instructional approaches we studied actually help learners very much. Our conclusion is that statistically significant group differences in the range of +1 to +7 NCEs are noteworthy and educationally important. In demonstration or experimental studies, considerably larger effects have been reported, but in such settings, results can be demonstrated by experimental methods that permit a large number of relevant factors to be controlled. The results from this study are correlational: They indicate that when a variety of other relevant variables are taken into account, the instructional approaches under examination have consistent, positive associations with outcomes. They do so even when numerous other variables known to be related to learning (e.g., teacher expectations) are inconsistently or not at all linked to outcomes (see the discussion below of other influences on outcomes). The fact that teaching for meaning has consistent effects in such circumstances strikes us as educationally significant.

Differences Between High- and Low-Performing Children

Meaning-oriented approaches to mathematics, reading, and writing instruction would not make so much sense in high-poverty classrooms if they

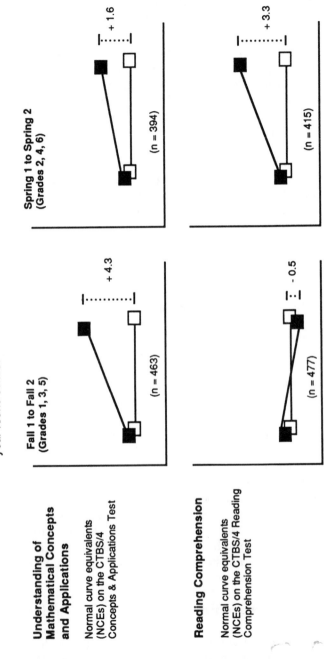

FIGURE 7–4. Sustained mastery of advanced skills: Comparing outcomes

Differences in scores at the end of a 12-month period, controlling for initial differences in achievement and poverty level, and for participation in a year-round school

Understanding of Mathematical Concepts and Applications

Normal curve equivalents (NCEs) on the CTBS/4 Concepts & Applications Test

Reading Comprehension

Normal curve equivalents (NCEs) on the CTBS/4 Reading Comprehension Test

Fall 1 to Fall 2 (Grades 1, 3, 5)

+ 4.3

(n = 463)

- 0.5

(n = 477)

Spring 1 to Spring 2 (Grades 2, 4, 6)

+ 1.6

(n = 394)

+ 3.3

(n = 415)

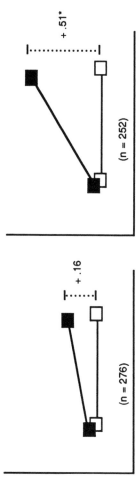

**Competence in
Written Composition** [a]

z-score units on writing
assessment [b]

(n = 276)

+ .16

(n = 252)

+ .51*

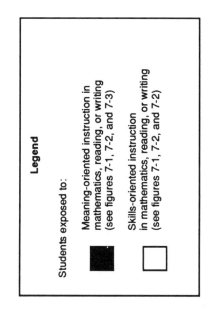

Legend

Students exposed to:

■ Meaning-oriented instruction in
mathematics, reading, or writing
(see figures 7-1, 7-2, and 7-3)

□ Skills-oriented instruction
in mathematics, reading, or writing
(see figures 7-1, 7-2, and 7-2)

a   Based on analysis of classrooms in
grades 3-6 only.

b   See Appendix A for explanation of
writing assessment measurements.

*   Statistically significant at p < .05.

Figure reads: "By comparison with their counterparts in
classrooms focusing on arithmetic computation skills,
students exposed to meaning-oriented mathematics
instruction performed an average of 4.3 NCEs higher at
the beginning of the next school year (taking into account
initial differences in poverty level and achievement, and
participation in a year-round school). . . ."

worked well only for the brightest children in these schools. To discover whether this was the case, we divided the overall student population into thirds based on levels of achievement at the beginning of the school year and then ran parallel analyses for each third.

The results, summarized in Figure 7-5, offer clear evidence that alternative practices work at least as well for low-performing students as for high-performing students. In all three subject areas, instruction aimed at meaning appeared to work as well for students at the low end of the achievement distribution as for those at the high end. In both years, the incremental difference attributable to alternative practices was positive for both groups, and in half the instances it was statistically different from zero at the .05 level. The weight of evidence thus inclines toward the assertion that, on average, after initial differences among them are taken into account, low-performing children increase their grasp of advanced skills at least as much as their high-achieving counterparts when both experience meaning-oriented instruction. And for both groups, this approach to instruction produces results superior to those of skills-oriented practices.

MASTERY OF DISCRETE SKILLS

Our outcome data for assessing the effects of instruction on children's grasp of discrete skills are somewhat less complete than for investigating effects on understanding, reasoning, and composing skills. Measures of discrete skills attainment were available for only one of the two years in mathematics and reading and, in the latter case, only for children in the lower three elementary grades. Nonetheless, some patterns of association can be discerned.

Overall, evidence presented in Figure 7-6 suggests that meaning-oriented practices do not impede the mastery of discrete skills and may facilitate it. In mathematics, children extensively exposed to teaching for meaning performed substantially better on measures of computational ability than students being taught arithmetic skills only — the very skills that were tested. In reading and writing, extensive exposure to instruction aimed at meaning generally produced positive differences in all but one instance (word-attack skills in year 1), although these differences were not statistically different from zero at the .05 level. Therefore, children's learning of discrete skills was no worse in classes that departed from conventional practices than in those that were oriented toward discrete skills learning.

Additional analyses indicated that, with regard to writing, a single-minded pursuit of discrete skills learning through heavy doses of instruc- tion in language mechanics skills does not significantly improve students' grasp of discrete skills. In reading, however, there is some evidence that such instruction does boost discrete skills scores, at least in the early grades.

OTHER INFLUENCES ON OUTCOMES

We considered other factors that could have influenced results, both be- cause they might offer alternative explanations for the apparent effects described above and because they might provide important insights into the components of effective practice. We did so by running the preceding outcome analyses with additional variables in the equation that indicated the amount of instructional time, the degree of attention paid to discrete skills, the teacher's general proficiency at managing instruction, and other background characteristics of the teacher.

These analyses indicated that the association between approach to instruction and students' capacity to understand what they read, reason mathematically, and compose was largely unaffected by the presence of these variables in regression equations. In other words, it appears that our results cannot be accounted for solely by the amount of time spent in instruction, the attention paid to discrete skills teaching, or various char- acteristics of the teachers. At the same time, many of these variables were themselves significantly linked to variation in outcomes, and in the direc- tions one might expect. In particular, the amount of time spent in instruc- tion was positively associated with outcomes, as was the teacher's general proficiency in managing instruction. Interestingly, the amount of instruc- tion in discrete skills (which meaning-oriented teachers did in varying degrees) was also positively linked to outcome scores on advanced skills.

Independent of instruction in any given year, characteristics of the students themselves were also powerful predictors of achievement out- comes. In all our analyses, two factors — poverty level and initial achieve- ment level — were consistently and powerfully linked to outcome scores (and, in statistical terms, they accounted for most of the variance in out- come measures). This result was hardly surprising; decades of educational research have uncovered similar associations. In other words, children's learning reflects the influence of various conditions linked to poverty level — differential access to school resources, inconsistent home support for learning, lack of familiarity with the culture of the school (combined with the school's lack of familiarity with the child's culture), or inade- quate nutrition. In a similar way, what a learner knows at the end of the

FIGURE 7-5. Mastery of advanced skills: Comparing outcomes of meaning-oriented and skills-oriented instruction for high- and low-performing students

Differences in scores at the end of the school year, controlling for initial differences in achievement and poverty level

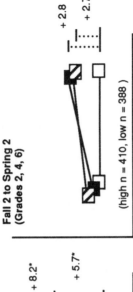

Fall 1 to Spring 1
(Grades 1, 3, 5)

+ 8.2*

+ 5.7*

(high n = 379, low n = 355)

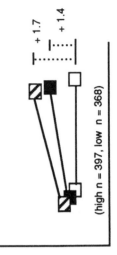

Fall 2 to Spring 2
(Grades 2, 4, 6)

+ 2.8

+ 2.7

(high n = 410, low n = 388)

Understanding of Mathematical Concepts and Applications

Normal curve equivalents (NCEs) on the CTBS/4 Concepts & Applications Test

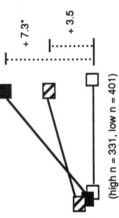

+ 7.3*

+ 3.5

(high n = 331, low n = 401)

+ 1.7

+ 1.4

(high n = 397, low n = 368)

Reading Comprehension

Normal curve equivalents (NCEs) on the CTBS/4 Reading Comprehension Test

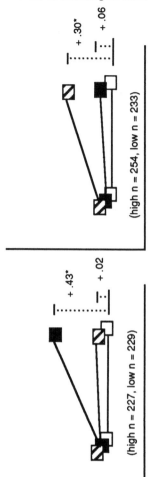

Competence in Written Composition [a]

z-score units on writing assessment [b]

+ .43*

+ .02

(high n = 227, low n = 229)

+ .30*

+ .06

(high n = 254, low n = 233)

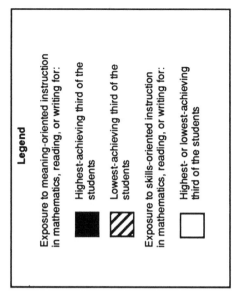

Legend

Exposure to meaning-oriented instruction in mathematics, reading, or writing for:

Highest-achieving third of the students

Lowest-achieving third of the students

Exposure to skills-oriented instruction in mathematics, reading, or writing for:

Highest- or lowest-achieving third of the students

a   Based on analysis of classrooms in grades 3-6 only.
b   See Appendix A for explanation of writing assessment measurements.
*   Statistically significant at p < .05.

Figure reads: "By comparison with their counterparts in classrooms focusing on arithmetic computation skills only, high-achieving students exposed to meaning-oriented mathematics instruction performed an average of 5.7 NCEs higher at the end of the school year, while low-achieving students performed 8.2 NCEs higher (taking into account initial differences in poverty level and achievement). Both of these differences are statistically different from zero at the .05 level. . . . "

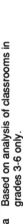

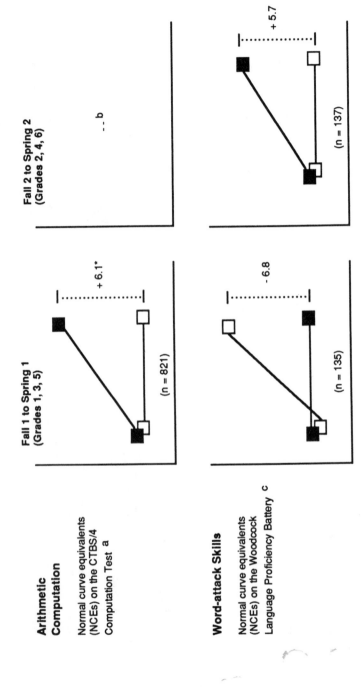

FIGURE 7–6. Mastery of discrete skills: Comparing outcomes of meaning-oriented and skills-oriented instruction

Differences in scores at the end of the school year, controlling for initial differences in achievement and poverty level

Arithmetic Computation

Normal curve equivalents (NCEs) on the CTBS/4 Computation Test [a]

Word-attack Skills

Normal curve equivalents (NCEs) on the Woodcock Language Proficiency Battery [c]

Mechanical Correctness of Writing [a]

z-score units on writing assessment [d]

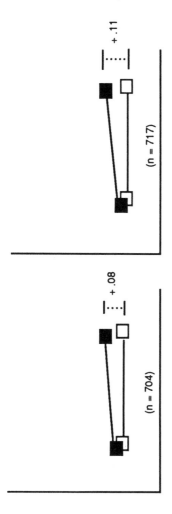

(n = 704)   + .08

(n = 717)   + .11

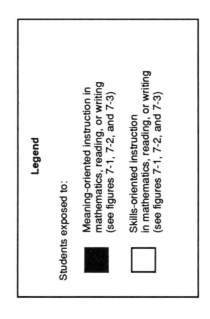

Legend

Students exposed to:

■ Meaning-oriented instruction in mathematics, reading, or writing (see figures 7-1, 7-2, and 7-3)

□ Skills-oriented instruction in mathematics, reading, or writing (see figures 7-1, 7-2, and 7-3)

a   Based on analysis of classrooms in grades 3-6 only.
b   Data unavailable in year 2.
c   Based on analysis of classrooms in grades 1 and 2 only.
d   See Appendix A for explanation of writing assessment measurement.
*   Statistically significant at p < .05.

Figure reads: "By comparison with their counterparts in classrooms focusing on arithmetic computation skills, students exposed to meaning-oriented mathematics instruction performed an average of 6.1 NCEs higher on a test of arithmetic computation at the end of year 1 (taking into account initial differences in poverty level and achievement). This difference is statistically different from zero at the .05 level. . . ."

school year is in part a function of what he or she knew at the year's beginning, which reflects the cumulative effects of teaching in earlier years, level of innate ability, self-image of the learner, or the pattern of response to the culture of the school.

SUMMARIZING AND INTERPRETING LINKS TO STUDENT LEARNING

The kinds of analyses we did only begin to explore the complicated questions of relationships between teaching for meaning and student learning. But at a minimum, our analyses established the following for the classrooms we studied:

- The more classrooms focused on teaching for meaning—that is, geared mathematics instruction to conceptual understanding and problem solving, reading instruction to comprehension, and writing instruction to composing extended text—the more likely students were to demonstrate proficiency in problem-solving ability, reading comprehension, and written communication, all other factors being equal.
- Approaches to mathematics, reading, and writing instruction that emphasized meaning were likely to work as well for lower-achieving children as for higher-achieving ones, and sometimes better.
- Students in classrooms emphasizing teaching for meaning acquired a grasp of "basic" arithmetic computation, decoding, and writing mechanics (e.g., handwriting, spelling, punctuation, grammar) that was at least as good as that of students in classrooms in which these skills, taught out of context, were the main focus of instruction.

These propositions assert relationships that run counter to strongly held beliefs about instruction in high-poverty classrooms. But there are good reasons, beyond the technical soundness of the statistical procedures, for believing that the results of our analyses make sense: Logic and intuition, supported by a good deal of recent theory and some demonstrations (noted in Chapter 1) related to these areas of instruction, suggest that the first proposition, at least, *should* hold. Interpreted at face value, this proposition asserts that the more students are asked to reason mathematically, the better they become at such activities; the more they are guided toward deeper understandings of what they read, the more likely it is that their reading comprehension will improve; and the more they write, the better they will write. Added to these is the obvious fact that, in effect, students in meaning-oriented classrooms have been "taught to the test" (even though the teachers we studied did not know what kinds of tests we would use to assess their students' grasp of advanced skills).

But there is more to it than the sheer amount of exposure to nonroutine mathematical problems, the number of times comprehension strategies are taught, or the number of pages students compose. Our observations made it clear that, in the average meaning-oriented classroom, something was *qualitatively* different about the way students encountered mathematical problems, written text, or writing tasks. Teachers who focused on extended text writing illustrate the point: Typically, they had in mind a certain kind of communication as the goal of instruction — elaborated text addressed to a particular audience, in which students had to compose coherent thoughts in prose — and they constructed a learning environment in which students were explicitly taught how to do this, through the means described in Chapter 5. In addition, through the medium of written communication, students were encouraged to connect their school-based learning with their lives outside of school, as discussed in Chapter 2.

The second proposition — that teaching for meaning works as well for low-performing learners as for high-performing ones — flies in the face of intuition at first glance; yet there, too, a plausible connection exists between instructional approach and the outcomes we found. For example, although it is true that high-poverty classrooms are populated by many children who appear to lack facility with Standard English — the very ones who are typically at the low end of the classroom performance continuum — it does not necessarily follow that more drill and practice with the discrete components of Standard English will help these learners see how the components fit together into coherent expression that they might read or compose. It is just as plausible — and our findings strongly suggest it — that individuals who are performing below their peers are *most* in need of opportunities to see how the discrete pieces of literacy learning cohere into a communicable whole.

The third proposition is not so obvious and, in some respects, runs counter to intuition. Skeptical educators (including a large number of the teachers we studied) are likely to wonder why a focus on advanced skills should facilitate mastery of basic skills. Don't the "basics" still have to be taught skill by skill? Based on our results, the answer is a qualified yes and no. It is clear from our data that being in a meaning-oriented classroom did not adversely affect students' learning of discrete skills and in some instances clearly helped it. There are probably two reasons for this result. First, most meaning-oriented teachers, in effect, hedged their bets by including a good deal of arithmetic computation drill, decoding exercises, or writing mechanics skill teaching in the daily learning diet (put another way, most teachers sincerely believed that both goals, understanding and discrete skills mastery, were important). Orienting instruction toward meaning thus did not preclude an emphasis on discrete skills. Second, as argued by the literature on teaching for understanding (see Means & Knapp, 1991) and as suggested repeatedly by our classroom observations, teaching for meaning appeared to offer learners a context for understanding each skill they were learning—that is, seeing how the skill might be used and grasping the importance of mastering it.

But if there are good grounds for believing the results of our analyses, there are also reasons to be cautious. For one thing, our research did not investigate the full range of learning outcomes that teaching for meaning may produce. For another, our measures and analyses of discrete skills mastery were quite limited and should be thought of as suggestive rather than definitive. Third, as we explore more fully in Chapter 8, we investigated the effects of teaching for meaning in a restricted range of high-poverty classroom settings that excluded teachers who were apparently less capable, experienced, or committed to their profession. We therefore have more to say about the results of teaching for meaning under more favorable conditions rather than under the full range of conditions that appear in high-poverty classrooms across the land.

CHAPTER 8

Forces Inside the Classroom Linked with Teaching for Meaning

Michael S. Knapp

Each classroom represents a unique set of individuals and conditions that, together, produce an environment for academic learning over a school year. First of all, there are the students, with their individual characteristics, personal histories, and learning styles or needs, as well as the classroom group — an entity that is more than the sum of its parts, with its own distinctive character. Then there is the teacher, with his or her singular mix of training, experience, and background characteristics. The classrooms sit within schools and districts, each with policies, norms, and support mechanisms that can influence what teachers and students do in various ways. Finally, each school sits within a state context, which may set expectations or requirements regarding who can teach, what is taught, and how it is taught.

Previous chapters presented contrasting patterns of instruction among the classrooms we studied and documented their apparent effects on students' learning. In so doing, we established that, in most respects, teaching for meaning produces greater learning, other factors being equal. We now consider the forces and factors that drive classrooms toward, or away from, an emphasis on teaching for meaning.

We start in this chapter with forces at work within the classroom, by looking at the associations between student and teacher characteristics and the degree of emphasis on teaching for meaning. In the following chapter, we turn to forces outside the classroom, first within the school environment and then within the district and state context, paying special attention to features of the "policy environment" that impinge on the instructional choices teachers make. Because there is striking consistency across subject areas, we do not tell a separate story for mathematics, reading, and writing instruction. Rather, we discuss the most important forces at work inside or outside the classroom, noting their influences on the way teachers construct and offer learning opportunities to the children they face each day.

There are some limitations on our ability to identify all the forces at work inside each classroom: We did not do an exhaustive study of each teacher's professional development history or of the cultural, linguistic, and cognitive makeup of each class of students. Nonetheless, by considering crude indicators regarding the students and teachers in each room and augmenting this information with case material from our intensive study of some classrooms, we can suggest several patterns.

THE MAKEUP OF THE CLASSROOM GROUP

It is easy for educators to assume that the more impoverished the student population, the less appropriate are instructional approaches that depart significantly from a discrete skills orientation. This assumption lies at the heart of the conventional wisdom discussed earlier: Because children from low-income backgrounds are more likely to lack school-related skills and supports, this argument asserts, they need more structure, more practice with discrete skills, simpler tasks, and so on. If this were true, it would be reasonable to expect teachers in classrooms serving a more indigent clientele to opt for skills-oriented instruction, and perhaps to do so in classrooms typified by other student characteristics, such as cultural diversity or lower achievement levels, that are typically linked with poverty. Moreover, such teachers might also be expected to shy away from teaching for meaning when faced with other classroom conditions that are common in high-poverty settings, such as overcrowding or student mobility, which multiply the problems teachers face.

Earlier chapters in this book clearly established that, when student characteristics such as poverty or initial achievement level are taken into account, teaching for meaning still produces superior results. But it is still worthwhile to examine the likelihood that teachers would even try to emphasize meaning when faced with what are generally viewed as more difficult teaching conditions.

A quick answer comes from a consideration of the crude indicators of poverty, achievement, and the racial composition of each classroom: These indicators did not differ greatly between classrooms that emphasized teaching for meaning and those that did not. By and large, among the classrooms we studied, the poverty level of students exposed to teaching for meaning was the same as, or *higher* than, that of children in classes exposed to more skills-oriented instructional approaches—for example, 64 percent of children in classrooms emphasizing comprehension in reading as compared to 60 percent in classrooms focusing on discrete reading skills. In some instances (e.g., mathematics instruction in year 2), students exposed to meaning-oriented instruction started out the year somewhat higher in achievement (50 NCEs as compared to 45), but more often the differences between these groups were small or nonexistent. Small differences related to student racial background existed as well, but they were largely an artifact of the demographics of districts selected for the study. Thus, although classes receiving instruction with the greatest emphasis on meaning tended to have fewer minority children than those receiving the most conventional instruction in mathematics, reading, and writing, these differences were not particularly large—13, 19, and 10 percent fewer, respectively—and were attributable primarily to one district with a 95 percent minority population and virtually no examples of teaching for meaning in any subject area (the reasons for this have much to do with the school and district policy environment, discussed in the next chapter).

Still, there is evidence that the nature of the student population in certain high-poverty classrooms dissuaded some teachers from attempting to emphasize meaning in their instruction (or else dissuaded principals from assigning these classes to teachers who would be likely to pursue such instructional practices). At the same time, student characteristics accounted for fewer differences among classrooms than one might have expected.

Management of the academic learning environment offers a case in point: Classroom demographics help explain why some teachers had difficulty establishing order or why some maintained order through tight, restrictive control of classroom interaction, but they do not tell the whole story. Consider three obvious characteristics of the classroom group—class size, degree of poverty, and mobility. Smoothly run classes tended to be on the small side or to have at least one aide for part of the day, thus reducing the pupil-teacher ratio; most of the classes in which there was a constant struggle for order were large (more than 27 students). Yet some of the most effective managers had large groups of students, and the most chaotic classroom of all had only between 14 and 18 students during the year. In a third of the intensively studied classrooms (in year 1), 100 percent of the children received free or reduced-price lunches; these classrooms were just as likely to offer orderly, enabling learning environments as they were to provide limited or minimal learning opportunities. Classrooms with the highest student mobility rates were not necessarily the ones most likely to experience management problems.

Consider, as well, ethnic and linguistic heterogeneity, which in many teachers' views compounds the task of constructing successful learning environments. Homogeneity of classroom composition—by ethnicity or language background—was not necessarily an advantage in the quest for successful management. Although the all-white schools in one rural district had no poorly managed classrooms, several all-white classrooms elsewhere exhibited a variety of management problems. Conversely, although some of the classrooms with the most serious management issues were culturally diverse (and large), many of the most heterogeneous classrooms were among the most orderly and productive. As described in Chapter 2, teachers who approached cultural diversity constructively found ways to use it as a resource for the learning of all the children in the room.

There were many instances in which the nature of the classroom group predisposed teachers to adopt a particular approach to constructing and enacting learning environments in mathematics, reading, and writing. Moreover, other characteristics of the students in the classroom, not reflected in the measures discussed above, might encourage or discourage teaching for meaning. The obstacles to academic learning experienced by low-income families in the rural areas we studied differed from those we encountered in several violent, inner-city neighborhoods. These factors also had their effect on what was taught and how. For example, teachers were especially reluctant to assign homework in the inner-city schools, primarily because they thought that it would not get done.

There is no way to escape the conclusion that under extreme conditions—for example, where class size is large, student mobility is high, and the individual problems stemming from the stress of poverty are concentrated—teaching for meaning is less likely to be found. Our research cannot distinguish whether this is so because such instructional practices are hard to implement under such conditions or because teachers don't believe that they can manage such approaches with the clientele they are facing. But it is clear that high concentrations of students from low-income backgrounds typically present teachers with a greater number of special obstacles to overcome. These obstacles appear to play an important role in shaping curriculum and instruction, and, understandably, some teachers gravitate toward more routine, more structure, more skills-based instruction, and the path of least resistance—principally, it seems, for their own psychic health. The result for children is a more restricted curriculum and a narrower range of learning opportunities.

TEACHERS' PREPARATION, KNOWLEDGE, AND BELIEFS

Just as it is tempting to assume that high-poverty conditions in the classroom make teaching for meaning untenable, it is also easy to assume that such approaches are appropriate for only the most capable teachers. It is no secret that the approaches to teaching mathematics, reading, and writing on which this book concentrates demand a lot from teachers. Therefore, it is logical that the "best" teachers would be the ones most likely to engage in teaching for meaning (in the same breath, one could assert that whatever combination of qualities made these teachers the "best" might explain why their students did better on assessments of problem solving, comprehension, or composition).

To shed light on the role that teachers' characteristics might play in bringing teaching for meaning to high-poverty classrooms, we conducted a limited investigation of three things: (1) teachers' preparation related to the subject matter they were teaching, (2) their familiarity with and expectations of the kinds of students they were teaching, and (3) their capacity to "do it all" — that is, be innovative, manage the learning environment expertly in all areas, motivate all kinds of children regardless of need, and make a personal investment in teaching children from impoverished backgrounds.

What Teachers Know and Believe About Their Subject Areas

What teachers know and believe about the subject areas they are teaching stems from various sources, among them their prior preparation through degree work and in-service professional preparation, their ongoing interaction with colleagues, and their own discoveries while preparing for instruction and interpreting the apparent results in the classroom. The cumulative result of these experiences over time is a slowly evolving set of beliefs about what is to be taught and how to go about it.

Subject-related professional development. Among the 140 teachers we studied, the sheer amount of subject-related professional development was not consistently related to a tendency to emphasize meaning. In mathematics, for example, year 2 teachers emphasizing a broad range of mathematical topics and conceptual understanding had somewhat *lower* indices of professional development in mathematics than those teaching arithmetic skills only; the opposite was true for year 1. Regarding literacy teaching, teachers emphasizing meaning-oriented instruction exhibited slightly higher indices of subject-related professional development, but the differences were often small (e.g., from 0.2 to 1.1 on a 6-point scale — see Appendix A). A similar pattern pertained regarding graduate-level training. Although meaning-oriented teachers in mathematics and writing were slightly more likely than skills-oriented teachers to have attained a master's degree (e.g., 31 percent as opposed to 26 percent in year 2), their counterparts in reading were much less likely to have done so. This is not surprising when one considers that many teachers in the study sample received their master's degrees at a time when "basic skills" instruction was more in vogue and more widely believed to be the best thing for "disadvantaged" students.

These figures, however, give only the crudest picture of the extent of prior preparation among the teachers. By themselves, these data indicate little about what teachers knew and believed about the subject areas they were teaching. A more fine-grained understanding of the issue comes from examining the kinds of professional development teachers had in particular subject areas, based on the intensively studied classrooms. Among these teachers, it was clear that few had been offered a particularly rich diet of professional development related to teaching for meaning. Some with apparently sound credentials and many continuing education credits overall knew little about recent pedagogical developments in each subject area, such as the National Council of Teachers of Mathematics standards or integrated approaches to literacy instruction; others, who had less apparent exposure to staff development overall, were knowledgeable about alternative practices in one or more subject area.

The critical factor appeared to be that certain individuals engaged in a more extensive search for professional development in particular subject areas, combining what was routinely offered with what they could glean from other sources. Mathematics is a case in point. Most teachers in our sample (and indeed, nationwide) have not been exposed in any intensive way to alternative approaches to mathematics instruction. It is not surprising, then, that many teachers focus on arithmetic computation with little emphasis on underlying concepts. Teachers in classrooms that focused on conceptual understanding as well as arithmetic computation had often sought out special training to improve their skills in teaching mathematics. The same cannot be said for individuals making arithmetic computation their sole or primary goal in mathematics instruction. For example, among teachers in the conceptually oriented group, one first-grade teacher enrolled in a graduate credit course on teaching mathematics. She was observed to make less and less use of the textbook as her confidence and knowledge about mathematics instruction grew. A third-grade teacher had attended workshops on mathematics put on by a state group. Two other first-grade teachers in one school had developed a mathematics curriculum combining textbook, manipulatives-based activities, and a conceptually oriented mathematics program; they described themselves as having participated in every mathematics workshop they could get to over the past eight years.

The pattern of teacher preparation just described reflects not only the individuals' drive to prepare themselves but also the availability of training. The differences across schools (discussed in the next chapter) regarding the likelihood of adopting meaning-oriented practices are in part a function of access to training. Nonetheless, as the examples above suggest, there is clear evidence that teachers in high-poverty schools must want the professional development—in some instances, want it badly—before the requisite experiences begin to accumulate over time.

Beliefs about the subject area and how to teach it. Out of their professional development experiences, background knowledge, and formal preparation, teachers forge an image of the subject area they are teaching and how it should be conveyed to the students they are working with. These conceptions of the subject area and beliefs about how it should be taught appeared to be very strong among the teachers in our sample and had much to do with what transpired in their classrooms.

Beliefs about writing are an obvious example. We detected four basic conceptions of writing among the teachers we studied. The first two, which treat writing as a necessary tool for learning and as a means of communicating thoughts and ideas, were strongly associated with the pattern of instruction in classrooms offering frequent opportunities to write extended text. The third, which treats writing as a system of rules to be mastered, was closely linked to the pattern of instruction that prevailed in classrooms where students did little or no writing of extended text. The fourth view, of writing as an outlet for self-expression, was more evenly distributed across the spectrum of writing classes, though it was not particularly prevalent in classrooms offering little opportunity for extended text writing.

The four views of writing are not mutually exclusive. Some teachers held more than one view, but no one held all four. In most cases, one view dominated a teacher's thinking and was subsequently expressed in the way he or she carried out the writing program.

- *Writing as a tool for learning.* Some teachers saw writing primarily as a process that facilitates the individual's ability to clarify thinking, analyze information, solve problems, and develop or demonstrate understanding. In this view, writing is not an adjunct to other subject areas but a necessary tool for the full understanding of content presented in any area of the curriculum. Accordingly, the teachers who articulated this belief tended to encourage a great deal of extended text writing in all areas of the curriculum.

- *Writing as a means of communication.* Other teachers saw writing, along with reading and oral communication, as a vehicle for the exchange of ideas, opinions, and feelings. Teachers holding this belief tended to provide opportunities for students to communicate in writing and believed that the mechanics of writing would be learned mainly through use of the language. Some teachers in classrooms offering moderate to extensive opportunities for writing extended text held this belief.

 • *Writing as a system of rules.* A larger proportion of teachers viewed writing as the mastery of writing mechanics. Almost all taught in classrooms where little extended writing took place, and a great deal of time was spent learning and practicing discrete writing skills. Although such teachers might acknowledge communication as the ultimate purpose of writing, they took as their primary goal the teaching of the skills that they believed would enable communication to flow.

 • *Writing as an outlet for self-expression.* Several teachers placed less emphasis on writing as communication with other people and more on writing as a means of expressing personal thoughts, feelings, and experiences. Teachers holding this view of writing tended to offer numerous opportunities for extended text writing, often through journal writing.

These views of writing are powerful predictors of the kind of opportunities that will be provided to students. Although external factors such as textbooks and district assessment policies played an important role, as described in Chapter 9, there were many ways for teachers to build writing into their academic programs, regardless of external constraints. Given the freedom, they tended to build and implement curricula that were consistent with their views of writing.

In reading and mathematics, similar sets of beliefs about the subject area existed among the teachers in our sample, although these beliefs tended to be less clearly formed and articulated. In mathematics, many of the teachers appeared to believe—as do most adults, probably including a majority of parents and even principals—that for young students, mathematics *is* arithmetic. Following this belief, arithmetic *should* be the dominant focus of elementary mathematics instruction, and drill with routine exercises is an appropriate way to teach computational skills. This belief was common among teachers who took the most skills-oriented approach to mathematics teaching.

With regard to reading, teachers in our sample held a number of views in common and did not display the extreme positions that are part of the current debate about reading instruction. Virtually all the intensively studied teachers believed in teaching decoding skills and in engaging children's interest in, and understanding of, the written word through experiences with highly motivating text. But the priority they placed on acquiring discrete decoding skills and attempting to comprehend text differed. The roots of their differences seemed to lie in strong preconceptions about what the skill of reading consists of, derived from their own education or preparation for teaching (now in the dim past for some veterans). Thus, there were some strong phonics advocates among the teachers we studied, particularly at the first-grade level. (Only one school in the sample mandated a phonics-based approach to reading, but it also offered a daily period of integrated language arts instruction.) Yet, for the most part, even the most ardent phonics proponents did not believe that children learn to read by phonics alone. They saw knowledge of sound-symbol relationships as an essential tool that helps students become independent readers.

Interestingly, the teachers most committed to "whole language" principles incorporated some phonics into their reading instruction programs, typically by interspersing some traditional phonics drills throughout activities in an integrated language arts block. As we noted in Chapter 4, the teachers who concentrated on comprehension were not defensive about the amalgam of strategies they employed to bring children along in reading. If some phonics instruction was indicated, they did phonics lessons for a period of time. At the higher grade levels, the same was true for vocabulary development and word-attack skills. No apologies were involved. Activities aimed at discrete skills were simply viewed as part of a sensible, comprehensive reading program.

What Teachers Know and Believe About the Children They Are Teaching

Teachers' subject matter knowledge and beliefs are not applied in a vacuum. Teachers draw on these resources as they fashion and execute an instructional program for a particular group of children, and, as we have already noted, the groupings of children one is likely to encounter in high-poverty classrooms pose a considerable set of challenges for teachers. Several questions arise: Are the teachers who are most familiar with the students also the ones who attempt to teach for meaning? Do teachers at the meaning-oriented end of the instructional continuum expect more of their students, compared with other teachers? How do their knowledge and beliefs about the children affect the curriculum and instruction they offer?

A first set of answers came from looking at crude indicators of teachers' expectations for student success and their familiarity with the backgrounds of the students they taught (both based on a rough indicator from teacher questionnaire responses—see Appendix A). A similar indicator of teacher experience (e.g., the number of years teaching in high-poverty classrooms) also provided some clues.

Generally speaking, the teachers in the study sample held high expectations for student performance, regardless of their approach to teaching mathematics, reading, and writing. Such a result was not surprising, given the way we selected teachers for the study (see Appendix A); in other words, the sampling process yielded comparable numbers of teachers at each end of the instructional approach continuum who believed that all or most of their students could succeed by yearend. But not all teachers held the same conceptions of what "succeeding" meant. The nature of a meaning-oriented curriculum sets a different and, in some ways, more demanding standard for student success.

Teachers who were engaged in meaning-oriented approaches to mathematics and writing had a somewhat higher self-reported familiarity with students' backgrounds than teachers adopting conventional approaches to these subject areas (curiously, there was no difference for reading instruction). The index we used was a simple count of different ways that teachers had become familiar with students' backgrounds (e.g., making home visits, doing volunteer work in the neighborhoods in which children lived, having regular communication with parents). Although familiarity might reflect the teachers' years of experience working with this kind of student population, the data suggest that what teachers taught and how they taught it were not related straightforwardly to how long they had been doing so. On average, the teachers we studied were relatively seasoned, having taught between eight and ten years on average, once again reflecting our sampling criteria. Except in mathematics, where meaning-oriented teachers were considerably more experienced, teachers emphasizing meaning in their teaching had only slightly more years of experience, on average, than those pursuing skills-oriented approaches.

But as the discussion in Chapter 2 made clear, much more is involved in teaching students from diverse backgrounds than years of experience or familiarity with these backgrounds. A combination of factors leads some teachers to value and build on student backgrounds, while others pay little attention to students' lives out of school or, in some cases, allow their beliefs about these backgrounds to limit what they offer certain students. The continuum described in Chapter 2, ranging from actively nonconstructive responses to student differences to those that are actively or proactively constructive, represents the central range of differences among the teachers we studied.

Ultimately, what teachers did with their awareness of student backgrounds seemed to make the biggest difference in how they taught (and what results their students achieved). Those who emphasized meaning in mathematics, reading, and writing were more likely to draw on students' backgrounds as a resource for learning in all three subject areas, although not necessarily to an equal extent. In reading and writing, for example, teachers who actively incorporated student background into their teaching were at least twice as likely as teachers who ignored student background (or focused on it in nonconstructive ways) to emphasize understanding in reading or offer students extensive opportunities for extended text writing. The same was not quite true of mathematics, though clearly a constructive response to cultural differences was still associated with teaching for meaning.

Teachers' Capacity to "Do It All"

Perhaps the easiest — and least useful — explanation for the presence of teaching for meaning in high-poverty classrooms assumes that these approaches to instruction are the province of "superteachers." This argument assumes that, faced with the conditions that prevail in high-poverty classrooms, only the "best" teachers would take on the challenge of teaching multiple mathematical topics with attention to conceptual understanding, employ instructional strategies in reading that maximize comprehension, or provide numerous opportunities for extended text writing. In short, this explanation asserts that teaching for meaning is likely to be found in the classrooms of teachers who can "do it all," who can work magic with difficult classrooms. By the same token, for the majority of instructional staff who appear to possess less innate talent (or who are willing to devote only eight hours a day to their teaching careers), these approaches to instruction are not particularly feasible or appropriate.

What we learned sheds light on this notion, but the answers are not simple. At the extremes, the patterns were clear. There were a few (very few) superteachers in the schools we studied, and they were likely to gravitate toward instructional approaches that aim at meaning. Similarly, among the few teachers (in our sample) who had not yet mastered the difficult art of teaching — in any pedagogical tradition — most gravitated toward instruction aimed at discrete skills (though a few struggled to make teaching for meaning happen in their classrooms), probably because this approach seemed to offer a path of least resistance. The majority of teachers in our study fell in between the extremes; by and large, they would be deemed good but not exceptional by a wide range of observers. These teachers were fairly evenly divided between those who were attempting to teach for meaning in some respect and those who placed greater emphasis on the acquisition of discrete basic skills.

The predominant pattern, displayed in Figure 8-1, was this: If teachers chose to emphasize meaning (and almost three-fifths did), they did so in only *one* of the three subjects we studied. In the other subjects they

FIGURE 8–1. Likelihood of teaching for meaning in more than one subject area

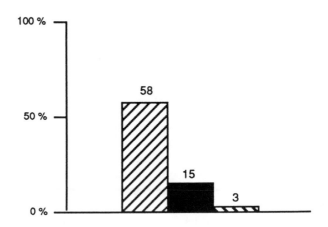

Percentage of teachers [a] emphasizing meaning
in one or more subject areas, two or more,
and all three, respectively

a   Based on analysis of 40
     classrooms studied
     intensively during
     year 1

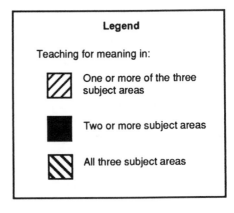

Legend

Teaching for meaning in:

One or more of the three
subject areas

Two or more subject areas

All three subject areas

adopted either a highly skills-oriented approach or a hybrid with some elements that would be considered meaning-oriented along with much that was not (as earlier chapters explained, many classrooms exhibited a "moderate" emphasis on meaning-oriented strategies or a mixed approach that combined elements of both instructional philosophies). Practically no teachers in our sample (3 percent) consistently emphasized meaning in all three subject areas we studied, and relatively few (15 percent) did so in two areas. (A similar pattern, not shown in the figure, appears when one considers the teachers who placed the greatest emphasis on discrete skills instruction: Only 10 percent chose a consistently skills-oriented approach to all three subject areas, and barely a fifth did so for two of the three subjects.)

In other words, teaching for meaning was a matter of specialization for the great majority of teachers we studied, rather than the exclusive province of a few highly talented teachers. Some schools capitalized on this fact and organized instruction so that teachers could specialize in particular subject areas for much of the day through teaming and departmentalized arrangements; in such instances, teachers were able to offer a richer menu of learning opportunities in the subjects they taught. More typically, however, teachers taught their "strong" subjects alongside all the other parts of the curriculum.

There are various possible explanations for this pattern. Teachers may have been more interested in one subject area than another and emphasized meaning in accord with their personal interests. Or perhaps the difficulty of mastering these approaches to teaching meant that, given the relative newness of this form of instruction, most were concentrating on a particular subject area until they were confident they could handle it. Alternatively, the sheer demand on time and preparation implied by teaching for meaning may have forced teachers to choose the one subject they felt they could maximize within the constraints imposed by the elementary school day.

Thus, from the point of view of teaching for meaning, there were few teachers who could "do it all." At the same time, there were not many who made *no* attempt to teach for meaning in *any* of the three subject areas: Few teachers in the study sample exhibited the most conventional forms of instructional practice in more than one of the three subject areas. This fact refutes what could easily be assumed—namely, that teachers who approach one subject area in a skills-oriented manner are likely to conduct all their teaching in this mode.

Nonetheless, as suggested in Chapter 1, the better managers of classroom learning environments were more likely to teach for meaning in one or more areas and somewhat less likely to make discrete skills mastery their primary instructional goal. For example, among the year 1 classrooms in which meaning was emphasized in one or more subject areas, 56 percent exhibited orderly, enabling environments, and only 18 percent experienced ongoing difficulties with classroom order. In skills-oriented classrooms, by contrast, a nearly opposite pattern pertained: Only a small percentage (14 percent) exemplified highly productive, orderly learning environments, and more than half (53 percent) displayed continuing struggles over classroom order, in some instances paralyzing most of the learning opportunities.

In sum, we offer a several-faceted answer to questions about the association between good teachers and teaching for meaning. To use these approaches well requires more of teachers than skills-oriented teaching; those who have mastered other aspects of the teaching craft are likely to master these approaches more quickly. But as a group, the teachers we observed who attempted to focus their instruction on teaching for meaning spanned the spectrum of teaching competence, and the results reflected varying degrees of skill. Not all were successful, but most had found some way of enriching their prior teaching repertoires by adopting this kind of approach. By the same token, the teachers attempting to teach for meaning had no corner on pedagogical expertise: We observed many skills-oriented teachers who were clearly masters of their chosen approaches to reading, writing, or mathematics instruction.

In considering whether teaching for meaning can be handled only by superteachers, it is important to take note of teachers' personal commitment to their work and to their students. More than their colleagues who emphasized the mastery of basic skills, teachers who taught for meaning invested a considerable amount of personal energy, time, and even resources in teaching. Although we have no systematic quantitative data in this regard, our qualitative analyses suggest that the teachers who emphasized meaning tended to do so at some personal cost to themselves. Several examples of meaning-oriented reading teachers illustrate this point. One veteran first-grade teacher commented that her husband had started to give her a hard time about the number of evenings and weekends she committed to preparation as she experimented with an approach to reading and writing instruction that integrated the language arts. She also acknowledged spending "a small fortune" on professional books and periodicals. A third-grade teacher in another district acknowledged thinking of her class each year as the children that she and her husband (a retired school principal) had never had. She "spoiled" her classes with personal expenditures to enrich the classroom environment. Another teacher, although nearly burned out after over 30 years of teaching, was intent on exposing her students to as many experiences as possible. The year we observed her classroom she directed her fifth graders in a production of *Macbeth*, in addition to organizing many field trips to local cultural institutions.

Teachers in meaning-oriented classrooms were also likely to be risk takers in some degree. This was not surprising, given that the conventional wisdom in the districts we studied and in the teaching profession as a whole still holds that high-poverty classrooms are likely to benefit most from a highly structured diet of discrete skills. Understandably, at a time when meaning-oriented teaching was not yet widespread in the schools we were studying, teachers who were willing to try new things were the ones one would expect to experiment with alternatives to the conventional wisdom.

REFLECTING ON THE ROLE OF STUDENTS AND TEACHERS

The contents of this chapter constitute a partial set of answers, at best, to questions regarding how the characteristics of students and teachers interact to produce meaning-oriented teaching in the classroom. To go farther, we would have to explore teachers' instructional choices at a more microscopic level, taking into account decisions made about particular children or subgroups within the classroom. We would also need to look more closely at what teachers actually know about each subject area and their "pedagogical content knowledge" (Shulman, 1986) — not to mention the process over time by which they learn how to teach for meaning — to get at the precise role that knowledge and beliefs about teaching play in developing practices that place a high priority on meaning. Other kinds of studies are far more adept at exploring these matters than ours.

But we can say several things with reasonable certainty. There is no simple way that the nature of student groups in high-poverty classrooms precludes teaching for meaning, though under extreme conditions, it seems unlikely that teachers would try to teach this way or succeed if they did try. Rather, many teachers faced with a high-poverty clientele — including the cultural diversity and range of personal needs that this classroom population implies — are opting to emphasize meaning in their teaching and are finding success.

We can also be confident that teaching for meaning is not the sole province of the "best" teachers in the system. Although teaching for meaning clearly demands a lot of teachers in terms of knowledge and professional development support, teachers from across the spectrum of teaching competence are likely to be drawn to these approaches, and many appear able to enrich their teaching repertoires.

CHAPTER 9

The School and District Environment for Meaning-Oriented Instruction

Michael S. Knapp
Patrick M. Shields
Christine Padilla

Academic instruction does not take place in a vacuum. Although it is clear from the preceding chapter that the presence of teaching for meaning within a high-poverty classroom reflects the attributes of the teacher and the group of students, the teacher's choices among instructional approaches are constrained and guided by events and conditions outside the classroom. There are many ways that these external forces make their way inside the classroom door. To begin with, assignment policies are partially responsible for the size and composition of the student group and for the presence of a particular kind of teacher in the room. The broad contours of the curriculum taught in the room, as well as the materials available to the teacher, are generally determined externally, though teachers exercise various degrees of discretion in how they enact the intended curriculum. Other forces are also relevant to the way teachers and students go about academic work, among them testing requirements and the operation of supplemental instructional programs (discussed in Chapter 6).

In short, the "environment" of policies, constraints, resources, and other conditions that surround the classroom may be important to an understanding of teachers' efforts to teach for meaning. To identify the most important forces in this organizational environment, we consider their sources at different levels—first in the school as a whole, and then in the district and state.

THE SCHOOL ENVIRONMENT FOR ACADEMIC INSTRUCTION

Among the schools we studied, something about the school as a whole appeared to support or inhibit certain approaches to academic instruction.

As Figure 9-1 indicates, schools differed tremendously, both within and across districts, in the percentage of sample classrooms that emphasized meaning in mathematics, reading, and writing instruction. Take Schools 1 and 2 in District 1: Both had nearly identical percentages of classrooms emphasizing meaning in reading and writing yet were vastly different with regard to mathematics — approximately three-quarters of the classrooms in School 1 displayed meaning-oriented approaches to mathematics, but barely a tenth of those in School 2 did so (the percentages, not shown in the figure, of teachers adopting the most conventional approaches to mathematics differed in a similar way — none in School 1, compared with nearly half in School 2). Certain schools appeared to concentrate on meaning-oriented instruction in one particular subject area, such as writing in School 3. Occasionally, as in School 1, a high proportion of classrooms featured meaning-oriented instruction in all three subject areas; conversely, in a few schools, we encountered a high proportion of classrooms emphasizing discrete skills.

What accounts for these differences? Why does teaching for meaning take root in one school and not another? Our data point to a number of forces and conditions within the school that exert a telling influence on the teachers' approach to instruction in mathematics, reading, and writing. Five sets of forces seemed most important: staffing and student assignment, the organization of the instructional day, subject-specific instructional leadership, collegial and administrative support, and the degree of professional autonomy granted to teachers.

Staffing and Student Assignment

The discussion in the preceding chapter made it clear that in some ways the presence of teaching for meaning in a classroom reflects the nature of the teacher and the student group. Decisions made at the school level are responsible for placing particular teachers with particular groups of students. We encountered various situations in which school-level staffing or student-assignment decisions made it easier or more difficult for teachers to teach for meaning in one or more subject areas. As noted in Chapter 8, departmentalized arrangements and the assignment of resource specialists to particular grades were among the devices used to maximize the possibility that particular teachers with interest and relevant expertise would emphasize meaning in a particular subject area. Conversely, assignment of overly large student groups (more than 27) to a single teacher reduced the likelihood that teaching for meaning would be attempted.

To be sure, these decisions are not solely a reflection of staff desires and priorities at the school level. Teacher-pupil ratios are obviously constrained by district-level resources. The kinds of children who attend the

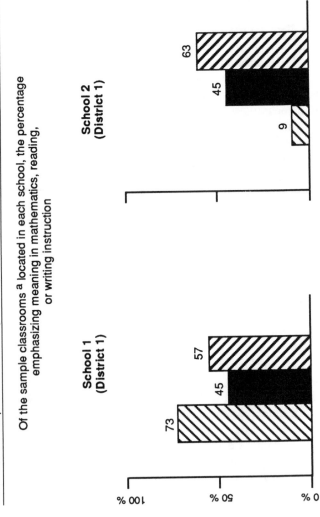

FIGURE 9–1. Emphasis on teaching for meaning in selected schools within the study sample

Of the sample classrooms [a] located in each school, the percentage emphasizing meaning in mathematics, reading, or writing instruction

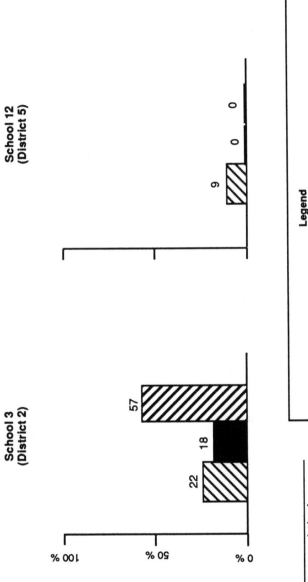

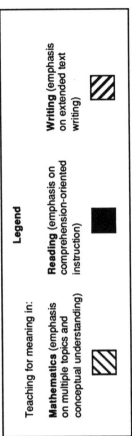

School 3
(District 2)

School 12
(District 5)

100 %

50 %

0 %

22

18

57

9

0

0

Legend

Teaching for meaning in:

Mathematics (emphasis on multiple topics and conceptual understanding)

Reading (emphasis on comprehension-oriented instruction)

Writing (emphasis on extended text writing)

a   Based on an analysis of 11 classrooms in each of the four schools.

school reflect the larger social forces that give communities served by the schools their cultural and socioeconomic character. Also, schools are not completely free (sometimes not free at all) to select teachers, which limits their capacity to recruit individuals with an interest in teaching for meaning. Ultimately, large-scale conditions related to the profession of teaching, the desirability of particular settings for teaching, and salaries — to mention only a few of the most salient — have something to do with the presence or absence of particular kinds of people in the teaching pool of a given school.

Organization of the Instructional Day

The analysis of learning outcomes in Chapter 7 made it clear that the amount of time devoted to a subject area during the school day was associated with the degree of emphasis on meaning. Not surprisingly, teachers who discussed the meaning of reading with students, had them write extended text in class, or taught nonroutine problem solving in mathematics alongside discrete skills practice were likely to devote a large portion of their school time to these purposes. Their ability to do so was in part a function of the school schedule, which might or might not provide blocks of uninterrupted instructional time.

Many of the classrooms we studied followed the traditional pattern of students remaining with one teacher for most or all of the day, thereby offering large blocks of time for whatever subjects the teacher might choose. Other schools were departmentalized for mathematics or literacy instruction, rotated the students in "circles" for different subjects, offered instruction in special subjects away from the home classroom, or featured a number of pullout programs for designated students within the classroom. As the discussion in Chapter 6 showed, the programmatic connections between pullout services and regular classroom instruction were often weak or nonexistent.

The net effect of these organizational matters was that the school day could become quite fragmented in logistical or programmatic terms, or both. In ways that are both obvious and subtle, such conditions do not encourage teaching for meaning. In the most fragmented organizational structures, found in schools within one district that placed a great deal of emphasis on discrete skills teaching, there was little if any emphasis on meaning in the three subject areas. Given the amount and complexity of student movement during the school day, only an exceptionally skillful and creative teacher could have found a way to engage students in meaning-oriented activities on a regular basis in this setting. Short-term worksheets and other skills-oriented instructional devices fit more easily into the small slices of time available for instruction in any particular subject.

Subject-Specific Instructional Leadership

Although the organization of the school day could be a general constraint on teaching for meaning in any subject area, specific messages about a particular subject and how it should be taught could be communicated by individuals in positions of instructional leadership. Principals and resource specialists were the most obvious candidates for this sort of leadership, and the schools we studied displayed some clear examples of such individuals pushing teachers toward, or away from, teaching for meaning.

The principals in the sample schools varied a great deal in their approaches to guiding instruction in particular subject areas. The strongest principals offered a clear sense of direction to teachers, but generally in only one subject area. One principal insisted on a phonics-based approach to reading, even though the district mandated a new language arts curriculum that deemphasized phonics (her resistance set in motion a pitched battle with district authorities, which she won). Two other principals took a particular interest in writing (including the principal of School 3 in Figure 9-1); one had chaired the district's writing curriculum committee and was a strong proponent of teaching writing process skills and giving students numerous opportunities to write text in different genres. Other principals had less strong ideas about content and pedagogy or chose to communicate them less directly. In a few instances, principals explicitly disavowed any role in subject-specific instructional guidance, arguing that this was the realm of the teachers or staff developers. In such cases, teachers were on their own.

Resource staff could have a direct influence on the use of particular approaches to instruction. In School 1, the mathematics specialist made himself available to all teachers in the elementary grades on a regular basis to discuss their teaching of mathematics, respond to their concerns and questions, and push them to incorporate problem-solving strategies more explicitly into the curriculum. The work of this individual in the school went a long way toward explaining the high proportion of classrooms orienting mathematics instruction toward multiple topics, conceptual understanding, and the solving of nonroutine problems. Permanent resource staff of this sort were not common in the study schools; a few had reading specialists who were conversant with meaning-oriented instruction, and elsewhere, "mentor teachers" filled this role. District-level staff could also play a similar role, as in the district in which itinerant specialists (supported by the Chapter 1 program) came to each school to provide demonstration lessons and in-service staff development related to integrated language arts approaches. The teachers in these schools gained a greater appreciation of meaning-oriented language arts techniques from these professional development experiences, and several made substantial changes in their teaching approaches as a result, even though by training and basic convictions they were more sympathetic to skills-oriented instruction in language arts.

Collegial and Administrative Support

Regardless of their instructional orientations, teachers expressed (in questionnaire responses) comparable levels of satisfaction with the support they received from others in the school. The nature of that support, however, clearly differed from school to school. In explicit and implicit ways, colleagues and building administrators made teachers feel more or less comfortable engaging in a particular approach to instruction such as teaching for meaning.

Collegial support. In one sense, a school — or subunits within a school, such as grade-level teams or other groupings of staff — can be thought of as a collection of teachers that develops a unique "climate of peer support." Some schools have cohesive staffs that support their members in various ways; other schools do not. The schools we studied varied tremendously in this respect.

In schools with the most supportive staff climates, teachers were more likely to approach instruction with an emphasis on meaning. Elsewhere, individual teachers might make the choice to teach in a way that was at odds with conventional approaches, but they did so out of personal conviction and sheer willpower. Colleagues thus offer a first level of support to teachers in their efforts to change what they do in the classroom. In a variety of informal ways, the teachers in our sample used their colleagues as a source of advice, consolation, materials, troubleshooting, and curricular direction. Occasionally, the relationship was formalized, as in the case of teacher pairings in one school; teachers in the same grade level were given coordinated schedules and encouraged to plan and develop curriculum together (many pairs had taken good advantage of this opportunity).

Of course, peer "support" can discourage rather than encourage departures from conventional wisdom, and on more than one occasion, we heard staff-room commentary that subtly undercut the intentions of meaning-oriented curricula that were in the process of being adopted.

Moreover, in principle, school staffs might be as united around and mutually supportive of instructional goals that gave the mastery of discrete skills the highest priority. Several schools in District 5 approached this state of affairs, although their staffs could hardly be described as cohesive.

Administrative support. The climate of peer support reflects many things, among them the tone set by school leaders and the talents, interests, and other qualities possessed by the teachers in the school building. Some of the schools we studied were apparently more effective than others at attracting and retaining a group of teachers who were likely to experiment with alternative instructional approaches. Among other things, the ability of particular schools to "hold" teachers over time reflected the capacity of school leaders, especially the principal, to protect staff from external pressures or to provide material or staff assistance when needed. In addition, by communicating approval for the experimentation implied by attempts to build an emphasis on meaning into classroom practice—even when doing so meant failures as well as successes over the short term—administrators did much to encourage wavering teachers to try alternatives to the familiar patterns of practice.

Administrative support also meant managing external pressures such as curricular mandates or testing policies, which often had direct consequences for pedagogy. Some principals chose to buffer their teaching staffs against these pressures, as in the case noted above of the principal who bucked the new district mandate for a language arts curriculum deemphasizing phonics teaching. In another school in a different district, the principal encouraged teaching for meaning in language arts by telling certain faculty who were trying out these approaches that it was unimportant whether the children scored high on district-administered standardized tests emphasizing discrete language skills. More often, administrators did less to mitigate these conditions; teachers were directly affected by such pressures (as described later in the chapter) and had to choose between capitulation and subversion.

Administrators were central players in ensuring teachers' access to key resources, especially materials and support staff. The importance of adequate materials is self-explanatory, and its effect is most apparent in the negative case, as in the school where there were not enough textbooks to go around, let alone in-class libraries, reference materials, and the like. Such resource-poor settings were among the least likely to engage in teaching for meaning. Teaching for meaning did not automatically require a greater stock of materials than other approaches to teaching, but it often did, such as when teachers took seriously the need to represent mathematical ideas with physical objects, make use of calculators in class, or expose their students to trade books or other reading matter not in the approved textbook.

The way school resources (funding) translated into adult time and attention in the classroom, by itself, did not change the capacity of particular classrooms to emphasize meaning in any of the three subject areas. In fact, classrooms emphasizing meaning had slightly *higher* pupil-staff ratios than those exhibiting a more conventional approach to instruction, when support staff were included in the calculation. The reasons for this pattern were numerous and especially obvious when visiting the schools. Many schools, for example, received additional funding as part of desegregation-related policies (e.g., a consent decree between the district and the local court). In some of these schools, the funds contributed directly to additional instructional staff who were worked into the routine of the regular classroom. In other cases, the money contributed more indirectly to instruction in the regular classroom, as when supplemental program staff provided instructional leadership or professional development opportunities.

Degree of Professional Autonomy Granted to Teachers

"Support" from school leaders could range from gentle encouragement to strong suggestions—in some cases, heavy-handed requirements—that teachers adopt particular approaches to instruction. In doing so, leaders had to balance their impulses to lead instruction in certain directions against their desire to protect and enhance the professional autonomy of their teaching staffs. Our questionnaire data suggested that there was a link between professional autonomy and the choice by teachers to engage in teaching for meaning. Although the differences in our index of autonomy were slight, they consistently indicated that teachers opting for meaning-oriented instruction perceived themselves to have greater autonomy over curricular and instructional decisions than those who pursued instruction dominated by the mastery of basic skills. Because the different types of classrooms tended to cluster by school, there is some basis for asserting that the school, in addition to the individual, was responsible for the degree of autonomy teachers felt. The point was made forcefully by teachers in schools that were dominated by principals with a directive, even dictatorial, style of decision making. One such teacher complained at the end of the year:

> I love teaching here. The children are wonderful; I have only 16 students in my first-grade class, a full-time aide, all the materials I

need, and plenty of time for planning and collaboration with the other first-grade teachers. But sometimes I feel as though I am being treated like a child myself, and I find myself trembling at the thought of the principal coming through the door and discovering that my students don't know a vocabulary word.

The teachers' perceptions of autonomy must be interpreted in several different ways. On the one hand, as suggested in Chapter 8, these perceptions probably say something about the teachers themselves. Individuals who took on new approaches to instruction were risk takers who were likely to find ways to be creative regardless of constraints imposed on them. On the other hand, it was also clear that school leaders could enhance or inhibit these tendencies by the way they treated their staffs. For example, the teacher quoted above, whose teaching was characterized by a meaning-oriented approach to mathematics instruction, resigned from the school after the first year of the study rather than face the intrusive pressure of her principal for another year.

DISTRICT AND STATE POLICY ENVIRONMENT

Although school leaders may attempt to enhance or dampen the influence of external forces on academic instruction, they do not control events in the district and state policy environment that may be linked to the kind of instruction taking place in the classrooms of a given school. The result is a set of pressures on teachers that can affect whether teaching for meaning prospers or not. The basic pattern appears in Figure 9-2: Each of the six districts displayed a distinctive profile of classrooms engaged in teaching for meaning that could not be attributed solely to student characteristics, teachers' capabilities, or school-level forces or conditions. Rather, district-level policies about curriculum, textbooks, testing, and professional development — and the corresponding policies at the state level, where these existed — appeared to play a prominent role in determining the presence or absence of different types of instruction.

As noted in earlier chapters, some districts actively discouraged, or simply did not encourage, teaching for meaning in one or more subject areas, and the results are apparent in the figure (see, e.g., writing in District 4 or all subjects in District 5). Others did the opposite, such as District 6, which actively focused on the quality of reading instruction. District 1 had introduced curriculum revisions emphasizing meaning-oriented instruction in all three subject areas. Once again, the patterns

FIGURE 9–2. Emphasis on teaching for meaning in the six districts within the study sample

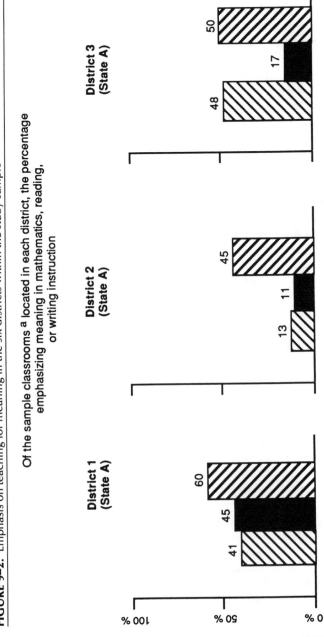

Of the sample classrooms [a] located in each district, the percentage
emphasizing meaning in mathematics, reading,
or writing instruction

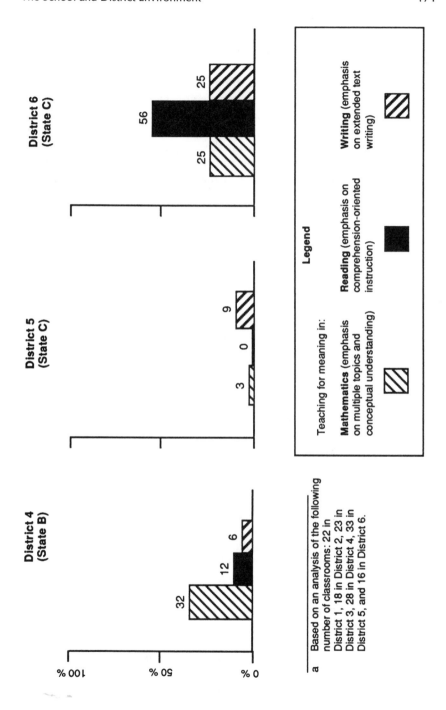

in the figure suggest that, although many factors at all levels may have contributed to these patterns, district- and state-level decisions and actions left their unmistakable stamp.

Sometimes these district-level forces acted as constraints, which limited the vision or flexibility of principals and teachers or simply the resources at their disposal. For example, in a district that did not pay for copying machines in the schools, the principals had to spend large amounts of time and energy raising money for this purpose. In other cases, district and state policies created the opportunity, if not the explicit expectation, for teachers to attempt some form of meaning-oriented instruction. The most influential forces derived from policies governing curriculum, textbook adoption, assessment, and professional development.

Curriculum Policies

Every district we visited set policies governing curriculum and instruction in reading, writing, and mathematics. These policies set forth specific expectations about the content of instruction in each of the three subject areas. As the discussion in Chapter 8 implied, not all teachers heeded such policies in the same way, but in most instances, the very existence of the guidelines was a major feature on the teachers' landscape. For example, teachers attempted to broaden the array of topics in the mathematics curriculum beyond arithmetic only in districts where there was some encouragement, or an explicit mandate, for this to happen. Often, but not always, this encouragement originated at the state level, as in the case of Districts 1, 2, and 3, which were located in a state that was pushing strongly for mathematics education reform. Virtually no teachers in the sample adopted such a curriculum in the absence of some strong urging from above; few would have opted for such a curriculum without such leadership.

Guidelines or policies regarding the teaching of writing—an often neglected element in elementary school literacy curricula—provide an even more dramatic illustration. The most significant policy in this subject area was a declaration by district (and state) authorities that writing must be taught and that students at each grade level should master particular kinds of writing (such a policy was often accompanied by an assessment requirement, as described later in the chapter). In the three districts we studied in which such policies were in place, 45 percent or more of the high-poverty classrooms featured meaning-oriented writing instruction, as compared with 25 percent or fewer in the other three districts, in which district guidelines deemphasized the importance of writing. In one of these latter districts, writing was explicitly treated as an optional element of the curriculum, to be included if reading skills were being mastered at a reasonable rate. More often than not, writing was ignored in the classrooms we visited in this district. The contrast was striking between these classrooms and those we visited in the districts with mandatory writing instruction, many of which showed signs of considerable writing activity — for example, walls were typically covered with students' written work, which changed as the year went on.

Aside from the subject-specific expectations they proclaimed, district curricular policies varied in the degree to which they detailed the content, sequence, and timing of what was to be taught in each subject area. The most prescriptive policies favored basic-skills-oriented instruction. In one district, the reading curriculum was set out in two-week units, each of which was accompanied by a test that had to be successfully completed before the next unit was started. In stark contrast, another district fit all its annual objectives for reading instruction onto several photocopied pages and left it to the teachers and schools to determine how and when to reach the objectives. As might be expected, teachers in the first district felt more constrained than those in the second; it is probably not a coincidence that few teachers in the first district were engaged in language arts teaching that deviated much from the discrete-skills-oriented curriculum advocated by the central office.

In conjunction with the way each school organized its instructional day (discussed earlier), the specific expectations and prescriptions of district curricular policies affected the degree of curricular cohesion the children experienced. Some of the districts and schools had devised an overall curriculum that either tried to do too much or subdivided what children had to learn into too many discrete boxes; this was especially evident in the teaching of language arts. The result was fragmentation of the school day into a series of unrelated segments. In some classrooms, no activity ever lasted more than 10 minutes; by definition, then, there was no time to read whole stories or even short articles, much less compose a letter, poem, or short essay. In other instances, the daily and weekly reading instruction schedule was quixotic because so many other social and curricular goals had been inserted into a finite amount of time — drug education, clubs, assemblies, and so on. The impression children got was that learning to read was equally important as talking with Officer Friendly about bicycle safety.

The manner in which curricular policies were introduced — ranging from central office mandate to participatory planning — affected the teachers' receptivity to policies that called for a departure from conventional practices and thereby influenced the likelihood that teachers would attempt meaning-oriented instruction. In one district, where change in the language arts curriculum occurred by fiat, most teachers were straining to understand what was expected of them during the time the study was taking place; many had given up halfway into the first implementation year. In two other quite disparate districts (one urban, one rural), planning for a major curricular change in language arts had been a much longer process that included much more participation by classroom teachers. Several teachers in one of these districts told us that they felt a personal responsibility for the new language arts curriculum. In the other district, a five-year plan for implementing an integrated language arts curriculum offered teachers some choice about when they would begin to change their teaching and how quickly they would proceed. In both instances, the decision to revise the district's approach to reading instruction had come from the top, but because the means to the end had been more participatory and more flexible, teachers in these two districts seemed to have a greater investment in seeing it succeed.

Textbook Policies

Textbook choices go hand in hand with overall curricular decisions and were typically the province of the central district office, although textbook choices were made at the school level in some cases. As noted above and in earlier chapters, textbooks play an important role in each of the subject areas, especially in mathematics. The conception of mathematics implicit in the textbook was usually the one the teachers tried to enact in their own instruction; most followed the textbook closely. The situation was not greatly different in reading, although teachers in the sample classrooms were somewhat more willing, on average, to depart from basal readers than from their mathematics textbooks.

In writing, teachers tended to be freer from the dictates of the writing assignments contained in language arts textbooks. However, the influence of these texts depended in part on school or district policy about textbook use and in part on how closely the teachers' basic beliefs about writing matched the approach taken in the textbook. In some schools, teachers were required to use a specific textbook that followed a certain approach to teaching writing. In other schools, a textbook was available, but teachers could choose to develop their own curricula. One way or another, teachers who had strong views about the teaching of writing tended to find ways to "work around" the curriculum presented in the textbook if it did not conform to their thinking.

The choice of textbooks by school or district does little by itself to make up for teachers' lack of experience with the approach contained in the textbook. In many of the classrooms we studied, teachers had just started to use a new textbook series based on the integration of reading and writing. Most tried to follow the textbook, but many felt unsure of themselves and approached the textbook's writing lessons selectively and in a more limited way than was intended by the textbook authors.

Assessment Policies

Testing of various kinds was an ever-present feature of the classrooms we studied, and this fact influenced both content and pedagogy in many ways. In effect, district and state assessment policies put varying degrees of pressure on teachers (and school administrators) to produce evidence of learning in particular areas of the curriculum but not in others. These pressures worked both for and against meaning-oriented instruction.

The effects of testing pressure were especially clear in the case of mathematics. In the most extreme case, district assessment policies greatly reduced the likelihood of teaching for meaning. Nearly all the mathematics classrooms we observed in this district emphasized arithmetic computation only; the few that did more still stuck closely to arithmetic and did not venture into other mathematical topics or skill areas. Not surprisingly, the district's assessment policy stressed the frequent use of criterion-referenced tests that focused primarily on students' arithmetic computation skills. The district's approach to assessment even made specific demands on instruction itself, such as the requirement that teachers "pretest" each chapter of the mathematics textbook (which had been selected by the district). Taken together, these policies strongly reinforced a skills-oriented view of mathematics teaching and learning, which the majority of teachers had come to accept.

In other districts, a number of teachers felt free enough to design less conventional approaches to the mathematics they were teaching. These teachers did not seem to perceive as much pressure that their students perform well on standardized tests that emphasized proficiency in arithmetic computation. To be sure, there was some pressure, but it was far less common.

The most obvious effect of mathematics testing — which, at the time of our study, was heavily oriented toward discrete arithmetic skills — was to limit the possibilities for meaning-oriented instruction. Teachers in one school (which was in a "problem area" of the city) placed great emphasis on tests because they hoped to increase the status of the school by raising its test scores. Furthermore, believing that students would do better on the test if they were exposed to as wide a range of material as possible, these teachers emphasized "covering" the math textbook, at the expense of understanding or mastery. In a school in another state, large amounts of time were spent on test preparation, in anticipation of state-mandated standardized mathematics tests as well as three separate administrations of the district's own criterion-referenced tests. One teacher, who was conversant with meaning-oriented approaches to teaching mathematics, explained that she stuck to the skills-oriented curriculum in a rigid fashion because she knew that the district tests were tied to material she was supposed to teach, and if she didn't cover the material, she would be held responsible for her students' poor performance.

Not all teachers succumbed to the pressure to emphasize discrete skills stemming from district and state mathematics testing. In three of the districts we studied, all of which had skills-oriented tests in place, a third or more of the classrooms provided meaning-oriented mathematics instruction. Somehow the testing pressures on these teachers were less onerous or were counterbalanced by other forces at the school and district levels (e.g., peer support, subject-specific instructional leadership) that pushed in the opposite direction. In addition, the usual procedure of reporting mathematics test results by school may have given teachers a sense of freedom that was lacking in the heavily tested district described above in which test scores were reported by classroom.

With regard to writing, district assessment policies exerted an equally strong influence and engendered even more teaching to the test. But in this subject area, testing could either inhibit or promote teaching for meaning. On the one hand, within districts in which the testing package assessed mastery of language mechanics and other discrete writing skills, there was clear evidence that teachers emphasized these skills at the expense of composing extended text. In the district mentioned above, students' mastery of language mechanics skills was also tested on a regular schedule, along with arithmetic computation. Not surprisingly, teachers taught these skills and, for the most part, ignored instruction involving extended writing tasks. In another district, which used a popular standardized achievement test designed to assess language mechanics but not the ability to compose text, teachers devoted considerable time in late winter and early spring to preparing students for the multiple-choice language arts section of the test. During the six to eight weeks of intensive preparation for testing, teachers paid little attention to extended writing.

On the other hand, assessment policies that appraised students' written composition holistically—that is, through samples of extended text writing—appeared to encourage writing instruction in which composing extended text was a priority. Three of the districts in our sample were in a state that had established this type of writing assessment program. The matrix sampling technique used in this assessment program meant that students in the same classroom could receive prompts eliciting different genres of writing; accordingly, teachers felt obliged to give their students composition tasks relevant to each of these genres. At the time of our study, the writing assessment program had been in place for a few years at the secondary level and was soon to begin at the sixth-grade level. Teachers in some of our sample schools were beginning to gear their instruction toward this fact.

As the preceding discussion and examples imply, the influence of assessment policies on academic instruction is not straightforward. Rather, a complex interaction occurs involving (1) the content of the tests, (2) their frequency during the year, (3) the incentives or consequences associated with test results, (4) the unit (classroom, school, or district) to which incentives or consequences are attached, (5) the degree of alignment between tests and the district or school curriculum, and (6) the ability of schools or individuals to resist or counteract the inevitable pressures of the testing situation.

It is tempting to conclude from this analysis that assessment represents a powerful lever for policy makers who might wish to encourage teaching for meaning. Although in some respects this may be true, there can also be unfortunate side effects of the inevitable ratcheting up of testing pressure. A feeling of powerlessness often manifests itself in such situations, leaving teachers feeling torn between conflicting goals. One fifth-grade teacher who had an interest in increasing her focus on conceptual understanding and who had sought out appropriate professional development opportunities noted that both her district and the required textbook put a high priority on computational skills. Knowing that this was what would be tested, she commented at one point, "I dread how my students are going to do on the California Achievement Test in a couple of weeks." Thus, despite a clear desire to shift the focus on her instruction, she felt an uncomfortable pressure — to which she succumbed — to devote full time to arithmetic computation skills.

Professional Development Policies

Our information base regarding the six districts' professional development policies was too sketchy to offer a full analysis of this aspect of the policy environment. But what we did learn, from the perspective of individual teachers, was sufficient to demonstrate that professional development opportunities related to meaning-oriented instruction (1) were in considerable demand among the teachers we studied and (2) were generally insufficient to meet the demand. For various reasons — among them, budget crises and the press of other topics on the staff development agenda — districts typically offered few workshops or other sessions related to meaning-oriented instruction in reading, writing, or mathematics. In the most extreme case, in a district that had introduced a new language arts curriculum featuring the integration of reading and writing, the only district-sponsored staff development in the first year of curriculum implementation was a single day's introduction to the textbook series provided by the publisher.

We did encounter examples of more powerful and helpful professional development related to teaching for meaning, and more often than not these were school based. One case noted earlier in the chapter represents the most successful example: There, itinerant reading specialists supported by a supplemental instructional program visited each school in the district, gave workshops and demonstration lessons featuring integrated language arts approaches, and, in the process, made converts of teachers who had been resistant to the new curriculum at the outset. The informal, ongoing support of a resident resource specialist in one school in a different district represented another kind of powerful school-based professional development. Had there been these kinds of professional support at the other schools we studied, the new approaches to teaching might have been more widely and successfully implemented.

In the absence of a rich menu of professional development offered by the district, enterprising teachers sought out these opportunities elsewhere — at local colleges of education, professional meetings, county offices, or other such venues. For a number of them, the *total mix* of professional development experiences over time, including but not limited to what the district offered, provided the foundation for their venture into meaning-oriented instruction.

BALANCING SUPPORT, AUTONOMY, AND PRESSURE FOR CHANGE

As the analyses of this chapter make clear, district and state policy makers' choices about curriculum, assessment, and the support of instruction, in conjunction with the academic environment of the school itself, affect an individual teacher's actions in the classroom. Sometimes, all these forces push a teacher in a single direction, as in the case of one new teacher who found herself in a school that valued quiet, orderly classrooms within a district that placed little emphasis on writing instruction, mandated the teaching of reading through a structured phonics-based program, and regularly tested students' mastery of these skills. Although the teacher had been trained in integrated approaches to language arts and started the year emphasizing active student learning, she eventually yielded to the pressures and altered her style of teaching to bring it more in line with skills-oriented practices.

More typically in the classrooms we visited, policies and the school environment were not so clearly aligned to support or inhibit particular practices. As a consequence, most teachers received mixed signals about what to teach, as in the following case:

> *Ms. Valencia's response to unsupported, mandated change.* Ms. Valencia has been teaching in the primary grades in an inner-city school serving a student population of mixed ethnicity for six years. Her own training in language arts emphasized a basic skills approach, with which she is comfortable and which she believes produces good results with her pupils. In the year of our visits, however, the district adopts a new, integrated language arts curriculum, virtually bans the use of ability grouping in reading, and requests that teachers introduce students to the writing process. At the beginning of the year, Ms. Valencia and her colleagues are introduced to the new curriculum in a two-day training session; they are handed new books and are told by the principal to implement the new program. Ms. Valencia's reaction — a combination of excitement, fear, and confusion — is typical of many teachers in the study who faced similar circumstances. Although attracted by the idea of the new language arts approach, she is uncertain about how to put it into practice. For example, in one writing lesson, she urges the students to focus less on sentence structure and spelling and more on communicating their ideas. As she walks around the room, however, she cannot help pointing out grammar errors and even berates a child for writing ideas that have strayed too far from the meaning of the story. Ms. Valencia is sending her students a mixed message about writing because of her own uncertainty about the best way to teach it and her lack of training in new techniques. Moreover, both the district and state tests focus on spelling, punctuation, and grammar. Within this context, she tries to teach both ways.

The story of Mr. Fulton, who taught at a different school within the same district, illustrates how teachers can develop new ways of teaching when school-based support reinforces a higher-level policy mandate.

> *Mr. Fulton's gradual implementation of a new curriculum.* Mr. Fulton has been a primary teacher for five years and has taught third grade in his present school for two years. Like Ms. Valencia's, his training in language arts emphasized skills-based instruction, and he

too begins the school year faced with the formidable task of taking on the new district-mandated language arts curriculum. However, Mr. Fulton's principal gathers the faculty on the first day of school, informs them of the district mandate, and makes it clear that no one should feel pressure to implement the program more quickly than he or she feels prepared to. Moreover, she appoints a small committee composed of a reading specialist and two mentor teachers (all with extensive training in integrated approaches to language arts instruction) to lead the faculty through a review of the curriculum, to make recommendations, and to serve as resources to the other teachers. As the year progresses, Mr. Fulton incorporates more of the new program into his teaching, spending less time on skills-only teaching and more time providing students opportunities to write and manipulate extended text. At the same time, he retains several aspects of his former teaching approach (e.g., spending time each day reviewing phonics) because, in consultation with the reading specialist, he has decided that his students can benefit from some skills-focused instruction.

The contrasting cases of Ms. Valencia and Mr. Fulton underscore the complexities involved in creating the conditions necessary for teachers to adopt alternative instructional approaches, especially when such approaches depart significantly from a teacher's own training and experience. These cases highlight three interrelated aspects of policy that are central to the adoption of meaning-oriented instruction:

• *Pressure for change.* It is unlikely that either Ms. Valencia or Mr. Fulton would have adopted alternative practices in language arts in the absence of external pressure to do so. They experienced such pressure because they taught in a district that had adopted a curriculum emphasizing an integrated approach to language arts instruction, reflecting in large part the emphasis of state curricular frameworks.

• *Room to exercise discretion.* The two cases differ markedly in the degree of professional autonomy the teachers were offered as they struggled to change the teaching approach. Mr. Fulton's principal buffered him from district mandates, encouraging him to implement the new program at a pace that he felt comfortable with and to the degree that he thought appropriate for his students. In contrast, Ms. Valencia was simply handed the new curriculum and told to put it in place. Although she sometimes deviated from the new curriculum, she did so with the fear that she would be discovered.

• *Professional support.* Mr. Fulton received much more assistance in devising a new approach to language arts instruction. He had regular access to a reading specialist and two mentor teachers who had been charged with the task of helping classroom teachers integrate the new program into their repertoires. Ms. Valencia received no such support. Her school's language arts specialist did not provide technical support for teachers but instead pulled students out of classes for extra help.

Adopting instructional strategies that emphasize meaning typically means that teachers must fundamentally rework their conceptions of the subject they are teaching and their approaches to it. Mandating changes without giving teachers considerable professional support and the flexibility to adapt the mandate to their particular circumstances can often be counterproductive. In such instances, many teachers become confused and embark on new approaches without understanding them, resulting in ineffective teaching.

As Mr. Fulton's and Ms. Valencia's cases make clear, the school is often the front line of support for teachers struggling to make changes. Principals, mentor teachers, and specialists can play an important role in encouraging certain instructional practices and providing guidance on how to adapt such practices to the particular circumstances of the school. Just as important, principals can buffer teachers from the demands of zealous state and district reforms by providing them the freedom to experiment with new practices.

Districts can exert strong pressure on the academic program through curriculum guidelines, textbook adoptions, and testing. The district's conception of "improvement" may favor or reject the premises underlying alternative practices such as teaching for meaning. The power of district policies is illustrated by the virtual absence of teaching for meaning in District 5 (see Figure 9-2), where upgrading students' performance in discrete skills has been an overriding policy aim.

Although more indirectly, state frameworks and assessment practices also influence classroom practice. Mr. Fulton's and Ms. Valencia's confrontation with a new language arts curriculum was initially set in motion by a new district curriculum framework and a concurrent change in state textbook adoption policies. The relatively high proportion of teachers adopting meaning-oriented instruction in Districts 1, 2, and 3 reflects the fact that these districts are located in a state with a curriculum framework and testing that encourage these instructional practices.

These two examples and the broader study findings suggest that policy makers have to find a balance between pressuring teachers to change their practices and providing sufficient room for discretion and professional support to make that change meaningful and appropriate. Among the districts and schools we studied are those that have made important strides toward striking this balance. The two examples also highlight the power of alignment among different kinds of policies at various levels, both those favoring teaching for meaning (e.g., in writing as a result of curricular frameworks, assessment policies, and school-level professional support) and those inhibiting it (e.g., in all subject areas within District 5, as a result of district-level curricular, testing, and accountability policies). The accomplishments of the teachers in settings with a favorable balance and alignment among policies indicate that, even in the often difficult circumstances encountered in high-poverty classrooms, teachers can be helped to bring new meaning to the education that large numbers of students receive. This is an achievement that policy makers can be proud of and that all educational leaders should strive toward.

CONCLUSION

Teaching for Meaning in High-Poverty Classrooms

Michael S. Knapp
Patrick M. Shields
Brenda J. Turnbull

The starting point for this book—and for the research on which it is based—was a long-standing contention about effective instruction for students from low-income backgrounds. This view is captured in a review of research from a decade ago, which asserts that children from low-income backgrounds

> need more control and structuring from their teachers: more active instruction and feedback, more redundancy, and smaller steps with higher success rates. This will mean more review, drill, and practice, and thus more lower-level questions. Across the school year, it will mean exposure to less material, but with emphasis on mastery of the material that is taught and on moving students through the curriculum as briskly as they are able to progress. (Brophy & Good, 1986, p. 365)

This statement hints at a set of assumptions about teaching in classrooms with large concentrations of children from low-income families—assumptions about learners and learning, effective instruction, and the kind of curriculum that is appropriate for such situations. For many years, this perspective on teaching in high-poverty classrooms—with its emphasis on learning deficits, tightly controlled direct instruction, repetitive practice, and the mastery of discrete "basic" skills—has held the status of conventional wisdom among large numbers of practitioners, bolstered by a good deal of research, particularly in the "process-product" tradition.

There are many reasons to question this view of teaching in high-poverty classrooms. Sparked by work on constructivism, cognitive processes, and cultural discontinuities and, most recently, captured in a growing literature on "teaching for understanding" (e.g., Brooks &

183

Brooks, 1993; Brown, 1993; Cohen, McLaughlin, & Talbert, 1993; "Teaching for Understanding," 1994), a number of educators and scholars have raised doubts about the premises of the conventional wisdom and pointed the way toward promising alternatives. By concentrating on assets rather than deficits, these scholars argue, teachers are predisposed to see more potential in the children they are teaching and are able to treat the children's experiences and backgrounds as resources for learning rather than constraints on it. By developing more varied instructional routines, which by stages increase student control over learning activities, teachers can decrease learners' dependence on their teachers and broaden the range of learning experiences children encounter. The argument goes on to assert that, by deemphasizing (though not eliminating) repetitive practice of discrete skills, teachers may limit the monotony and lack of meaning that attends much instruction in high-poverty classrooms and elsewhere. Finally, by concentrating early on the "advanced" skills of reasoning, problem solving, comprehension, and composition, teachers can engage children from the beginning in academic learning that has meaning and application in their lives both inside and outside of school.

In support of this argument, some provocative small-scale demonstrations suggest that alternatives to the conventional wisdom have merit (e.g., Resnick, Bill, Lesgold, & Leer, 1991; Palincsar & Klenck, 1991; Bryson & Scardamalia, 1991). The research on which this book was based took the next logical step, by launching the first large-scale, systematic attempt to examine meaning-oriented and skills-oriented instruction in a wide variety of high-poverty classrooms at the elementary school level.

The findings of our research form an integrated three-pronged argument about teaching for meaning in high-poverty classrooms in elementary schools. First, teachers who emphasize meaning construct and maintain rich and responsive academic learning environments. These environments are simultaneously orderly and varied; in managing them, teachers respond actively and constructively to the students' diverse cultural, linguistic, and socioeconomic backgrounds.

Second, these teachers give meaning a high priority in their mathematics, reading, or writing instruction by posing cognitively demanding tasks from the earliest stages in learning, teaching discrete skills in the context of their use, and connecting academic learning to the children's experience base. Approaching instruction in this way produces superior learning of "advanced" skills and comparable or better learning of "basic" skills by *both* high and low achievers.

Third, teachers are likely to attempt and sustain this form of teaching given the right combination of conditions and supports. At the school level, these conditions include subject-specific instructional leadership, a climate of peer support, and organization of the school day to permit uninterrupted blocks of instructional time. At the district and state levels, policies governing curriculum, assessment, and professional development must strike a balance among pressuring for change, guaranteeing some autonomy for teachers, and providing professional resources.

CONSTRUCTING RICH AND RESPONSIVE LEARNING ENVIRONMENTS

High-poverty classrooms present teachers with difficult combinations of learning needs. In such situations, the task of establishing classroom order — that is, sustained engagement by learners in an instructional program — is often formidable, and it is not surprising that teachers resort to curricula and techniques that appear to promise continuous control over potential chaos.

Among the classrooms we studied, the majority had succeeded at chaos control. Although some exhibited an ongoing struggle between teacher and students over order — a pattern frequently attributed to high-poverty classrooms — most could be characterized as orderly. To the casual observer, these classrooms were places where the business of schooling was going on: Students treated one another and the teacher with respect, were engaged in academic tasks most of the time, and were clearly acquiring academic skills. However, as we discussed in Chapter 1, a subtle but pronounced distinction emerged among the orderly classrooms: Those we labeled "restrictive" had a more limited range of learning routines and constant tight control by the teacher; in those we characterized as "enabling," the routines were more varied and students assumed more responsibility for aspects of their own learning. The differences between the two kinds of classrooms translated into differences in pacing, motivational strategy, feedback to students, approach to dealing with disruptions, and balance of teacher and student talk, among other aspects of instructional management.

Classrooms varied in the way teachers responded to differences in background among the children, especially differences stemming from the ethnicity, poverty status, or English language proficiency of the children's families (see Chapter 2). Some teachers approached these differences in ways that were not constructive for children from nonmainstream backgrounds; others dealt with background differences more constructively. At the nonconstructive end of the continuum, teachers either ignored student differences or, in a few instances, actively marginalized nonmainstream children. At the constructive end, teachers acknowledged differences and, in varying degrees, drew on children's backgrounds in the design and conduct of lessons. The way teachers responded to student differences had a clear impact on the engagement of students in academic work: Especially in literacy instruction, the more teachers connected instruction to students' backgrounds, the more consistently and continuously students were engaged in learning tasks.

In sum, the ways in which teachers manage the learning environment and respond to student diversity shape the quality of learning opportunities in the classroom. Furthermore, students' actual engagement with academic tasks derives in part from the combination of flexibility and routine in the learning environment and the degree to which children sense a connection between the world they know outside of school and the culturally different world of school-based academic work. Together, the learning environment and the sense of connectedness provide a foundation for meaning-oriented instruction in particular subject areas.

EMPHASIZING MEANING IN INSTRUCTION

Regarding the teaching of mathematics, reading, and writing, the classrooms we studied fell along a continuum — from those we characterized as skills-oriented, in which teachers adhered most closely to the conventional wisdom described above, to those in which meaning and understanding were central priorities. Many classrooms located in the middle of the continuum displayed a mixture of priorities, though typically they presented a narrower range of approaches to instruction and, consequently, a restricted range of learning opportunities. Classrooms were characterized separately for each of the three subject areas. Thus, the same classroom could be considered skills-oriented for mathematics and meaning-oriented for writing or reading instruction, or vice versa. Many classrooms displayed such differences. In fact, few if any fell at one end of the continuum for all three subject areas.

The argument we are advancing rests on the following conception of *meaning* in teaching and learning. Put most simply, we assume that, from the students' perspective, meaning (in the context of a skills-oriented curriculum) derives from perceiving the relationship of the parts (concepts, discrete sills) to the whole (a large body of knowledge; the application of skills in holistic, higher-order ways to communicate, comprehend, or reason). By emphasizing the whole and continually developing students' grasp of the parts in the application of their use, teachers provide learners with the tools to make sense — to *create* meaning — out of the world around them, for example, by posing and solving mathematical problems for themselves, grasping what written communication might say to them, and, in turn, communicating important thoughts to valued audiences. This perspective on teaching and learning further assumes that (1) learners are active meaning makers rather than passive recipients of knowledge, no matter what teachers do; and (2) knowledge itself is negotiated and jointly constructed by teacher and learner. Presumably, teachers can facilitate the learning process by making higher-order thinking a central goal, constructing challenging tasks, engaging students in discourse about what they are doing, and providing rich opportunities to demonstrate understanding.

We made no assumptions about whether these principles would be fully realized in any of the classrooms we studied. Instead, we anticipated that an orientation toward meaning might take a more limited form in the hands of teachers who, for the most part, were relatively new to this way of thinking about instruction. The contrasts embedded in the sample of 140 classrooms afforded a unique opportunity to establish what meaning-oriented instruction actually looked like in high-poverty classroom settings and determine its relative contribution to student learning.

In mathematics instruction, teachers at the meaning-oriented end of the continuum focused on conceptual understanding (though not to the exclusion of algorithmic skills) and did so with a wide range of mathematical topics in addition to arithmetic, including geometry, estimation, logic, graphing, and probability (see Chapter 3). In meaning-oriented mathematics classes, students encountered nonroutine problems — puzzles and complex story problems — as well as the more routine story problems that, along with sheets of arithmetic practice problems, formed the mainstay of skills-oriented classrooms.

In the teaching of reading, described in Chapter 4, meaning-oriented approaches to instruction placed a high priority on comprehension in various ways. Children were given extensive opportunities to read text and were taught various strategies for comprehending what they were reading. They also had numerous opportunities to talk over what they had read and to integrate their reading with writing. In skills-oriented classrooms, however, learners spent large amounts of time on decoding and other basic reading skills and significantly less time on the act of reading and making sense of what was read.

In writing instruction, teachers placed emphasis on meaning by maximizing opportunities for composing extended text (as compared to non-composed writing such as copying or dictation and the more restricted composition called for by fill-in-the-blank or short-response exercises). As detailed in Chapter 5, other aspects of writing instruction supported the emphasis on meaning, in particular, teaching about writing processes, embedding lessons about mechanical skills in the context of writing text, integrating writing with reading and other aspects of the curriculum, and encouraging student-student interaction while writing. These features were not in evidence in skills-oriented writing classrooms; there, little or no composition took place, and the bulk of instructional time was spent teaching the correct mechanical skills of writing — punctuation, grammar, spelling, and so on.

Evidence from the classrooms we studied, summarized in Chapter 7, suggests that instruction oriented toward meaning pays off in student learning. In particular:

- At the end of the school year, students exposed to instruction emphasizing problem solving and conceptual understanding in mathematics, comprehension in reading, and competence in written composition performed between 1 and 6 normal curve equivalents (NCEs) higher on measures of these mathematics and reading skills than their counterparts in skills-oriented classrooms (when controlling for academic performance levels at the beginning of the year and the students' socioeconomic status). (Comparable results occurred for competence at written expression, although outcome analyses employed a different metric.) And though the evidence was somewhat less consistent, these effects appeared to hold across the twelve-month period (including the summer months) from one fall or spring to the next.
- Meaning-oriented instruction appeared in most instances to promote the learning of advanced skills as much or more for low-performing students as for high-performing ones who might be assumed to be more ready for "advanced" work. (However, there was no easy way to pinpoint the effects of the supplemental instruction that many of these low-performing children received.)
- As far as our evidence base permitted analysis, students in classrooms in which meaning was emphasized mastered discrete basic skills as fast or faster than students in skills-oriented classrooms.

We took pains to consider other possible explanations and checked for associations between the learning of advanced skills and other conditions in the classroom, especially the amount of time available for teaching any particular subject area, the attention paid to discrete skills, the teacher's level of formal professional development, and the teacher's overall level of competence (to the extent that this could be represented with crude quantitative indicators). Although these conditions were associated in some degree with the learning outcomes, the basic patterns held up when we controlled for these factors in statistical analyses.

The picture of attempts to teach for meaning in high-poverty classrooms is complicated by the variety of supplemental instructional services targeted to various categories of children, especially those at the low-achieving end of the performance continuum. As a result of these services, the regular classroom teacher's efforts were supplemented, in reading and mathematics primarily, by remedial or compensatory instruction offered by specialists, aides, and others. Offered either inside or outside the regular classroom for identified groups of low-performing or otherwise needy children, supplemental instruction appeared to have a curious relationship with teaching for meaning. As we argue in Chapter 6, most of the supplemental instruction we observed reinforced discrete basic skills instruction, though in some instances supplemental classes were designed to help children with the aspects of their academic work that focused on meaning — for example, solving nonroutine mathematical problems or writing extended text. And in some schools, supplemental instruction was at the forefront of the school's venture into meaning-oriented practices, through the efforts of specialists who provided subject-specific leadership, offered professional development opportunities, and built meaning into the learning diet of students served by supplemental programs. Most often, supplemental instruction differentiated instruction for children of varying abilities by offering the low performers something that was different, and often disconnected, from what was available in the regular classroom. Based on what we learned in this study, we cannot say whether this differentiation of curriculum is, on balance, helpful or harmful to students who are having trouble in the regular classroom learning situation. But what we learned raises the possibility that supplemental instruction may unwittingly limit the learning of target children as much as it helps them.

SUPPORTING TEACHERS' ATTEMPTS TO TEACH FOR MEANING

Located in schools and districts that typify many of the conditions surrounding high-poverty classrooms nationwide, the elementary school classrooms we studied represent the range of such settings where meaning-oriented instruction might take root. By contrasting cases in which this rooting had and hadn't happened, we were able to identify forces and conditions inside and outside of classrooms that appear to encourage or discourage teachers' attempts to engage in this kind of teaching.

Inside the classroom, the nature of the student group and the characteristics of teachers had something to do with the presence of meaning-oriented instruction, though the influences were less strong than one might expect and, in some instances, were negligible. Teaching for meaning appeared regardless of the socioeconomic composition of the student group (which ranged from roughly half to all the students in a class coming from low-income families). Teachers' decisions to emphasize meaning apparently did take into account the size of the student group, however: The largest classrooms (those with more than 27 students) were somewhat less likely to feature meaning-oriented instruction than classrooms with fewer students.

What teachers knew about the subject matter and about the students they were teaching was also related to attempts to emphasize meaning. Teachers who did so held richer conceptions of the subject area they were teaching than those who emphasized discrete skills. Not surprisingly, those who found more complex meanings in the subject itself found ways to make meaning a central priority in teaching. Those with a richer understanding of numbers and number operations, for example, were more comfortable helping learners see how these concepts were part of estimation, graphing, geometry, and other mathematical topics. Teachers who saw, in written text, more than a system of grammatical rules were more inclined to engage learners in the construction and revision of extended compositions. Alongside what they had learned about the subject areas, teachers' views and knowledge of the learners in high-poverty classrooms were also linked to the approach they took to mathematics, reading, and writing instruction. Although most of the teachers we studied held high expectations for their students, those with the greatest self-reported familiarity with their students' backgrounds (from whatever source—community work, years working at the school, approach to lessons, and so on) were most likely to make meaning a high priority in academic instruction.

Outside of the classroom, conditions in the school—the immediate institutional environment surrounding high-poverty classrooms—and the district or state "policy environment" were linked to the presence of meaning-oriented instruction. We encountered meaning-oriented classrooms in all the schools we studied, but clearly some school environments were more hospitable to this kind of teaching or, to put it another way, to the teachers who would be most likely to undertake such instruction. Though diverse in setting and structure, schools with the largest proportion of classrooms (i.e., a third or more) emphasizing meaning in one or more of the three subject areas shared certain attributes: one or more individuals (not always the principal) who provided subject-specific instructional leadership; a collegial climate that encouraged communication among teachers; a degree of autonomy that permitted teachers to experiment with curriculum and teaching; an organization of the instructional day that permitted large blocks of time to be devoted to core subject areas; and adequate administrative support, including the provision of resources and protection from outside influences. In addition, the mere fact of assigning student groups of a certain size and character to particular teachers, and assigning teachers with subject-area expertise to particular teaching roles, could increase or decrease the chances that meaning-oriented instruction would take place.

Similarly, among the six districts we studied, some clearly encouraged — and were lodged in state contexts that favored — teaching for meaning; others discouraged in varying degrees this approach to academic instruction. Of particular relevance were district (and state) policies that prescribed particular curricula, set the means by which student learning would be assessed, held teachers or schools accountable for learning outcomes, and provided for staff development. In obvious ways, all these policies could work together to make teaching for meaning a higher or lower priority of teachers; just as likely, different policies could send mixed messages about what to teach and how to teach it. Cutting across all types of policies was the manner in which districts or states formulated and implemented policies. In this regard, the districts we studied varied greatly in the degree of control from the top. The most actively controlling district favored instruction aimed at discrete skills that could be specified, sequenced, and tested at regular intervals. Not surprisingly, under such circumstances, few teachers dared to emphasize meaning in instruction. In several other districts, where proportionately larger numbers of teachers engaged in meaning-oriented teaching, district policies were less prescriptive but still insistent about particular curricular or instructional priorities.

Considering the joint effect of these external conditions on teachers' instructional decisions, we can conclude that meaning-oriented instruction is most likely to take root where the policy environment does not explicitly contradict the premises of meaning-oriented instruction; a delicate balance has been struck among external directives, protection for teachers' autonomy, and professional supports of various kinds; and policies affecting different aspects of the classroom (e.g., curriculum, assessment, textbook adoption) are reasonably well aligned with one another.

IMPLICATIONS FOR EDUCATION AND EDUCATORS

It is important to reflect on what our claims may mean for educational practice. Specifically, we offer comments about the meaning of this book's argument for students from low-income families, for teachers who work in high-poverty classrooms, for educators who provide initial and continuing education to such teachers, and for policy makers concerned about the quality of learning opportunities in these classrooms. We frame our comments in terms of questions that concerned educators may raise about curriculum and instruction in high-poverty settings.

Significance for Students from Low-Income Families

The first set of questions concerns the nature and extent of the contribution made by meaning-oriented instruction to the schooling of students from low-income families:

- Has teaching for meaning proved its worth in elementary school classrooms that serve large numbers of children from low-income families?
- Will teaching for meaning really work in the full range of high-poverty classrooms?
- Will the learning gains that come from meaning-oriented instruction close the gap that separates more and less affluent children in the schools?

The worth of teaching for meaning in high-poverty classrooms. What we learned suggests that the family of instructional approaches we refer to as teaching for meaning has a clear place in elementary school classrooms that serve children from low-income families. At a minimum, our investigation suggests that these children will progress more rapidly toward mastery of advanced skills at the same time that they develop their grasp of basic skills.

This assertion is not without important qualifications, however. First, as noted in earlier chapters, our measures of learning outcomes did not tap all the dimensions of student understanding that teaching for meaning seeks to affect and were especially limited with regard to effects on discrete skill learning (see Chapter 7). Furthermore, some important outcomes were not assessed at certain grade levels (e.g., competence in written composition in first and second grades). Second, there are some anomalies in our results, for example, regarding the superior performance of students in year 2 classrooms with "moderate" (as contrasted with "high") exposure to meaning-oriented reading instruction. Finally, the limitations of our student sample allowed us to make more confident claims about short-term outcomes — those apparent at the end of the school year — than about effects across a twelve-month period or longer. These qualifications notwithstanding, the weight of evidence unmistakably points to the value of orienting instruction toward meaning in high-poverty classrooms.

Our argument does not claim that this instructional approach is relevant only for students from a certain socioeconomic stratum. Because we did not compare the impact of such instruction on students from affluent and low-income backgrounds, we have no empirical way to determine whether these practices are uniquely suited to the children of poverty. But we can comment on the appropriateness of teaching for meaning and understanding for the segment of the population on which this study concentrated.

Above all, our findings dispelled one myth that has been around for a long time regarding the children of poverty: that, because of their presumed or apparent deficiencies in relevant skills, academically challenging work should be postponed until they are "ready," that is, until they have mastered all relevant basic skills. Approached in this way, that time of readiness may never arrive for many children.

In fact, it is plausible that teaching for meaning is *especially* appropriate for children from low-income families because of the cultural discontinuity they experience in schools that largely reflect the mainstream of American society. In the classrooms we studied, meaning-oriented instruction helped children connect their academic learning with the world they knew outside the school, a world in which the routines, activities, and discoveries of the classroom often seemed out of place. Meaning-oriented approaches to writing, for example, gave children from these backgrounds numerous avenues of expression that they would otherwise have been denied. Strategies aimed at maximizing understanding in reading encouraged children to go beyond the literal meanings of words to deeper understandings. These are important opportunities for disenfranchised groups, for whom the disjunctures between the world they know outside of school and the world they encounter within school walls are hard to make sense of. The more chances and tools they have to do so, the better.

Applications in the full range of high-poverty classrooms. The legitimacy of our claim that teaching for meaning can work in the full range of elementary school classrooms serving children from low-income families depends in part on how that range is defined. Perhaps the most telling way to define the range—and the way that confronts the teacher from the moment class begins—is in terms of the mix of cultural backgrounds, experience with schooling, and intellectual capacities among the children in the class.

From this perspective, the results of this study suggest that teaching for meaning has wide applicability. The cultural diversity of students is a case in point. The configurations of student backgrounds and needs found in the 140 classrooms we studied were among the most typical now encountered in high-poverty settings across the nation. Although we did not systematically vary the approach to instruction by type of student population (as might have been the case in a planned variation study), we found teachers attempting to teach for meaning in classrooms with students of varying cultural backgrounds (African American children in urban and suburban settings; Hispanic children in urban, suburban, and rural settings; Asian children, both recent immigrants and those whose families had lived in the United States for more than a generation; white children in inner-city and suburban settings; and so on). Many of these classrooms were highly heterogeneous culturally, and others were homogeneous. For example, in several inner-city classrooms, all the students came from low-income, white Appalachian families; several others were populated entirely by African American children participating in the free or reduced-price lunch program.

With regard to the range of student abilities and specialized learning needs, one may reasonably argue that teaching for meaning is appropriate for all ability levels. In doing so, we acknowledge that we did not assess outcomes in classrooms taught bilingually and in special-needs classrooms (e.g., resource rooms for handicapped children, Chapter 1 program pull-out rooms). But, short of convincing outcome evidence, a reasonable case can still be made regarding the potential of meaning-oriented instruction in such settings. We saw high levels of engagement in bilingual classrooms and in some Chapter 1 pullout rooms in which students were being taught with meaning-oriented instruction. In the regular classrooms, we documented effects of meaning-oriented instruction that were equally positive for children at the low- and high-performing ends of the achievement continuum. Furthermore, the results in the regular classrooms seemed to underscore the importance of forging a sense of connection between the school-based learning environment and the home environment. These clues point to the conclusion that instruction that emphasizes meaning should work well with children whose performance is below average (as is true in Chapter 1 rooms) and whose cultural backgrounds make school a strange place to be (which is especially true of children who do not speak English well).

To be sure, our claims about meaning-oriented instruction are, in part, a reflection of the kinds of schools and teachers we chose to study. We intentionally studied apparently successful schools and seasoned teachers. We did so because our primary goal was to learn about the potential of certain approaches to curriculum and instruction, not the many other conditions in high-poverty schools that compromise the quality of education. In troubled schools where the principal source of chaos is teacher burnout, inexperienced teachers, a vacuum of leadership, or misassignment of teaching staff, meaning-oriented instruction may not be applicable.

Implications for the gap between more and less affluent children. It is tempting to be optimistic about the role that teaching for meaning can play in improving the educational prospects for children from low-income families. After all, more conventional forms of instruction appear to place unnecessary intellectual limitations on these children. Would not instruction that expands their intellectual horizons more rapidly offer these children the chance to catch up with their more advantaged counterparts elsewhere?

We feel compelled to address the matter more cautiously. We suspect that if teaching for meaning were widely adopted and competently implemented, it would change the learning experience for many *individuals* from low-status backgrounds, giving them more reasons to participate in schooling and the means to carry their schooling farther than they might have otherwise. This is not the same, however, as saying that the gap between the haves and the have-nots would diminish as a result.

A number of other forces and conditions would have to change for there to be a lessening of *group* differences reflected in the gap between children who are from affluent backgrounds and those who are not. First, if teaching for meaning is widely adopted by teachers in schools serving the affluent — and there is every reason to believe that this will be the case — then students in high-poverty classrooms will be at no comparative advantage. There is little reason to believe that they would make greater strides forward in learning than children anywhere, all other things being equal. Furthermore, the relative differences in achievement among more and less affluent children can be traced to many sources, only some of which are reflected in curriculum and teaching (see Knapp & Woolverton, forthcoming). These forces include the many clear obstacles that impoverished circumstances impose on any child, whatever his or her abilities — less adult attention, nutritional deficiencies, and the lack of space and time to work on academic lessons outside of school. In addition, there are pervasive social forces that encourage schools to channel children from low-status backgrounds into learning and career paths that ensure a large and compliant workforce for relatively low-level jobs. Young people develop an image of their capabilities and their futures from many sources, only one of which is school.

Significance for Teachers and Teacher Educators

A second set of questions arises regarding implications for teaching, teachers, and teacher educators:

- Should teachers abandon skills-oriented teaching, either in the regular classroom or in supplemental programs?
- Will teachers who incorporate teaching for meaning into their repertoires be "better" teachers? In all subject areas?
- To emphasize meaning in their practice, what must teachers learn, and what sort of learning process will help them do so?

Implications for the continuation of skills-oriented teaching. Some readers may see in our findings convincing evidence that skills-oriented teaching is less effective than teaching for meaning and should therefore be abandoned. Such a conclusion is unwarranted and oversimplifies our argument regarding alternatives to conventional wisdom. In our view, the core deficiency of instruction aimed at discrete basic skills is not that it is ineffective at achieving all instructional goals—far from it. When competently practiced (and we saw a lot of competent skills-oriented instruction), it succeeds admirably at its primary purpose—inculcating discrete basic skills. We are arguing that the chief limitation of such approaches to teaching reading, writing, and mathematics is that they unnecessarily limit the intellectual growth of the young people who populate high-poverty classrooms and reduce their sense of meaningful connection with schooling.

Teachers can increase the emphasis they place on meaning and understanding without abandoning discrete basic skills. Indeed, we saw many ways in which teachers tried to combine both approaches, sometimes with apparent success, and sometimes with a sense of confusion and mixed messages. Although instruction aimed at meaning and understanding rejects many conventional premises, teachers in the study sample did not typically view themselves as choosing between incompatible pedagogical philosophies. More often than not, teachers combined conventional modes of instruction with alternative practices. For example, many teachers who taught multiple mathematical topics with an emphasis on conceptual understanding also gave students considerable practice in arithmetic computation. Reading teachers typically taught reading mechanics alongside activities designed to maximize understanding.

In part, this tendency to combine old with new reflects teachers' learning curve: It is easier to learn new approaches by incrementally adjusting or adding to an existing repertoire than to start fresh with a whole new set of instructional routines. But the pattern may also reflect a sensible approach to teaching under any circumstances. Even though it is clearly effective to have students do a lot of reading with a focus on comprehension, the need for practice with decoding does not disappear. Alternative approaches to reading stress the need to encounter, learn, and practice decoding in context, and we observed a great deal of this in the classrooms we studied. But given that many students in this population have clear weaknesses in basic reading skills, there still may be an important role for additional practice in decoding done the old-fashioned way. Our findings about discrete skills teaching in reading are especially suggestive of this need (see Chapter 7).

Instruction that emphasizes meaning calls into question many assumptions underlying conventional practice—the place of basic skills in the overall curricular sequence, the usefulness of focusing on complex tasks (writing, reading, unfamiliar mathematics problems) from early on, and so on. But for high-poverty classrooms, instruction that appropriately *subsumes* conventional practices within an instructional framework guided by alternative assumptions may have the most to offer. Thus, the prospect for teachers is not to abandon what they have been doing—and often doing exceedingly well—but to expand their repertoires to teach a more challenging curriculum.

In short, though fundamental changes in perspective on teaching are involved in making meaning-oriented instruction come alive in high-poverty classrooms, this perspective need not dominate everything children do in class. Discrete skills still need to be learned, and the evidence from our investigation suggests that the explicit attempt to teach these skills is still necessary in high-poverty classrooms. Put another way, understanding is not the only worthy educational goal, and it would be short-sighted to make such a claim. In addition, there may be many ways in which understanding is enhanced by, and ultimately requires, proficiency in discrete skills.

Implications for the quality of teaching. Expanding instructional repertoires to include an emphasis on meaning is no guarantee of better teaching in a particular subject area, nor does mastering teaching for meaning in one subject area naturally transfer to other subject areas. It may seem that giving priority to meaning would naturally lead teachers to a mode of teaching that works better in terms of the teachers' comfort level, the students' engagement in academic learning, and the outcomes of instruction. In the classrooms we studied, however, teaching for meaning was implemented well in some instances and poorly in others; during the two years of the study, we saw numerous instances of bad meaning-oriented teaching.

In extreme cases, teachers lost control of their classrooms in search of a more flexible structure, greater student responsibility for learning, more opportunities for expression, or flexible grouping arrangements. For example, of the 23 classrooms studied intensively in year 1 that emphasized meaning in one or more subject areas, four had serious problems with basic levels of classroom order, and two exhibited learning environments we classified as dysfunctional. (Of course, problems of classroom order were not unique to meaning-oriented teachers — two classrooms in which all subjects were taught in the most skills-oriented way were also classified as dysfunctional.) More frequently, teachers attempting to put meaning-oriented principles into practice "got the words but not the tune" — that is, they undertook new kinds of learning activities without understanding them or exploiting their opportunities for learning. Many, perhaps most, of the teachers categorized as moderately engaged in meaning-oriented practices taught their classes this way. Such teachers might ask probing comprehension questions to get at deeper meanings of a reading passage but neglect to listen, probe, or respond to students' answers. Or they might use manipulatives, ostensibly to motivate students' learning of arithmetic, without helping them make important conceptual connections (or even understanding the connections themselves). In writing instruction, extended composition tasks might be assigned or completed without any attempt to teach students that revision is part of writing.

Partial implementation of new practices is understandable as teachers struggle to master new ways of conceiving the material they teach and new ways of orchestrating children's engagement with it. But when teachers think that they understand alternative practices fully but grasp only part of the story, they may unintentionally defeat the very purpose they are trying to accomplish.

Even when teachers make teaching for meaning work in one subject area, this does not automatically transfer to other subjects. This point is underscored by the small number of teachers (only 15 percent of all we studied) who placed consistent emphasis on meaning in two or more of the three subject areas. In all likelihood, the pattern reflects several things. First, elementary teachers are not likely to be deeply immersed in all the subject areas they teach or the associated pedagogical content knowledge, which is, after all, subject specific. Their training is unlikely to have emphasized deep immersion in any area of the curriculum, and the fact that they have become expert in one area probably represents personal preference and the availability of continuing education opportunities. Second, time for instruction in the elementary school curriculum is fixed. Teaching for meaning takes time, as the preceding chapters have made clear; maximizing meaning in writing instruction may thus impinge on the time available to invest in meaning-oriented reading or mathematics, not to mention other aspects of the already full elementary school curriculum. Integration of curriculum is a partial answer (and we saw some of this in the natural integration of reading and writing), but trade-offs in time, energy, and attention are still inevitable. Third, most teaching assignments in elementary schools discourage specialization (supplemental program teaching and some teamed or departmentalized arrangements are exceptions). Even if they want to develop meaning-oriented approaches to multiple areas of their curricula, the pressures of teaching a variety of other subjects and managing other aspects of the school day are more likely to encourage teachers to improve their breadth of competence in all areas rather than their depth of competence in several. Finally, teaching for meaning is hard work. Teachers have understandable limits on the number of areas in which they are willing to invest the extra time and experience the increased ambiguity that meaning-oriented instruction entails.

What we learned about teachers' efforts to master teaching for meaning within and across subject areas was, of course, a reflection of the time frame surrounding our research. We studied high-poverty classrooms during a period (the 1989–90 and 1990–91 school years) when many policy makers at the district and state levels were attempting to encourage changes in instruction that shifted the emphasis toward meaning and understanding. For many teachers we observed, meaning-oriented instruction was a relatively unfamiliar thing, and it meant substantial changes in their practices. Therefore, we have more to say about teachers' initial attempts to incorporate these new ideas about teaching and learning than about the fine-tuning of their understanding over the long term. But even so, the timing of teachers' encounters with meaning-oriented instruction does not change the fact that teaching for meaning is hard to do well, and learning to do so in one subject area is unlikely to shortcut the learning that must take place in other areas.

What teachers need to learn and how they can learn it. From watching teachers at varying stages in their attempts to incorporate teaching for meaning into their repertoires, it is possible to comment on the nature of the learning challenge and ways to address it. In brief, to embrace meaning-oriented instruction, teachers in high-poverty classrooms need to learn new things about learners, subject matter, and academic learning environments. In each case, they need to transcend a set of misconceptions that are easy to come by and widely held.

The teachers who placed the greatest emphasis on meaning in their instruction had made two significant shifts in their thinking about learners — the first from a view of learners as passive recipients to one of learners as active participants in learning, and the second from a primary focus on learners' deficits to an asset model of the learner that highlights the strengths and resources children bring to the learning situation. This shift was most visible in the way certain teachers responded to cultural diversity (described in Chapter 2): By treating cultural background as a resource for learning and actively or proactively addressing cultural dimensions of instruction in mathematics, reading, or writing, teachers were able to sustain children's engagement with academic work and more explicitly connect the children's world of experience to the world of school-based learning. Not all teachers were successful in this regard, nor did all try to forge such connections; but those that did achieved a higher level of meaning in their work.

Teachers who placed the greatest emphasis on meaning in mathematics, reading, or writing were the ones who had the broadest and deepest grasp of these subject areas. They had developed pictures of the content and skills they were teaching that were rich and detailed and that typically subsumed other more limited conceptions of the subject area. Compare, for example, those who treated mathematics as the routine application of arithmetic algorithms with those whose view of mathematics combined routine arithmetic with nonroutine problem solving, geometric representation of ideas, and logical reasoning (see Chapter 3). Similarly, the teachers of writing who approached this skill area as a system of grammatical rules held a much more limited view of writing than those who, without denying a role for such rules, saw in it a means of communication and a tool for learning (as noted in Chapter 8). In each case, teachers who emphasized meaning in their instruction had moved beyond a rule-based conception of the subject area to one that subsumed rules within a larger conceptual terrain. Teachers holding these conceptions viewed curriculum in much less linear terms.

Teachers who emphasized meaning had transcended a view of classroom order that called for tight and continuous control by the teacher in favor of a conception of order that permitted a wider range of learning activities and modes of participation. In addition, as described in Chapter 1, such teachers were more likely to appreciate the interconnections between decisions about order and decisions about subject-specific pedagogy.

These shifts in thinking and approach to instruction have profound implications for professional development efforts. If we learned anything from two years of watching teachers experiment with meaning-oriented instruction, it is that the learning process requires rich and continuing forms of professional support. Most of the teachers we studied did not receive such support, though nearly all had some access to relevant opportunities. According to the individuals who displayed the most meaning-oriented approaches to instruction, their learning was acquired from diverse sources and took place over time: Advice from trusted colleagues, modeling by peers and mentors, discoveries in the classroom, explicit teaching, reading in journals, exposure at professional conferences, one-shot workshops inside and outside of the district, and other forms of in-service training (including graduate work for some) were all part of a balanced diet of professional development experiences.

The most powerful forms of professional development we observed were those that were available "at the teachers' elbow" on an ongoing basis, through resident specialists and peers who had developed particular expertise in an area of teaching. These examples do not exhaust the possibilities for effective professional development (nor was it our purpose to systematically study questions of professional development), but they do highlight qualities of professional exposure and reinforcement that educators should aspire to recreate through whatever means available.

Whether teachers will find — or seek out — the appropriate mix of learning opportunities over time depends, in part, on their own initiative and, in part, on conditions that lie outside their control but potentially within the reach of policy makers.

Significance for Policy Makers

We live in an era of well-intentioned attempts to reform education, so leaders in district or state offices of education who are concerned about the quality of learning opportunities in high-poverty classrooms naturally raise questions about the roles they can play:

- Should school districts or state agencies mandate teaching for meaning? If not, how can higher-level policy makers who believe in the principles that underlie meaning-oriented instruction create conditions that support this form of teaching?
- Should schools be restructured to encourage teaching for meaning? If so, how should they be restructured?

The role of curriculum mandates and associated policies. Given evidence or simply the belief that meaning-oriented instruction improves learning, it is tempting for policy makers to require teachers, through some form of curriculum mandate and associated textbook selections, to adopt this approach. In several of the districts we studied, that is exactly what had happened shortly before the study began. It is just as tempting to dismiss such policy actions: After all, simply telling teachers to emphasize meaning will not change their minds about learners, subject matter, and academic learning environments. And if the "pedagogy of policy" is at odds with the approach to instruction being mandated, then teachers may well keep following familiar pathways and mistake superficial adjustments for deep change (Cohen, 1990; Cohen & Barnes, 1993). Under these circumstances, the potential for such a mandate to backfire seems substantial — by breeding resentment among teachers who feel unprepared to take on a new and difficult approach to their work, by multiplying the number of instances in which teachers think they are teaching for meaning but aren't, and so on.

Our view of mandates is somewhat more complicated. Although it is clear that curriculum mandates by themselves will not bring about a fundamentally different way of approaching teaching, they are an important element in the mix of conditions and incentives that stimulate teachers to attempt new ways of teaching. It is obvious from our research that pressure for change from school-level instructional leaders, district policy makers, and state agencies helped encourage — and sometimes pushed — teachers to try new ways of teaching mathematics, reading, and writing.

At the same time, curriculum mandates do not happen in a vacuum; they are part of a set of policies emanating from both district and state levels that converge on the classroom and form a policy environment in which teachers plan instruction and guide learning. Of particular relevance to meaning-oriented instruction is the convergence of — or discrepancy among — policies governing curriculum, student assessment, the accountability of teachers and schools, and professional development.

Implications for school restructuring. Restructuring is a broad and inclusive term, subsuming attempts to change many aspects of the school, including its organization, staffing, budgeting, decision-making processes, curriculum, and community interface. Not all of this broad agenda is implicated in the development of teaching for meaning. We saw meaning-oriented instruction flourish in a variety of school environments, many of which were not engaged in restructuring (by anyone's definition). Nonetheless, what we learned has implications for changing the way school staffs organize and carry out their work.

At a minimum, our findings point to certain schoolwide features that influence the growth and longevity of meaning-oriented instruction. To the extent that these conditions are not present and would require substantial changes in order to put them in place, a restructuring of sorts is called for. First, the structure of the school day must yield blocks of time for extended engagement with a single subject area; this is not a tall order in many elementary schools, but neither is it a foregone conclusion. Second, a minimal quality of conversation among teachers must be in place, supporting the notion that teaching and learning are intellectual endeavors and that efforts to promote academic learning in all its forms should be prized. Ideally, the school's collegial climate would provide for a richer conversation, based on opportunities to exchange ideas and give feedback. Third, the size of classes and the assignment of teachers to them need to be carefully considered to keep from creating classroom climates that defeat meaning-oriented instruction. Although hampered by resource constraints, school and district policy makers have some flexibility in the overall size of classes. They also have options in assigning teachers to schools and classrooms that may maximize the possibility for meaning-oriented instruction (although not a panacea, teaming and departmentalized arrangements offer some obvious advantages in this regard). Finally, teachers need access to expertise — that is, to individuals who know what meaning-oriented instruction looks like in the classroom and who can be consulted on an ongoing basis as teachers try to learn what this form of instruction requires. There are various ways to ensure these conditions, and, depending on the school and its history, not all imply major changes in organization, decision making, budgeting, and so on.

CLOSING THOUGHTS

Our overall conclusion is this: Instruction that emphasizes meaning, as interpreted and implemented by the teachers we studied, has proved its worth in high-poverty classrooms. Across a wide range of settings — and even in the absence of sustained support or focused promotion — these methods of conducting academic instruction have shown that they belong in the repertoires of teachers working under the varied and often difficult conditions that pertain in high-poverty elementary schools. They deserve serious consideration by all teachers who work in such settings and by the full array of educators — school leaders, curriculum designers and coordinators, compensatory program specialists and directors, district and state policy makers, teacher educators — who create the environment in which teachers work.

Readers should leave this book with no illusions about what teaching for meaning demands of teachers. As is increasingly recognized in current discussions (e.g., Brandt, 1994), such approaches to instruction are hard work. The teachers we observed who made teaching for meaning a priority persisted for many reasons, but they were all willing to push themselves to master the subtle art of giving children who have ambivalent feelings about school more responsibility for learning, orchestrating academic tasks that ask more of students, and sustaining engagement in learning among children who bring widely varying backgrounds and capacities to the classroom.

In closing, we hope that educators who are concerned about high-poverty classrooms will explore the possibilities of teaching for meaning but resist making meaning-oriented instruction a formula for the future — in other words, a new conventional wisdom. There is nothing formulaic about the way the most successful teachers we observed approached their task. No checklist of behaviors, questioning styles, instructional strategies, or ways of connecting instruction to students' backgrounds exists — or could exist — that would bring teachers closer to the goal of offering children from low-income backgrounds an academically challenging learning experience in elementary school. The argument of this book is best thought of as a series of challenges to often unquestioned assumptions. As long as educators continually challenge these as well as future assumptions underlying their craft, the children of poverty will be well served.

Notes on Methods and Measures

In this section, we review briefly the key features of the research strategy, the sample, the types of data collected (including qualitative data and quantitative measures), and the approach to data analysis. Readers will find more detail about these and other aspects of the study design in the second volume of the full technical report of the study (Knapp & Marder, 1992).

RESEARCH STRATEGY

The study on which this book is based set out to identify effective practices in classrooms with high concentrations of children from low-income families. In that context, we were particularly interested in the form, extent, and impact of instruction that emphasized meaning in some fashion. Although meaning-oriented instruction had been shown to be effective in demonstration settings (cited in the Introduction), no research had examined the existence or viability of such approaches across all three subject areas among a wide range of classrooms that typify the schooling available to the children of poverty. Given that the ideas motivating meaning-oriented instruction had been widely disseminated in professional journals and networks, we assumed that many teachers would have tried such alternatives in some form or other. If so, lessons about effective practice could be derived by comparing those teachers with others whose assumptions about learners, curriculum, and approaches to teaching favored discrete-skills instruction.

The search for natural variation implied that we would follow a correlational research strategy rather than one in which experimental controls could be predetermined, as is the case in planned variation designs. Thus, we assumed that instructional practices within and across schools would be sufficiently varied to demonstrate, through correlational analyses, associations between certain kinds of practices and learning outcomes.

We designed the study in such a way that we could arrive at conclusions about effective practice within and across subject areas by combining qualitatively based understandings about a small number of classrooms with quantitatively based insights about many classrooms. In attempting to do so, we drew on two research traditions that are not normally joined together: the process-product tradition (Gage & Needels, 1989) and that of multisite qualitative research (e.g., Miles & Huberman, 1994).

Combining Research Traditions

The marriage of the two research traditions rested on certain assumptions and reflected some adaptations of each to accommodate the other. First, we assumed that something as complex and subtle as teaching and learning could best be grasped by intensive immersion of observers in the actual settings so that they could watch instruction take place on numerous occasions, interview teachers and students periodically, and examine the materials and curricula in use. To study instruction under a number of conditions and in a variety of classrooms, we employed this intensive strategy in multisite qualitative designs. Doing so made it possible to pay close attention to the intricacies of each classroom case, although some attention to the unique attributes of each case and its context had to be sacrificed to enable cross-site contrasts following a common analytic scheme, as is typically done in such designs.

The number of sites that can be studied through qualitative means is limited. In some scholars' views and in our experience, the returns diminish rapidly as one exceeds a sample size of 25 to 30 (Miles & Huberman, 1994). To enlarge the sample and provide a systematic way to relate attributes of instruction to student outcome measures, we turned to the process-product research tradition. Designs in this tradition have been in use for some time, primarily in research on generic aspects of teaching, such as approaches to classroom management. As typically employed, this research tradition assumes that key features of instruction (e.g., pacing, the amount of teacher talk) can be identified independent of the particular subject area, measured quantitatively, and associated with test outcome measures to provide evidence of more or less effective teaching practice. As in many quantitative research traditions, designs of this sort assume that a measurement has a relatively fixed meaning across different contexts and that the context for teaching is a relatively unimportant part of the story to be told. Although these assumptions can be (and have been) criticized (e.g., Erickson, 1986), a large segment of the educational research community accepts that certain regularities in the way instruction occurs can be identified and interpreted across contexts.

We adapted the process-product premises in several ways. First, we did not focus primarily on generic instructional practices, but rather developed different (though related) measures for each subject area we were investigating. In other words, we assumed that subject matter would provide an important context for instructional practices and might give these practices different meanings. Second, we did not approach the investigation with a discrete set of already validated measures, but rather developed measures and indicators that could be validated for the specific settings in which we were conducting the investigation. Third, we took pains in the analysis to consider a variety of possible contextual effects. Finally, in developing our conclusions, we relied as much on insights derived from systematic qualitative analysis as on the evidence yielded by the quantitative design.

Components and Levels of the Study Design

We fashioned a strategy for data collection that allowed us to investigate curriculum and instruction at several different levels. At one level, we studied the whole year's curriculum, as enacted in the sample classrooms. Information about the year's curriculum, derived from interviews, teacher logs, and examination of syllabi or materials, was necessarily somewhat superficial. We were simply unable to make a detailed record of everything that was taught during a 9-month period, nor would it necessarily have served the study purposes to do so. At this level, our goal was to provide a descriptive overview of what was taught and how it was taught during the school year.

At a second level, we examined curriculum and instruction in greater detail during selected observational periods (2 weeks long in year 1, and 1 week in year 2). Often, these periods coincided with defined instructional units; in other instances, we observed a slice of an instructional unit or simply a sample of an ongoing instructional sequence that was not organized into discernible units. In both years, we examined one period during each of the major time blocks of the school year — fall, winter, and spring. The data we collected about these time periods were derived from multiple sources: interviews, teacher logs, examination of materials or unit plans, and a descriptive writing sample collected at the end of the period. These sources permitted a more detailed description of what was taught and (to a limited extent) the instructional strategies used.

A third level of data collection was necessary to get a concrete picture of the actual content of instruction and the way academic instruction took place in the classrooms. Within each of the observational periods, we selected several days on which to observe instruction. To the extent possible, the days were chosen to represent the most central teaching and learning activities of the time period (testing days or review days, for example, were considered poor choices for observation). Observations were directed at both the whole classroom and targeted students within the room. By combining observational data with what we learned from semistructured debriefing interviews with the teachers (e.g., after each lesson), examination of the materials in use during the observed lessons, and interviews with target students, we were able to capture in considerable detail how teachers conducted instruction and how students responded to it.

Intensive observation of instruction required too many research resources to be carried out in all sample classrooms. Therefore, we did so in a subset of classrooms—in year 1, one of the two classrooms per grade in each school was studied intensively (a total of 44 classrooms); in year 2, one or two classrooms were chosen per school (for a total of 23 classrooms) to allow further investigation of special issues related to instructional strategies in particular subject areas. The other classrooms in each school were also observed, but not as frequently. For these classrooms, we relied more heavily on interview and log data.

To capture what students learned, we tested children twice each year, in October and May. A battery of tests was administered to all students in sample classrooms across a two-day period by members of the study team.

Three other sorts of data were collected from teachers or from school and district sources. First, from classroom rosters and school records, we gathered basic demographic information about the students in the sample. Second, in the second year, coded information from observational visits was supplemented by a survey of teachers to elicit information about their backgrounds and their attitudes regarding children, teaching, and the school setting (in year 1, this information came from teacher interviews). Third, we interviewed principals and district office staff on several occasions to collect information about school and district policies, ethos, resources, staff development, and other features of the school setting that might influence the classroom.

SAMPLE CONSTRUCTION

The sample was constructed in several stages. To identify school districts, we examined prior-year (1988–89) test score and demographic data for all school districts lying within a commutable distance (approximately 50 miles) of the three study team home bases (Washington, D.C.; Cincinnati, Ohio; San Francisco, California). All districts with high overall levels of poverty (as indicated by Orshansky percentile figures) were examined to determine which elementary schools in these districts (1) served student populations in which 50 percent or more of the children came from low-income backgrounds, and (2) performed better than average compared with other schools serving comparable populations. Six districts that contrasted on key contextual factors (urbanicity, ethnic or racial diversity), each with large numbers of candidate schools, were invited to participate in the study.

Once districts had agreed to participate, we selected schools in consultation with district officials. Fifteen schools were chosen on the basis of the two criteria. First, we picked schools serving student populations with large numbers of children from low-income backgrounds but that differed in socioeconomic and cultural makeup. Several schools served relatively homogeneous populations (e.g., all white or all African American students; 100 percent from low-income backgrounds), and others served more diverse populations (e.g., with different mixtures of white, African American, Hispanic, and/or Asian American children; with different percentages from low-income backgrounds). Second, although all were performing well compared with other schools in their districts serving similar student populations, the schools in the study sample varied considerably in test score performance the year before the study commenced. Schools' average test scores ranged from well above national averages in an absolute sense (e.g., above the 70th percentile) to the low end of the second quartile (approximately the 30th percentile nationwide). (The schools in the study sample differed in several other respects — for example, two were year-round schools, and several others contained magnet programs of one kind or other).

Within the fifteen schools, 150 classrooms were identified for study — 80 first-, third-, or fifth-grade classrooms in the first year, and 70 second-, fourth-, or sixth-grade classrooms in year 2 (as a result of attrition and excessive missing data from a few classrooms, most analyses were performed on 140 or fewer classrooms). Classrooms were selected for study based on four criteria: variation in instructional approach, the teacher's level of experience (inexperienced teachers were excluded), apparent proficiency at managing classrooms (wherever we could, we avoided classrooms that, by reputation, were experiencing serious management problems), and the teacher's willingness to participate. Our choices were heavily constrained by the small number of teachers per grade. At most, there were four teachers per school at each grade level; in some schools there were only two. In addition, our desire to exclude first-year teachers or those who were experiencing major problems in classroom management further limited our choices. In a few instances, we were unable to include more than one teacher per grade in the study sample.

A similar process was followed in the second year of the study, with the additional constraint that we tried to choose classrooms containing as many students from the first year as possible. In two school districts, elementary schools ended at the fifth grade; hence no sixth-grade classrooms were included in the study from the five schools located in these districts.

Criteria for selecting the subset of classrooms for intensive study were different in each year of the study. During year 1, one of the two classrooms per grade was included in this subsample to maximize the range of approaches to instruction that we could examine closely. The following year, we selected 23 classrooms that showed particular promise for probing more deeply into effective practices in one subject area. These 23 were approximately evenly divided among classrooms that were especially appropriate for examining meaning-oriented approaches to mathematics, reading, and writing instruction, respectively. In selecting these classrooms, we also took into consideration the potential for investigating questions related to classroom management and supplemental instruction.

QUALITATIVE AND QUANTITATIVE DATA

To capture instruction and its outcomes with sufficient depth and subtlety, we drew on a variety of qualitative and quantitative data sources.

Qualitative Data

The team that collected qualitative data consisted of the authors of this book and a group of researchers with extensive experience in qualitative research on schooling and instruction. Before each year of data collection began, the team met for an intensive week-long orientation to develop common strategies for research and agreements regarding how to interpret the data. In addition, during each year, team members met periodically in smaller groups (and once again as a whole study team) to discuss the progress of data collection and to share emerging insights.

We collected qualitative data at the classroom and school levels by observing lessons, examining instructional materials, and conducting semi-structured interviews with teachers and other school staff (see Knapp & Marder, 1992, for more detail on these procedures). Observations were focused yet open-ended: Rather than record behaviors in a checklist form (as is typical in process-product research), observers constructed a narrative record of lessons, focusing on those events that were of greatest relevance to the study's purpose (the nature of the academic task, the teacher's interaction with students, and so forth). We also examined instructional materials in use during the one- or two-week observation period; we collected examples of materials for use during analysis and maintained a field-note record of other materials. Interviews with teachers were semi-structured, following an outline of analytic topics related to the major issues addressed by the study. We interviewed teachers four or more times during the year — at least once during each of the three rounds of site visiting, and once at the end of the year. Others such as the principals, special program staff, or district-level coordinators were interviewed once.

Following each round of visits to classrooms, site visitors summarized in narrative form what they had learned about each classroom from all three data sources (observations, materials examination, and interviews), following a detailed analytic outline.

Quantitative Measures

Quantitative measures came from four primary sources:

- *Coding forms filled out following site visits.* Following each field visit, the observers entered information from observations, materials examination, and interviews onto a coding form. The form was divided into sections for language arts and mathematics and further subdivided into subsections corresponding to the actual observed lessons or the period within which these lessons took place. Some of the codes pertained to each observed lesson, others to the full one- or two-week period that was the focus of the visit.
- *Teacher surveys.* During the second year of data collection, a survey was administered to all regular classroom teachers to elicit information about their professional backgrounds, their attitudes about the children they were teaching, and their perceptions of the school setting in which they were teaching. The items in this survey had been included in the first-year coding form.
- *Student rosters/background data.* The school or the classroom teachers themselves provided information on student ethnicity, participation in supplemental programs, receipt of free or reduced-price lunch, and so forth.
- *Teacher logs.* Regular classroom teachers in the study sample kept daily logs of instructional activities in mathematics, reading, writing, and other language arts, using a structured form developed by the study team (see Knapp & Marder, 1992). Log forms were filled out from the time of pretesting (late October) to late May, a period that included approximately 120 instructional days.

These data sources yielded different kinds of measures for analytic purposes. Because outcome analyses concentrated on the whole school year and took classroom instruction as the primary unit, the following types of analytic measures were used: (1) percentage of the classroom's students with a given attribute; (2) of all instructional days, the percentage on which a given activity or event took place; (3) across all observed lessons (or observation periods), the percentage in which a certain instructional strategy or material was used; (4) across all observed lessons (or observation periods), the average ratings by observers of some aspect of instruction; and (5) across all observed lessons (or observation periods), an average count of something taking place in the classroom, such as the number of minutes students actually read text or the number of extended writing tasks assigned during the observation period.

All but a few variables were measured at the classroom level. In other instances, student-level data were aggregated to form classroom-level measures. Most of the observational data were collected by a single observer per classroom, but to assess interobserver agreement, we paired up observers (during year 2) and compared observation codes for particular days on which the pairs watched the same lessons. Coefficients of agreement were calculated as the ratio between agreements divided by total possible agreements: The average coefficient of agreement among pairs was .85; no pair had a coefficient less than .75.

The validity of measures used in analysis was established principally in two ways: first, by correlating what observers saw with what teachers coded in their logs for all items that were identical and, second, by comparing coded information and summary indices with qualitative case reports. Coefficients of agreement between teachers and the site visitors who watched their classes were calculated in the same way described above (agreements divided by total possible agreements). Average coefficients for the four sections of the log (reading, writing, other language arts, and mathematics) were .82, .91, .87, and .96, respectively. Values on various items were compared with qualitative reports to check their validity, and in constructing the variables indicating the predominant pattern of instruction, classroom reports were used extensively to identify the pattern in the first place and as a check on the meaningfulness of quantitative data used subsequently to classify cases.

We describe below the measures on which the analyses described in this book concentrated — that is, the measures highlighted in the figures accompanying each chapter. A larger number of measures, some of which are referred to in text, played a role in the study; for a complete description and specification of all measures, see Knapp and Marder (1992).

Student and teacher background measures. Regarding students, two background measures were used extensively in outcome analyses: poverty level and prior achievement level. The former measure, constructed at the classroom level, represented the percentage of children participating in the free or reduced-price lunch program. To represent prior achievement level, we used fall pretest scores on the Comprehensive Test of Basic Skills (CTBS)/4 Concepts and Applications, Computation, and Comprehension subtests, depending on the analysis being performed (because we had no consistent premeasure of writing ability, we settled for the CTBS/4 Comprehension test as a proxy for proficiency in writing-related skills; although not optimal, this choice seemed justified by the generally high correlations between reading and writing outcome scores).

Based on coding data in the first year and teacher survey data in the second year (using items that were virtually identical to the first-year coding form), we constructed several scales regarding teachers' backgrounds. First, we created an index of the richness of teachers' professional development history by summing different categories of professional development the teachers had experienced (e.g., undergraduate or graduate training in the subject area, training in subject-specific teaching methods as part of a degree or certification program, subject-specific professional development offered by the school district). The index went from 0 (least) to 6 (most). Second, we captured teachers' satisfaction with teaching through a 4-point Likert scale from 1 (very unsatisfied) to 4 (very satisfied). Third, a similar scale was created to represent the teachers' expectations of their students' academic potential, ranging from 1 (most will not be able to succeed) to 4 (all students can succeed at grade level). A fourth index scale, ranging from 0 (least familiar) to 7 (most familiar), represented the sum of different ways in which teachers indicated that they had familiarity with their students' backgrounds (e.g., grew up in the same community, had visited some of the students' homes, did community work in the neighborhood, lived in the neighborhood). A final scale summed the different aspects of curriculum and instruction over which teachers thought they had discretionary control (e.g., selecting the content and skills to be taught during the year, departing from the textbook chosen by the school or district, determining the timing and amount of homework).

Measures of curriculum and instruction in mathematics. The two broad strategies for emphasizing meaning in mathematics instruction were measured by indices summarizing data from the coding form or teacher's log. The index of teachers' focus on conceptual understanding and real-life applications was created by summing dichotomous (1, 0) codes indicating whether teachers focused on conceptual understanding in any way, applied mathematical concepts or procedures to nonroutine problems, or connected mathematical ideas to the life situations of students; sums were then averaged across all observed lessons during the year. The second index, representing the breadth of mathematical topics other than arithmetic, summed the percentage of days during the year on which the teacher reported focusing on each of five categories: geometry, measurement, graphs/data/statistics, logic problems/puzzles/problem-solving strategies, and other topics (which teachers specified).

By combining the two indices, we formed a 2 × 2 table with quadrants labeled as follows: focus on arithmetic, skills only (low on both indices); focus on arithmetic, emphasis on conceptual understanding (high on the first index, low on the second); multiple topics, skills only (low on the first index, high on the second); and multiple topics, emphasis on conceptual understanding (high on both indices). Cut points defining "high" and "low" on each index were set to maximize the fit with cases from 40 intensively studied classrooms in year 1, which were qualitatively classified by the conceptual definitions of the four quadrants.

Other measures of mathematics instruction were derived straightforwardly from coding forms or teacher log data. For example, the amount of time allocated to mathematics instruction was simply an average of the observer's count of the minutes elapsed during observed mathematics lessons. Indicators of manipulative or calculator use were derived from the teachers' logs, which asked whether or not the teacher had employed either on each day.

Measures of curriculum and instruction in reading. Indicators of the strategies for maximizing meaning in reading instruction came from the teachers' logs or observers' coding forms. In their daily logs, for example, teachers indicated whether (1) comprehension instruction focused on deeper understanding of text, (2) reading instruction was integrated with writing or other subject areas, and (3) students were given opportunities to discuss what they had read. Analytic measures for each were created by calculating the percentage of all days of language arts instruction on which each feature of instruction was present. Based on their observations and interviews, observers coded (4) the number of minutes students actually read text, either orally or silently; (5) whether or not there was some explicit teaching of a comprehension strategy (e.g., prediction, summarization, use of context clues); and (6) whether discrete reading skills were taught primarily out of context, in context, or through some combination of the two. Averaged across observed lessons, the dichotomous codes yielded the measures used in the analyses reported in this book.

A measure of the three instructional patterns described in Chapter 4 was derived from an index combining these strategy indicators. The measure was created by trichotomizing the strategy indicators, summing the trichotomized values into an index, and then trichotomizing the index. The cut points between "low," "moderate," and "high" emphasis on meaning-oriented reading strategies were set so that cases falling into each category corresponded with the qualitative classification of intensively studied classrooms.

Measures of curriculum and instruction in writing. Indicators of the strategies for maximizing meaning in writing instruction resembled those for reading. Two were derived from the daily logs, in which teachers reported whether they had (1) integrated writing with reading or (2) focused instruction on prewriting or revision. As in the case of reading, analytic measures for each were created by calculating the percentage of all days of language arts instruction on which each feature of instruction was present. Observers' coding forms afforded indicators of three other instructional strategies, based on data indicating whether teachers (3) encouraged or permitted student-student interaction during writing instruction; (4) explicitly connected writing instruction with students' backgrounds in any way; and (5) taught language mechanics skills primarily out of context, in context, or through some combination of the two. Averaged across observed lessons, the dichotomous or trichotomous codes representing each strategy provided analytic measures.

An index was created to represent the sixth strategy—the extent to which teachers offered opportunities for writing extended text—which was also used as the measure of the three instructional patterns described in Chapter 5. Ranging from 4 (little or no opportunity for extended text writing) to 12 (extensive opportunities for extended text writing), the index was created by trichotomizing four variables—the average number of extended text tasks during observation periods; the proportion of writing tasks that involved extended text during observation periods; the average number of minutes students spent actually writing text during observed lessons; and, based on teachers' logs, the percentage of instructional days on which students worked on their own text. Each classroom's score (1, 2, or 3) on each variable was summed to create an index score. Cut points were then set to distinguish classrooms according to the qualitative classification of intensively observed classrooms into the three patterns of writing instruction.

Measures of supplemental curriculum and instruction. Measures indicating the focus of observed supplemental instruction in language arts were created by averaging dichotomous codes for each visit, which represented whether discrete reading or language mechanics skills, reading of text, writing composed text, or oral communication was a focus of instruction. Separate measures were created for in-class and pullout supplemental instruction (pullout instruction was not observed on every visit; in these instances, site visitors relied on interviews with supplemental teachers to determine what was taught). In a few classrooms, more than one pullout program was operating; there, observers coded information for the program serving the largest number of children from the classroom. The analytic measure of each possible instructional focus was created by averaging the dichotomous (1, 0) codes for each observation visit and then dichotomizing the result (e.g., 1 = . . . was a focus of instruction on at least one visit).

A similar set of measures was created to indicate the focus of observed supplemental mathematics instruction, based on observers' codes for a focus on practice with arithmetic computation skills, practice with other mathematical skills, conceptual understanding of mathematics, and applications of mathematical ideas or procedures to unusual or unfamiliar problems.

Other measures of curriculum and instruction. Four variables played a central role in analyses, reported in Chapters 1 and 2, of the way teachers managed the academic learning environment and their response to differences in students' backgrounds. The first, which categorized classrooms according to their predominant approach to classroom order, was created solely on the basis of qualitative analysis of case reports regarding the classrooms that were studied intensively during year 1 (no coding form or log items in either year had the requisite data from which to construct a suitable index or indices). A second variable, created in a similar way for the intensively studied classrooms, distinguished classrooms by the teacher's predominant approach to student differences (actively nonconstructive, passively nonconstructive, and so forth, as described in Chapter 2). A third variable represented teachers' general proficiency in classroom management through an index ranging from 1 (least proficient) to 5 (most proficient), which summarized the three subject-specific measures of student engagement in academic tasks, described below. The combined engagement measure, constructed by averaging the three subject-specific measures, served as a proxy for the teacher's general proficiency in managing classrooms. A fourth variable summarized teacher efforts across subject areas to make connections between instruction and students' backgrounds. The measure was constructed by averaging the coding form items in each of the three subject areas and creating four ranges (0, >0–1, >1–2, and >2).

Measures of student learning and response to instruction. A measure of student engagement in academic tasks was created for each of the three subject areas. Ranging from 1 (consistent low engagement) to 5 (consistent high engagement), the scale was created by averaging ratings recorded by observers for each mathematics, reading, or writing lesson they watched. Their ratings were a global summary of both level of engagement and proportion of the class involved, based on a periodic scan of the classroom (e.g., every 10 minutes) during which the observer noted the number of disengaged students and the general character of engagement on academic tasks.

Outcome measures in each subject area were derived from standardized tests and from several alternative assessment measures. Appropriate levels of the CTBS/4 were used to capture students' grasp of mathematical concepts and applications, computation skills, and reading comprehension. Alternative measures were used to assess mathematical problem-solving proficiency, grasp of discrete reading skills, competence at written expression, and the mechanical correctness of students' writing.

To get at problem-solving proficiency (for students in grades 3–6), we used previously validated mathematical problem-solving "superitems"—sets of related items concerning a common problem, in which each successive item in the set requires a higher level of cognitive response—developed at the University of Wisconsin (Romberg, 1982). With these superitems we constructed two short (10-item) tests, one for third and fourth graders, and the other for fifth and sixth graders. Using validation data from the University of Wisconsin regarding item responses of 9- and 13-year-olds, we assembled a pool of items that appeared to be manageable for children in grades 3 through 6 if we dropped the items in each set that required the highest levels of cognitive response. The item pool was then subdivided by apparent difficulty into two subpools, from which we constructed a Version A test for third and fourth graders and a Version B test for fifth and sixth graders.

Our only measure of discrete skills in reading was furnished by the Woodcock Language Proficiency Battery, an individualized test that we administered to a subset of six children in each first- and second-grade classroom. These children were chosen to represent the range of proficiencies in the room, based on information available at the beginning of the year. Two subtests were used in analyses of basic skills: the word-attack test (in which children "read" increasingly complex nonsense words) and the word-letter identification test (in which children read increasingly complex syllables and words). Resource constraints dictated that the tests be given only at the end of each year; consequently, as with writing, we used the students' CTBS/4 Reading Comprehension pretest as a proxy for basic skills-related achievement at the beginning of the year. The Woodcock is a normed test with results convertible to normal curve equivalents (NCEs), which we employed as the basic analytic measure.

To capture students' proficiency at writing, we developed an assessment procedure that yielded a writing sample at the end of each school year (an additional writing sample obtained during the fall of the second year was used for longer-term analyses of instructional effects). Modeling our efforts on procedures used in several state writing assessments, we constructed an assessment in which students responded to one of two simple prompts (e.g., "Think about your favorite food. Describe your favorite food so that someone reading your description will understand why it is your favorite."). The first elicited a piece of descriptive writing, the second a piece of analytic writing. The writing prompts were field-tested, revised, and retested to ensure that they would yield appropriate data. In each year of data collection, prompts were randomly distributed to children within each classroom, who wrote for approximately 20 minutes.

Analytic measures were derived from holistic scoring of the writing samples, done by a team of trained raters. Each sample was scored by two different raters on a scale of 1 (lowest proficiency) to 6 (highest proficiency) for two different aspects of the writing: competence in written composition (not including mechanical correctness) and the mechanical correctness of written text. (In cases in which the two raters diverged considerably, a third rater was brought in.) The two raters' scores for each variable were summed to make a combined raw score ranging from 2 to 12. The raw combined score was not used in analysis, however, because all writing samples regardless of grade level were scored on the same criteria and scale. Consequently, to reflect the relationship of each student's work to a more relevant norm, we constructed within-grade z-scores, which indicate the degree of difference from the mean of all other students at that grade level.

ANALYSIS

We learned about teaching for meaning in two distinct yet complementary ways. First, we conducted qualitative analyses of curriculum and instruction in a subset of the classrooms during each year to determine the principal patterns of instruction in the classrooms and to identify the various influences on them. Second, using the quantitative measures described above, we performed multiple regression analyses with data from all classrooms in each year to determine what was most strongly associated with student outcome measures.

Qualitative Analysis

The analysis of qualitative data served three functions in the study: to validate quantitative measures (and in some cases to create them); to identify and describe different ways teachers approached instruction in the three subject areas, managed the academic learning environment, and responded to student differences; and to identify forces and conditions that influenced teachers' attempts at emphasizing meaning in instruction.

Qualitative analyses proceeded through within-case and cross-case stages, following an analytic tradition that is commonly used in multisite qualitative studies (Miles & Huberman, 1994). We produced two types of within-case qualitative analyses. At the end of the year, we developed a lengthy qualitative report on each of the intensively studied classrooms that combined the summaries from each period of observation. These reports presented narrative discussions of (1) classroom ethos and context, (2) the backgrounds and attitudes of all professional staff who worked in the classroom, (3) instructional approaches in each subject area and students' responses to them, (4) the nature and management of the academic learning environment, (5) the role of supplemental instruction, and (6) the influence of external forces emanating from the school, district, or elsewhere. To create these reports, site visitors drew on all the data sources at their disposal — principally, classroom observations, teacher interviews, and the examination of instructional materials.

A similar but shorter qualitative report was developed for each school by the team leader of the school's site visitors. This report synthesized what the site team had learned over the two years regarding (1) the general ethos and climate of the school, (2) the nature of the student population, (3) curricular organization and policies, (4) the organization of supplemental instruction, (5) the school as a workplace for teachers, and (6) the community and district context. This report combined what had been learned about the school from teachers with information gleaned from interviews with the principal and district office staff.

We conducted cross-case analyses by first generating assertions about patterns that might hold across cases (classrooms or schools) and then testing them against the qualitative reports of intensively studied classrooms or school context, as appropriate.

Quantitative Analysis

We approached the analysis of quantitative outcome data with a simple analytic model in mind. We assumed that variation in outcomes was associated with linear combinations of (1) student characteristics (e.g., poverty level, initial achievement level), (2) teacher characteristics (e.g., satisfaction with teaching, expectations for student success), (3) subject-specific instructional strategies aimed at advanced skills (e.g., teaching comprehension strategies in reading), (4) subject-specific strategies aimed at basic skills (e.g., decoding drills, computation practice), and (5) generic features of instruction (e.g., pupil-teacher ratio). Separate analyses were done for each subject area. Our analysis of outcomes was guided by an overarching hypothesis that emerged from past research and our own classroom observations: In schools serving high concentrations of children from low-income families, the more classrooms exhibit strategies aimed at maximizing students' grasp of advanced skills, the better the students' academic performance will be, other things being equal. The analysis explored issues related to this hypothesis by posing specific analytic questions related to the mastery of advanced skills at the end of the school year and over the longer term, the differences between high- and low-performing students, and the mastery of discrete basic skills.

In principle, the study design permitted some longitudinal effects to be investigated, but it was not longitudinal in the classic sense. A cohort of students was not tracked systematically over a period of years. The study focused instead on curriculum and instruction as enacted within classrooms — a phenomenon that is restricted to the school year. We conceptualized the effects of academic instruction as either short term — manifested at the end of a school year — or longer term — manifested over a 12-month period (from the fall of one year to the fall of the next, or from the spring of one year to the spring of the next, thus including any gains or losses over the summer months). Our ability to assess these longer-term effects depended, of course, on the number and nature of first-year students retained in the second-year classroom sample.

Decisions regarding approach to quantitative analysis. Given the continuous nature of the dependent variables, we chose a linear model for analysis. Linear regression is mathematically similar to analysis of variance (ANOVA, which can be used only for categorical independent variables) and analysis of covariance (ANCOVA), but it differs in results and flexibility. The advantage of regression is that it estimates coefficients that indicate the size of a change in the dependent variable associated with a unit change in each covariate, in addition to indicating the precision and significance level of each estimated coefficient (with standard errors and p values) as well as the goodness of fit of the whole model (R^2).

Based on our overarching hypothesis, we estimated models of short-term (fall to spring in both data-collection years) and longer-term (fall to fall or spring to spring) performance in each subject area. Most of the models we estimated were nested, beginning with simple models containing only instructional approach variables along with two student characteristics as control variables—poverty level (we used the percentage of students in the classroom who participated in the free or reduced-price lunch program as a proxy for poverty level) and achievement level at the beginning of the year (represented by the students' scores on the most relevant CTBS/4). To these models we added other independent variables to determine the coefficients for these variables and to examine any changes in coefficients for approach variables, once other factors were entered into the equation.

For many analyses, no meaningful gain score could be computed because measures were taken only at the end of the year. For this reason, we chose as our primary outcome indicator the level of performance at the time of the posttest, with the most relevant pretest measure used as a covariate. For analyses of performance level, we used NCE scores whenever possible. We chose these nationally normed scores rather than raw scores because they provide a useful relative meaning to students' achievement levels. Of the normed scores, we selected NCEs over percentiles or scale (expanded standard) scores because of their statistically desirable properties (e.g., a more nearly linear scale) and their wide currency among policy audiences. No national norms exist for the problem-solving superitems tests and writing assessments, so we relied on easily understandable transformations of the raw score (e.g., for mathematics, the percentage of answers correct; for the writing assessment, within-grade z-scores).

There are countless interaction effects that could be examined in this kind of study, and we resisted the impulse to go on a fishing expedition for possible interactions. Instead, we focused on those for which there was clear logical and observational grounding, in particular, grade-level instruction and the differential effects of instruction on high- and low-performing students. Because in some instances we had only classroom aggregate measures of free or reduced-price lunch (FRL) program participation, we had to attach to each student the mean FRL value for the classroom, thus controlling for the extent of poverty among students in the classroom.

Our conceptual model and overall hypothesis assert that classroom-level phenomena affect students' performance. Thus, we faced the questions of the appropriate level or levels of analysis to focus on and whether to use multistage or multilevel analytic techniques. In analyzing multilevel phenomena, neither the classroom nor the student level by itself is optimal.[1] Classroom-level analyses properly acknowledge the fact that stu-

---

1. There is a third important level—the school—to consider. In our sample, there were too few schools and too much confounding of instructional variables with school settings to permit school-level variables to be included meaningfully in regression equations. Instead, we did separate exploratory analyses with cross-tabulations and breakdowns to document possible school-level influences (see Chapter 9).

dents are nested within classroom groups and that a number of instructional variables are measured at the classroom level, but information about individual student variation is lost. The advantage of conducting analyses at the student level (e.g., by attaching to student records the corresponding instructional variables for the student's classroom) is that variation in student background characteristics and outcomes is retained, but such analyses may presume greater independence among cases than is in fact true.

We were well aware of the dangers of single-level methods. The student-level analyses, for example, violated the assumption that error terms are uncorrelated across cases, a necessary condition for the type of analyses we conducted. Nevertheless, no alternative was clearly better. Two-stage analyses, for example, would have meant estimating within-classroom models at the student level and then using results from these models in classroom-level models. Such multistage techniques have been criticized for several reasons, among them that the classroom-level analyses do not take into account the varying precision of within-classroom student-level estimates (Bryk & Raudenbusch, 1988). Recently developed single-stage methodologies (e.g., hierarchical linear modeling, or HLM, developed by Bryk and Raudenbusch) attempt to correct this problem by estimating models with variables of several levels. Although HLM-like techniques are gaining in acceptance, there is no consensus concerning the goodness of the empirical Bayesian estimators used in such multilevel models. Given these problems, the continuing lack of consensus, and the added expense of using HLM-like techniques, we concluded that the marginal benefit of such techniques did not make them worthwhile.

We approached the levels-of-analysis dilemma by running regressions at both the student and the classroom levels and comparing how coefficients were affected. Though a little cumbersome, this approach is a clean way of examining multilevel phenomena without invoking a problematic model or assumptions. Relatively few differences between levels emerged from these analyses, probably reflecting the fact that so much of the measurement occurred at the classroom level. The analyses summarized in this book are at the student level.

Adjustments due to sample attrition or missing values. There were significant problems of missing cases and data. We handled these problems in two ways. First, when a given classroom was missing values for a small number of variables relevant to a particular analysis, we imputed values as follows: We estimated a correlation matrix of all independent variables and then estimated a model, regressing the variable with the missing values on the variable with which it had the highest correlation. Values for missing cases were then imputed based on the results of the regression equation. When no variables were highly correlated with variables that had missing values for some classrooms, the mean of all cases was imputed to the cases with missing values. For some analyses, the imputed value was the mean for the full sample; in other cases, it was a within-grade-level mean. This imputation process did not create any new information, but it did enable us to retain cases in multiple regressions even when they were missing one or a few variables relevant to the regression.

Second, in several instances, we deleted cases that were missing data. Students who were absent from the posttest in both years were deleted from the database altogether. Students who were absent from the posttest in only one year were excluded from outcome analyses in that year. When a given classroom was missing values for a high proportion of variables, we deleted the case altogether rather than attempt to impute values.

Deletion of student or classroom cases raised the possibility that the missing cases differed systematically in some respects that had a bearing on the analysis in question, thereby biasing results. Fortunately, the number of deleted cases for analyses taking place within a given school year was relatively small. For example, about 12 percent of the classrooms in year 1 and approximately half that percentage in year 2 were dropped from analyses. Even so, we checked for possible biases by comparing the cases, as analyzed, with the original set of relevant cases on overall background variables (poverty level, initial achievement levels) that were strongly associated with outcomes. For short-term analyses, there appeared to be no major biases resulting from missing cases.

The problem for longer-term analyses, however, was more pronounced and was compounded by sample attrition across years. As noted earlier, sample attrition from year 1 to year 2 was large — approximately 50 percent of the students from year 1 were missing at the time of the year 2 pretest. There were various reasons for this: Students had been regrouped and reassigned, many into classrooms not included in the year 2 sample; others had transferred out of the school or district; two of the sample districts did not have sixth grade in their elementary schools (hence fifth graders from the year 1 sample in these schools did not appear in year 2). Our basic approach to assessing possible biases due to sample attrition was essentially the same as our way of handling missing values, described above.

Statistical Tables

The following tables provide results of selected regression analyses that underlie the findings reported in Chapter 7. Due to space limitations, we present only a single table for each of the three subject areas. The three tables show the regression coefficients in equations predicting selected student learning outcomes (understanding of mathematical concepts and applications, reading comprehension, competence in written expression) for three sets of independent variables: (1) pattern of instruction in mathematics, reading, or writing; (2) student characteristics (poverty level, prior achievement level); and (3) teacher characteristics (richness of teachers' backgrounds, teachers' expectations for student success, and teachers' satisfaction with teaching). These analyses represent the fully specified model on which the strongest conclusions are based, those related to advanced skills learning outcomes over the short term (fall to spring).

The tables offer a more technically complete picture of the analytic evidence on which our conclusions are based. However, not all information relevant to the assessment of regression results appears in the tables. Bivariate correlation matrices, for example, are not shown (however, these were checked to see whether multicollinearity would be a problem, but no variables were correlated higher than approximately .75, and all but a few variable pairs correlated at less than .50).

The coefficients shown in the tables differ slightly from those that appear in the figures shown earlier in the book, because the models reported here include characteristics of teachers as well as students. For example, Table B-1 shows that, by comparison with their counterparts exposed to arithmetic skills only, students in meaning-oriented mathematics classrooms (those emphasizing conceptual understanding and multiple mathematical topics) performed 6.0 normal curve equivalents (NCEs) higher at the end of year 1 and 2.4 NCEs higher at the end of year 2, taking into account initial differences in the students' achievement and poverty levels *and* differences in their teachers' backgrounds, expectations, and satisfaction with teaching. In an equation that does not include teacher characteristics — the one on which Figure 7-1 in Chapter 7 is based — these differences are 6.4 and 1.7 NCEs, respectively, for years 1 and 2. This example demonstrates the robust nature of the findings presented earlier in the book: Introducing additional variables into the regression equations did not substantially change the coefficient of relationship between instructional approach and outcomes.

Although analyses were done at the classroom and student levels, only the student-level analyses are shown here. Regression results were relatively similar across levels (probably reflecting the fact that nearly all measurements occurred at the same level — see Appendix A).

Readers wishing a more complete set of regression tables should consult Appendix H in Volume 2 of the full technical study report (Knapp & Marder, 1992).

TABLE B–1. Association between approach to mathematics instruction and mathematical understanding, controlling for selected student and teacher characteristics, over the short term (Fall to Spring)

Prediction Variables [a]	Unstandardized B-weights in multiple regressions	
	Year 1: Grades 1,3,5 (n = 1,061)	Year 2: Grades 2,4,6 (n = 1,172)
Approach to Mathematics Instruction [b]		
• Multiple topics with conceptual understanding	6.0 *	2.4 *
• Multiple topics, skills only	1.7	2.3
• Arithmetic with conceptual understanding	– 0.5	0.1
Student Characteristics		
• Initial achievement level: CTBS/4 Concepts & Applications test for fall 1 or 2	0.7 *	0.6 *
• Poverty level: Percentage of class participating in free or reduced-price lunch program	– 0.1 *	– 0.1 *
Teacher Characteristics [c]		
• Richness of teacher's background in mathematics (scale from 1 to 6)	0.0	1.4 *
• Teacher's expectations for students' success in mathematics (scale from 1 to 4)	1.1	– 0.1
• Teacher's satisfaction with teaching (scale from 1 to 5)	0.8	– 1.1 §
	$R^2 = .52$	$R^2 = .49$

[a]   These variables predicted spring outcome scores (in normal curve equivalents) on the CTBS/4 Concepts & Applications Test. Dummy variables for students' presence in different grade levels were also entered into the prediction equation. For year 1, the coefficients (B-weights) for presence in grade 1 (as contrasted with grade 3) = – 3.3 *; presence in grade 5 (as contrasted with grade 3) = – 2.8 *. For year 2, the coefficients for presence in grade 2 (as contrasted with grade 4) = – 3.9 *; presence in grade 6 (as contrasted with grade 4) = – 0.5.

[b]   Variable indicates students' presence in classrooms with each type of instructional focus, as contrasted with those in classrooms focusing on arithmetic skills only.

[c]   These measures are described in more detail in Appendix A.

* $p < .05$ § $p < .10$

Table reads: "By comparison with their counterparts exposed to arithmetic skills only, students in classrooms focusing on multiple topics and conceptual understanding scored 6.0 NCEs higher at the end of year 1 and 2.4 NCEs higher at the end of year 2, taking into account initial differences in student and teacher characteristics at the beginning of the year. Both of these results are statistically different from zero at the .05 level...."

TABLE B–2. Association between approach to reading instruction and reading comprehension, controlling for selected student and teacher characteristics, over the short term (Fall to Spring)

Prediction Variables [a]	Unstandardized B-weights in multiple regressions	
	Year 1: Grades 1,3,5 (n = 1,068)	Year 2: Grades 2,4,6 (n = 1,123)
Approach to Reading Instruction [b]		
• Great emphasis on comprehension-oriented strategies	5.5 *	1.2
• Moderate emphasis on comprehension-oriented strategies	4.0 *	3.9 *
Student Characteristics		
• Initial achievement level: CTBS/4 Reading Comprehension Test for fall 1 or 2	0.6 *	0.7 *
• Poverty level: Percentage of class participating in the free or reduced-price lunch program	– 0.1 *	– 0.1 *
Teacher Characteristics [c]		
• Richness of teacher's background in language arts (scale from 1 to 6)	– 0.0	0.8 *
• Teacher's expectations for students' success in language arts (scale from 1 to 4)	1.0	0.9
• Teacher's satisfaction with teaching (scale from 1 to 5)	– 0.4	1.0
	$R^2 = .45$	$R^2 = .55$

[a] These variables predicted spring outcome scores (in normal curve equivalents) on the CTBS/4 Reading Comprehension Test. Variables for students' presence in different grade levels were also entered into the prediction equation. For year 1, the coefficients (B-weights) for presence in grade 1 (as contrasted with grade 3) = – 2.4 §; presence in grade 5 (as contrasted with grade 3) = – 2.3 §. For year 2, the coefficients for presence in grade 2 (as contrasted with grade 4) = – 2.1 *; presence in grade 6 (as contrasted with grade 4) = 1.3.
[b] Variable indicates students' presence in classrooms with each level of instructional emphasis, as contrasted with classrooms placing little or no emphasis on comprehension-oriented strategies.
[c] These measures are described in more detail in Appendix A.
* p < .05   § p < .10

Table reads: "By comparison with their counterparts exposed little to comprehension-oriented strategies, students in classrooms emphasizing these strategies scored 5.5 NCEs higher at the end of year 1 and 1.2 NCEs higher at the end of year 2, taking into account differences in student and teacher characteristics at the beginning of each year. The first of these results is statistically different from zero...."

TABLE B-3. Association between approach to writing instruction and competence in written composition, controlling for selected student and teacher characteristics, over the short term (Fall to Spring)

	Unstandardized B-weights in multiple regressions	
Prediction Variables [a]	Year 1: Grades 3,5 (n = 612)	Year 2: Grades 4,6 (n = 654)
Approach to Writing Instruction [b]		
• Great emphasis on extended text writing	.25 *	.31 *
• Moderate emphasis on extended text writing	.03	.15
Student Characteristics		
• Initial achievement level: CTBS/4 Reading Comprehension Test for fall 1 or 2 [c]	.02 *	.02 *
• Poverty level: Percentage of class participating in the free or reduced-price lunch program	– 0.0 *	0.0
Teacher Characteristics [d]		
• Richness of teacher's background in language arts (scale from 1 to 6)	.01	.03
• Teacher's expectations for students' success in language arts (scale from 1 to 4)	– .01	– .12
• Teacher's satisfaction with teaching (scale from 1 to 5)	.24 *	.16 *
	R^2 = .20	R^2 = .16

[a] These variables predicted spring outcome scores (in within-grade z-scores) on the writing assessment (see Appendix A for an explanation of writing outcome measures). Dummy variables for students' presence in different grade levels were also entered into the prediction equation. For year 1, the coefficient (B-weight) for presence in grade 5 (as contrasted with grade 3) = 0.2. For year 2, the coefficient for presence in grade 6 (as contrasted with grade 4) = 0.4.
[b] Variable indicates students' presence in classrooms with each level of instructional emphasis, as contrasted with classrooms placing little or no emphasis on extended text writing.
[c] Reading comprehension was used as a proxy for writing-related skills at the beginning of the year.
[d] These measures are described in more detail in Appendix A.
* $p < .05$

Table reads: "By comparison with their counterparts exposed minimally, or not at all, to extended text writing (and associated instructional strategies), students in classrooms placing great emphasis on extended text writing scored .25 z-score units higher at the end of year 1 and .31 z-score units higher at the end of year 2, taking into account differences in student and teacher characteristics at the beginning of each year. Both results are statistically different from zero at the .05 level. ..."

References

Brandt, R. (1994). Overview: It's not easy. *Educational Leadership, 51*(5), 3.

Brooks, J. G., & Brooks, M. G. (1993). *In search of understanding: The case for constructivist classrooms.* Alexandria, VA: Association for Supervision & Curriculum Development.

Brophy, J., & Good, T. L. (1986). Teacher behavior and student achievement. In M. Wittrock (Ed.), *Handbook of research on teaching* (3rd ed., pp. 328–375). New York: Macmillan.

Brown, R. G. (1993). *Schools of thought: How the politics of literacy shape thinking in the classroom.* San Francisco: Jossey-Bass.

Bryk, A., & Raudenbusch, S. (1988). Toward a more appropriate conceptualization of research on school effects: A three-level hierarchical model. *American Journal of Education, 97,* 65–108.

Bryson, M., & Scardamalia, M. (1991). Teaching writing to students at risk for academic failure. In B. Means, C. Chelemer, & M. S. Knapp (Eds.), *Teaching advanced skills to at-risk students* (pp. 141–167). San Francisco: Jossey-Bass.

Calfee, R. (1991). What schools can do to improve literacy instruction. In B. Means, C. Chelemer, & M. S. Knapp (Eds.), *Teaching advanced skills to at-risk students* (pp. 176–203). San Francisco: Jossey-Bass.

Calkins, L. M. (1980). Children's rewriting strategies. *Research on Teaching English, 14,* 331–341.

Cohen, D. K. (1990). A revolution in one classroom: The case of Ms. Oublier. *Educational Evaluation & Policy Analysis, 12*(3), 327–345.

Cohen, D. K., & Barnes, C. A. (1993). Pedagogy and policy. In D. K. Cohen, M. W. McLaughlin, & J. E. Talbert (Eds.), *Teaching for understanding: Challenges for policy and practice* (pp. 207–239). San Francisco: Jossey-Bass.

Cohen, D. K., McLaughlin, M. W., & Talbert, J. E. (Eds.). (1993). *Teaching for understanding: Challenges for policy and practice.* San Francisco: Jossey-Bass.

Delpit, L. (1988). The silenced dialogue: Power and pedagogy in educating other people's children. *Harvard Education Review, 58*(3), 280–298.

Dyson, A. H. (1983). The role of oral language in early writing processes. *Research in the Teaching of English, 17,* 1–30.

Erickson, F. (1986). Qualitative methods in research on teaching. In M. C. Wittrock (Ed.), *Handbook of research on teaching* (3rd ed., pp. 119–160). New York: Macmillan.

Gage, N. L., & Needels, M. C. (1989). Process-product research: A review of criticism. *Elementary School Journal, 89,* 253–300.

231

Garcia, G., & Pearson, P. D. (1991). Modifying reading instruction to maximize
    its effectiveness for "disadvantaged" students. In M. S. Knapp & P. M.
    Shields (Eds.), *Better schooling for the children of poverty: Alternatives to
    conventional wisdom* (pp. 31–60). Berkeley, CA: McCutchan.
Goodlad, J. I., & Keating, P. (1990). *Access to knowledge.* New York: College
    Entrance Examination Board.
Heath, S. B. (1983). *Ways with words.* Cambridge: Cambridge University Press.
Hillocks, G. (1986). *Research on written composition.* Urbana, IL: National
    Council of Teachers of English.
Knapp, M. S., Adelman, N. E., Marder, C., McCollum, C., Needels, M. C.,
    Shields, P. M., Turnbull, B. J., & Zucker, A. A. (1992). *Academic challenge
    for the children of poverty – Volume 1: Findings and conclusions.* Washing-
    ton, DC: U.S. Department of Education, Office of Policy & Planning.
Knapp, M. S., Adelman, N. E., Needels, M. C., Zucker, A. A., McCollum, H.,
    Turnbull, B. J., Marder, C., & Shields, P. M. (1991). *What is taught, and
    how, to the children of poverty: Interim report from a two-year investiga-
    tion.* Washington, DC: U.S. Department of Education, Office of Policy &
    Planning.
Knapp, M. S., & Marder, C. (1992). *Academic challenge for the children of
    poverty – Volume 2: Study design and technical notes.* Washington, DC:
    U.S. Department of Education, Planning & Evaluation Service.
Knapp, M. S., & Needels, M. C. (1991). Review of research on curriculum and
    instruction in literacy. In M. S. Knapp & P. M. Shields (Eds.), *Better school-
    ing for the children of poverty: Alternatives to conventional wisdom* (pp. 85–
    122). Berkeley, CA: McCutchan.
Knapp, M. S., & Shields, P. M. (Eds.). (1991). *Better schooling for the children
    of poverty: Alternatives to conventional wisdom.* Berkeley, CA: McCutchan.
Knapp, M. S., Turnbull, B. J., & Shields, P. M. (1990). New directions for
    educating the children of poverty. *Educational Leadership, 48*(1), 4–9.
Knapp, M. S., & Woolverton, S. (forthcoming). Social class and schooling. In J.
    Banks & C. M. Banks (Eds.), *Handbook of research on multicultural educa-
    tion.* New York: Macmillan.
McKnight, C. C., Crosswhite, F. J., Dossey, J. A., Kifer, E., Swafford, J. O.,
    Travers, K. J., & Cooney, T. J. (1987). *The underachieving curriculum:
    Assessing U.S. school mathematics from an international perspective.* Cham-
    paign, IL: Stipes.
Means, B., & Knapp, M. S. (1991). Cognitive approaches to teaching advanced
    skills to educationally disadvantaged children. *Phi Delta Kappan, 73*(4),
    282–289.
Miles, M. W., & Huberman, M. (1994). *Qualitative analysis: An expanded
    sourcebook* (2nd edition). Beverly Hills, CA: Sage.
Oakes, J. (1990). *Multiplying inequalities: The effects of race, social class, and
    tracking on opportunities to learn mathematics and science.* Santa Monica,
    CA: RAND Corporation.
Palincsar, A., Klenck, L. (1991). Dialogues promoting reading comprehension.

In B. Means, C. Chelemer, & M. S. Knapp (Eds.), *Teaching advanced skills to at-risk students* (pp. 112–130). San Francisco: Jossey-Bass.

Perkins, D., & Blythe, T. (1994). Putting understanding up front. *Educational Leadership, 51*(5), 4–7.

Peterson, P. L., Fennema, E., & Carpenter, T. (1991). Using children's mathematical knowledge. In B. Means, C. Chelemer, & M. S. Knapp (Eds.), *Teaching advanced skills to at-risk students* (pp. 68–101). San Francisco: Jossey-Bass.

Resnick, L. B., Bill, V. L., Lesgold, S. B., & Leer, M. N. (1991). Thinking in arithmetic class. In B. Means, C. Chelemer, & M. S. Knapp (Eds.), *Teaching advanced skills to at-risk students* (pp. 27–53). San Francisco: Jossey-Bass.

Romberg, T. A. (1982). *The development and validation of a set of mathematical problem-solving superitems — Appendix B: Superitems with technical data, comments, and response keys.* Madison, WI: Wisconsin Center for Education Research, University of Wisconsin.

Shields, P. M. (1991). School and community influences on effective academic instruction. In M. S. Knapp & P. M. Shields (Eds.), *Better schooling for the children of poverty: Alternatives to conventional wisdom* (pp. 313–328). Berkeley, CA: McCutchan.

Shulman, L. (1986). Those who understand: Knowledge growth in teaching. *Educational Researcher, 15*(7), 4–14.

Snow, C. E., Barnes, W. S., Chandler, J., Goodman, I. F., & Hemphill, L. (1991). *Unfilled expectations: Home and school influences on literacy.* Cambridge, MA: Harvard University Press.

Teaching for understanding [Thematic issue]. (1994). *Educational Leadership, 51*(5).

Tharp, R. G. (1989). Psychocultural variables and constants: Effects on teaching and learning in schools. *American Psychologist, 44*(2), 349–359.

Villasenor, R. (1990). *Teaching the first grade mathematics curriculum from a problem-solving perspective.* Unpublished doctoral dissertation, University of Wisconsin, Milwaukee.

Winfield, L. F. (1986). Teacher beliefs toward academically at risk students in inner urban schools. *The Urban Review, 18*(4), 253–267.

Zucker, A. (1991). Review of research on effective curriculum and instruction in mathematics. In M. S. Knapp & P. M. Shields (Eds.), *Better schooling for the children of poverty: Alternatives to conventional wisdom* (pp. 189–208). Berkeley, CA: McCutchan.

About the Authors

Michael S. Knapp is an Associate Professor of Educational Leadership and Policy Studies in the College of Education at the University of Washington. His scholarship and teaching concern policymaking processes, school reform, and the sociology of education, as well as methods of research and evaluation. Policies and programs aimed at "disadvantaged" groups have been a special focus of his attention over the years, culminating most recently with this book; two earlier volumes co-edited by Dr. Knapp deal with effective instructional practices for classrooms serving children who are at high risk of school failure—*Better Schooling for the Children of Poverty: Alternatives to Conventional Wisdom* (with Patrick Shields, published by McCutchan in 1991) and *Teaching Advanced Skills to At-Risk Students* (with Barbara Means and Carol Chelemer, published by Jossey-Bass in 1991). Dr. Knapp is currently investigating comprehensive, collaborative services for children and the connections between educational policy and the improvement of teaching.

Nancy E. Adelman is a Senior Associate with Policy Studies Associates in Washington, D.C., where she specializes in research and evaluation of education reform strategies. As a former elementary and middle school teacher, she welcomed the opportunity to once again spend extensive time in classrooms collecting the data on which this book is based. Dr. Adelman is currently working on studies of dropout prevention programs, systemic reform of mathematics and science education, time as a factor in the school reform process, and the development of state systems for school-to-work transition.

Camille Marder is a Senior Sociologist in SRI International's Health & Social Policy Division. For the past ten years, she has examined educational policies and programs, focusing primarily on the education of historically underrepresented groups, and the mathematics and science offered to all students. As part of a SRI team engaged in national longitudinal research, Dr. Marder contributed to a series of publications regarding the secondary school experiences and the transition from youth to adulthood of individuals with disabilities. Dr. Marder is currently examining the effects of various reform efforts in mathematics and science education.

Heather McCollum is a Senior Research Associate at Policy Studies Associates, where her research interests focus on the lives of youth at risk and how organizations can change to support them more effectively. She recently completed studies of bilingual family literacy programs and schoolwide reforms in schools serving concentrations of children from low-income families. She is currently co-directing an investigation of the effects of alternative assessment on teaching and learning in the classroom.

Margaret C. Needels is a Professor of Teacher Education in the School of Education at California State University, Hayward. Her interests include research on teaching, teacher education, the teaching of writing, gender differences in writing, and the ethics of social science research. She is especially interested in understanding how schools and teachers can best address the needs of students from diverse populations. Her current research focuses on possible factors influencing girls' and women's views of themselves as writers and how schools and teachers might enhance these views.

Christine Padilla is a Senior Policy Analyst at SRI International in its Health & Social Policy Division. Her 20 years of evaluation work have focused on governmental policies, program implementation, and school reforms, with a particular emphasis on federal- and state-supported programs for at-risk students. She has a particular interest in the connections between the improvement of learning opportunities for children from low-income families and the nature of the policy environment in schools, districts, and states. Ms. Padilla is currently involved in research on the cost effectiveness of early intervention services for children and the school-to-work transition process.

Patrick M. Shields is a Senior Policy Analyst and Manager of the Education Policy Studies Program within SRI International's Health & Social Policy Division. His research focuses on the analysis and evaluation of educational reform policies, especially those targeted on children from low-income families. With Dr. Knapp, he is the co-editor of *Better Schooling for the Children of Poverty: Alternatives to Conventional Wisdom.* Dr. Shields is currently coordinating a 5-year national study of the National Science Foundation's (NSF) Statewide Systemic Initiative (SSI) Program, which funds the efforts of 25 states to comprehensively improve mathematics and science education.

Brenda J. Turnbull is a Principal of Policy Studies Associates. She directs research and evaluation studies in education with a special focus on policy issues in the federal Title I (formerly Chapter 1) program and in federal strategies for school improvement. She was a member of the commission on Chapter 1 and has led numerous studies of Title I at the state, district, and school levels. Among her other major interests is the rethinking of federal policy for educational research, development, and dissemination, to promote more practitioner-centered methods of school improvement. She is pursuing this interest through an evaluation of the regional education laboratories program and through her writings on federally sponsored technical assistance.

Andrew A. Zucker manages the Mathematics and Science Education Program within SRI International's Health & Social Policy Division. His work at SRI encompasses research, instructional materials development, program evaluation, and policy analysis, primarily focusing on grades K–12. Dr. Zucker's print and video materials for teaching and mathematical problem solving in the middle grades, *Becoming Successful Problem Solvers* and *Making Money with Major Munchy: Explorations in Probability* (with Ed Esty, published by HRM Video and Silver Burdett), are widely used by thousands of teachers. Dr. Zucker has conducted various national studies of issues, practices, and programs in mathematics and science education, among them, an investigation of the U.S. Department of Education's Eisenhower Program, which supports professional development in mathematics and science education; and a review of NSF's investments in K–12 science education. With Dr. Shields, he is currently co-directing a 5-year evaluation of NSF's SSI Program.

Index